MY JOURNEY:
FROM THE BUSH TO
BANKER AND BACK

MY JOURNEY: FROM THE BUSH TO BANKER AND BACK

John Chatterton AM

First Edition: Xlibris

Second Edition: AJ Chatterton and VJ Chatterton

 A catalogue record for this book is available from the National Library of Australia

ISBN 978-0-6488617-4-4

Interior and Cover Layout: Pickawoowoo Publishing Group / www.pickawoowoo.com

Printed and Distributed: Ingram (AUS /US/UK/EUR)

Contents

DEDICATION

It is with a sense of great loss that I dedicate these writings to
the memory of both our precious daughter, Lisa,
and son, Andrew—they live on in our lives.

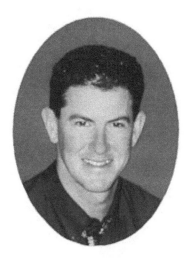

Lisa Jayne Chatterton   Andrew John Chatterton

ACKNOWLEDGEMENTS

During the long drawn-out process of writing this biography, I was assisted by various people in different ways.

At the head of this small list is the name of my dear wife, Valerie. I acknowledge her great contribution with much love. Without her continued support and encouragement, I doubt that I would have persevered through to its completion. Also, she deserves my deep gratitude for taking the time to read a number of drafts of the manuscript and offer suggestions for improvement. The inclusion of her own words in three appropriate places brings a softer female tone to those difficult sections of the writings.

Special thanks are due to historian Kay Fraser, who gently pushed me to conclude and publish these writings. Kay also contributed greatly to the process through her editing work, which has added considerably to the final outcome. Val and I value her friendship.

Finally, I wish to acknowledge and sincerely thank my sons Paul and Mark for their great support, helpful advice, and encouragement. It was through their encouragement, added to that of Kay Fraser's, that I was able to overcome my fear of the unknown world of publishing and to take the plunge.

INTRODUCTION

My intention in writing this story of my life is to document, for the benefit of my children, grandchildren, possibly their offspring, and anyone else who may be interested enough to read it, a life that I consider to be relatively unusual and successful. To all those who might choose to read this story, I must emphasise the fact that it is the story of my life as I recall it. Others may have a different memory of some events, but that is how they remember the occasion and is their story to tell.

Recalling accurately events that happened some fifty to sixty plus years ago is not always easy, yet many of those events, which occurred long ago, seem almost as clear in my mind today as they were then. Some memories have been lost too. I have endeavoured faithfully to tell the facts as I recall them. Others might dispute some of what I have said, but what is written here is my true recollection of events as I remember them.

I am proud of what I have achieved over the years, starting from a very humble beginning and with a relatively short formal education to support me. I feel that I owe much of my success to the excellent example my parents set me by establishing strongly in me values of respect for others, honesty, integrity, and a fair go for all. My other great support has been my dear wife, Valerie, who has stood firmly beside me at all times. Without her unquestioning love, wise counsel, and understanding, I doubt that I would have had the courage to press on in some of our darkest days.

Also, I feel that I owe a debt of gratitude to our children for what I perceive to be their suffering because of some of the impacts that my career moves had on their lives. They might not have all agreed with this assessment, because as a result of those moves they enjoyed many wonderful opportunities to see places and experience cultures that they might not have otherwise witnessed. However, I recognise with great sadness the downside that they endured, having to frequently forge new friendships at yet another new school as a consequence of my promotions to different locations. Although the move to Sydney was taken after lengthy deliberations between Val and me and with the very best interests of all of the family in mind, in hindsight I cannot help but think that its unsettling effect at that very important stage of the children's lives might have been a contributor in some way to the great heartache that those of us who have survived were left to endure.

Initially, I began to consider the idea of writing my life's story twenty or more years ago when I came to realise the enormity of the intergenerational gulf that existed between my childhood experiences and those of my children. It became clear to me that it was very difficult for them to understand, let alone believe, what I was talking about whenever my early years were the subject of our discussion. The life I experienced as a boy growing up on a dairy farm in Central Queensland during and soon after the 1939-1945 war was so vastly different from the world they had experienced in their youth in the 1960s-1980s era that they simply were unable to comprehend what I was talking about whenever I mentioned my life on the dairy farm. I had to acknowledge that within a period of just fifty years or so, times had changed so dramatically and had become so far removed from what I had experienced during my young lifetime that it was impossible for my children to picture in their minds what I was talking about and endeavouring to convey to them. When one thinks about the situation that I found myself facing, I expect it has possibly been ever thus from one generation to the next down through the centuries but with much greater emphasis on the dramatic changes taking place in all facets of our way of life since around the beginning of the twentieth century.

My story also encompasses a long period spent in the business world of banking. In 1955, I joined the Bank of New South Wales as Postage Clerk and under the bank's changed name of Westpac Banking Corporation had reached the top echelons of management by the time I retired in 1995. This is an insider's view of a period in Australian banking when big changes were happening. Interspersed in between the accounts of my business life and return to farming upon retirement, I document both the joys and tragedies that have accompanied our family through this period. Val has added her voice to my narrative of our personal family difficulties, providing a softer feminine picture.

John Chatterton AM

CHAPTER 1

Beginnings at Struck Oil

S truck Oil was where my family farmed for over three decades. It played an important part in my early development years and undoubtedly had considerable influence on the person I became and the manner in which I behave. In 1921, my grandfather, Robert Chatterton, purchased a farm of approx. fifty hectares (approx. 125 acres) at Struck Oil, near Mt Morgan in Central Queensland. There the family operated a dairy farm, kept a few pigs, and grew cotton and some other crops while at the same time Grandfather, who was a baker by trade, continued to work in the Mt Morgan mine. Prior to his marriage, he had enlisted in the Boer War in May 1902 at the age of twenty-six then enlisted again in the First World War in August 1914 at the age of thirty-eight years as a married man with a family. Details of his service record in World War I are in Appendix I.

Country life had always been part of my father's family. His grand-father James Chatterton, was from quite a wealthy family who were farmers, butchers, and wool-buyers in Theddlethorpe, Lincolnshire, England. He married Ann Wilson, who was the daughter of a groom at the Chatterton establishment. Apparently the marriage did not sit comfortably with the family because when James

Chatterton was drowned as a relatively young man, his widow, together with her seven youngest of her nine children including my grandfather Robert Chatterton, was 'shipped' out to Australia with what was then considered a large sum of money—£1,000. They eventually arrived in Bundaberg, Queensland, in 1883. Robert married Minnie Sutton in June 1904. Minnie was from Birmingham, Staffordshire, England and I believe she came to Australia via assisted passage on the *Duke of Norfolk* which arrived in Brisbane in 1901. It seems that she was born in a workhouse where her mother Emma Sutton (nee Ogden) was a domestic servant. For those who might be interested, I have included a brief family history in Appendix II.

Dad's birth date was registered as 11 September 1910 while his parents were residing at Mt Chalmers, near Rockhampton, Queensland, although his birthday was always celebrated on and believed to be 14 September. We did not find this out until a copy of his birth certificate was obtained at the time of this death in 1968. He was the fourth of eight children born to Robert and Minnie Chatterton. My mother's family name was Camplin and her family came from Theddlethorpe too. The two families knew each other both in England and in Australia. Mum's father, Ted Camplin, was a dairy farmer at Branyan, near Bundaberg in Queensland. Little wonder that all of my married life I have had a strong desire to own my own piece of land or farm.

Prior to his marriage, Dad had purchased a fifty-hectare dairy farm located next door to his parents' farm, with the assistance of a loan from the Commonwealth Bank of Australia. He bought it from a widow, Mrs Morgan, who was carrying on dairying by herself in a sort of fashion with help from her family. She must have been pleased with the sale arrangements as she remained a lifelong friend of our family. The farm was situated approx. twelve kilometres from Mt Morgan. The road to Mt Morgan consisted of about seven kilometres of rough gravel surface and the remainder was narrow but reasonable sealed surface. Moongan was the nearest rail siding approx. nine kilometres from the farm and was accessed by way of a rough gravel surface road. It was from here that cream was dispatched by rail in the early days to the Port Curtis Cooperative Dairy Association in Rockhampton to be made into butter. In those days, butter was sold at the equivalent of thirty cents per kilo. Dad batched (cooked and cared for himself) in the house at his newly acquired farm with the intention of getting married to my mother, Mavis Camplin, in about two years' time. It was her father's wish for the wedding to be deferred until then due to her young age. My grandmother, Minnie Chatterton, affectionately known as Ma to us kids, saw how lonely Dad was and how hard he was working without any support and apparently convinced Mum's father that they should be allowed to marry earlier than originally planned. They married on 25 January 1936 when Mum was just a few months short of twenty-one years.

My eldest sister, Elizabeth Merle, was born on 17 December 1936, and some eighteen months later, Mavis Joan was born on 8 June 1938. I was born in Mt Morgan hospital on 30 November 1939 at 1 p.m., weighing a healthy 4.1 kg (nine pounds) and went home some ten days later to Struck Oil to commence life as the son of a dairy farmer. My birth was registered in the name of Alan John, and like my two elder sisters, from day one my parents called me by my second Christian name. I have spent my adult life being called Alan by those people who do not know me and then having to explain why I was known as John when my first name was Alan. My two elder sisters suffer the same fate. I used to tell my elderly mother, who died recently at the age of ninety-nine years ten months, that she named me that way as payback for my refusing to enter the world until after midday on the day of my birth, which meant, by hospital rules of those days, she had to stay in hospital for another day. This of course is not the real situation at all; it was simply 'fashionable' in those days to name babies in this manner.

The name Struck Oil is that of a district. There was no village as such in my time other than a small State School and a rather austere galvanised ironclad World War I Memorial Hall built in 1921. I have lived all my life having to explain how the district got the name Struck Oil, and apparently, it was named after a theatre play written by the famous playwright J. C. Williamson. The play was an immediate success when it opened in Melbourne on 1 August 1874 and subsequently played in Sydney, and after touring Australia, it went on to India and eventually London.

Initially, Struck Oil district was heavily prospected for alluvial gold, with little success, until 1903 when a Gold Rush occurred with the discovery of many large alluvial gold nuggets in the Dee Ranges at the headwaters of the Dee River, just a short distance from where Dad's parents settled on their farm. The river actually formed part of the boundary along the northern side of their property, and we kids used to swim in some of its deeper waterholes after good rains. Over a thousand 'diggers' arrived in the area in the hope of finding their fortune. The broad gravel river bed near my grandparents' property was extensively mined with many dangerous shallow open shafts left behind. Once the gold petered out, the miners mostly drifted away. The few that remained turned to dairying, much of which was carried on at subsistence levels. Generally, the forest country was unsuited to dairying, but there were pockets of rich land where the rainforest scrub timbers were being felled, enabling dairying to be carried on successfully, given reasonable seasons. The majority of the property that Dad acquired was formerly good scrub land, some of which had been previously cleared for farming.

The nearby town of Mt Morgan was supported by the existence of the very large Mt Morgan open cut gold mine. The town's maximum population reached almost 10,000 in 1911 according to census data, but this number had reduced to approx. 4,500 around the time of my birth and currently stands at approx. 2,500 inhabitants. The property on which the mine is situated was originally owned by Donald Gordon, who sold it to three brothers named Morgan (not known to be related to the Mrs Morgan we knew) for £640 (£1 per acre). The mine was eventually acquired and worked by a syndicate named the Mount Morgan Gold Mining Company Ltd around the mid-1880s and was enormously successful, more particularly so in its earlier years. Vast quantities of gold, silver, and copper were won from its leases and the profits from the sale thereof made its syndicate shareholders very wealthy. In 1900, it headed the list of the twelve largest companies in Australia based on the market value of its ordinary shares. A major shareholder, William Knox D'Arcy, later became involved in oil exploration in Persia (Iran) and founded the Anglo-Persian Oil Company, now known as the mighty British Petroleum Company Limited or BP. Other major shareholders of the mining company were Walter Russell Hall together with various members of the Hall family. Many years later in 1996, through a quirk of fate, I became involved in a charitable trust named the Walter & Eliza Hall Trust which was established by Eliza in the memory of her husband.

Rockhampton was the nearest centre of any size to Mt Morgan, and in the 1940s to 1960s era, it was the unofficial 'capital' of Central Queensland, with a population of approx. 40,000 inhabitants (since then it has grown to around 75,000). It is situated on the Fitzroy River about forty kilometres north-east from our farm and was the major centre of shopping, commerce, and business, servicing town and country folk as far west as the Northern Territory border and for hundreds of kilometres north and south. It was then the port for Central Queensland, and extensive quantities of goods were shipped to and from the area via the Fitzroy River and Port Alma at the river's mouth.

The Struck Oil district was relatively small in size, and in my time there, the inhabitants consisted of approximately twenty families only, all of whom were trying to eke out a living from the land with most families having to subsidise their income from off-farm work in the mine at Mt Morgan. As I recall, they were rather a diverse group who spent lots of energy arguing among each other, which led to a lack of cohesiveness in the district. My parents initially attended and/or participated in sporting events, dances, and other functions at the local memorial hall. However, as neither drank nor wished to become embroiled in district arguments, they began to restrict their social intercourse with district members to chance meetings on the road or in the streets of Mt Morgan.

Our closest neighbours were Bob Neil, a widower, and his only son Matthew (Matt) who was a bachelor and who celebrated his thirtieth birthday on 8 August 1941, the day my younger sister Valmai was born. They were fruit and vegetable growers who supplied to the Mt Morgan and Rockhampton shops and markets. Their home was about 500 metres from ours, downhill and across open country and clearly visible from our house. Bob was a former ambulance officer and a delightful old man whose wife had died some years prior to my birth. Matt was a reticent chap; nevertheless, he loved walking around their extensive paddocks of various crops with us kids gathering the fruit and vegetables to fill the order that Mum frequently sent us to collect. The Neils were lucky to have two good sources of water on their property and as a result were excellent growers of a wide variety of produce and kept us supplied with all our needs. I remember the many happy times we spent going to the Neils' place to buy produce as varied as cabbage, cauliflower, radish, cucumber, lettuce, carrots, pumpkins, beans, peas, turnips, tomatoes, beetroot, rock melon, rhubarb, watermelon, pineapples, passion fruit, honey-dew and cobra melon, pawpaw, and bananas. As I recall, the only staple vegetable that they did not grow was the potato.

The style of life in the 1930s, 1940s, and 1950s throughout Australia was generally basic following on from the years of war, and for us it was even more so. Our parents worked unbelievably hard to carve out a good future for themselves and their family and had little time to provide us children with lots of attention. Discipline was strict, and one could not help but adopt a strong work ethic.

The farm house that Mum and Dad moved into at the time of their marriage could only be described as spartan in the extreme in today's terms. I remember it as being a small unpainted weatherboard structure on semi-high wooden stumps with a corrugated iron roof. Inside, there were two bedrooms and an eat-in kitchen-cum-lounge with well-worn linoleum floor coverings. There were neither ceilings nor linings anywhere in the house other than in the bedrooms, which meant that one could plainly see when a snake had taken up residence in the roof rafters. A small covered veranda ran along about two-thirds of the length of the front of the house. We kids bathed in a round tin bathtub either on the front veranda or under the awning of a nearby detached building that we knew as Jacky's shed (named after a young lad Jack O'Brien who worked for Dad on occasions). This shed was a two-room structure made from vertically standing split-slab round timbers with an iron roof, compacted dirt floor, and an iron roofed awning across the front. One room served as a storeroom and the other as a bunk room for itinerant labourers. The awning served as cover for the laundry tubs, while the wood-fired copper clothes boiler stood in the open.

Electricity and telephone supply was non-existent in those days, and the water supply was from a single 4,000-litre tank, which was recharged solely by rainwater runoff from the roof, if and when it rained. Frogs swam and died in it, wrigglers (mosquito larvae) thrived in it, and other nasties such as bird poo washed off the roof and mixed with the tank water. I guess my rather strong immune system was inherited partly from that source. Water was always a scarce commodity, and on bath night, which was not too frequent, we all went through the same water in the old round tin tub. The last one probably came out almost as dirty as they were when they went in. There was no such thing as reticulated water for a garden hose, and the few plants that were growing were either very hardy or very occasionally received a small drink by way of a bucket of grey water from the bath or when Mum finished washing.

Mum did all the cooking on a wood-fired stove which heated the kitchen area terribly in summer but was cosy in winter. Dad chopped and kept the wood supply up, but from relatively early years, I had to collect the kindling for starting the fire each morning. This was one of a number of such jobs that, as a young boy, I found far from enjoyable, and I recall a number of strappings for failure to fulfil orders. The wireless, as it was then known, was powered by two large (approx. 30 cm × 20 cm × 15 cm) dry-cell batteries and was the main source of contact with the outside world. In order to get reasonable reception, it required an extensive outside aerial stretched between two tall poles about twenty-five metres apart. Still, any small atmospheric change seemed to almost obliterate what was being broadcast. The ABC midday news broadcasts were essential listening as were serialised plays such as *Stumpy* and the famous *Blue Hills* by Gwen Meredith. At night, the family sat looking at the wireless (TV had not yet been introduced to Australia) and again listened to the ABC news and serialised plays before retiring to bed early.

One story that Mum recalls from their very early years of marriage was when they had a cat. On one particular evening, she observed the cat peering anxiously under the kitchen table at which Dad sat reading. Its fur was standing on end and its back was arched ready for action. She asked Dad what was wrong with it, and he quietly said to not move as there was a snake around his legs. Fortunately, it moved away and Dad was able to despatch it. It turned out to be a deadly poisonous tiger snake.

There was no electricity, so internal lighting at night was by way of kerosene lamps with tall glass globes. For outdoor use, there were tin framed hurricane lamps. There was a torch, but it was nowhere near as powerful as those available today. The lamps had to be refilled regularly, their wicks trimmed to ensure an even, non-flickering flame, and the globes cleaned of the black soot build-up on the inside, which, if left unattended, further reduced the already paltry light. School homework was always a trial for me during the whole of my school years, and I like to put the source of the problem down to the fact that I had to do homework at the kitchen table by the dim light of a kerosene lamp in the company of my sisters, which got me off to a bad start. That is my 'tongue in cheek' excuse anyway.

A visit to the toilet was another experience indeed—one only went when absolutely necessary. It was located about thirty metres from the house and was a harbour for poisonous red-backed spiders and snakes of all kinds. It is unbelievable to us in this day and age, but the toilet was actually situated at the front of the house, off to one side and completely in the open. It was not fenced off from the surrounding cow paddock and stood out like the proverbial 'country dunny'. Nor is it surprising, in view of where the toilet was placed, to find the barn building situated directly in front of the house about fifty metres distant. Obviously, aesthetics were not high on the list of priorities of the initial land owner. As a young child, it was a terrifying experience to have to visit the toilet at night by the light of a hurricane lamp, with the noises of the night outside and 'maybe' a big brown snake (highly venomous) under the toilet seat. There was no such service as the night-cart or a rubbish collection. Dad had the unenviable job of emptying and burying the contents of the toilet can and disposing of the household rubbish, other than food scraps, which were fed to the chooks. Papers were burnt in the stove fire and tins, bottles, and other hard rubbish were despatched in a 'tip' out of sight of the house. Food packaging was very simple at the time—only cardboard boxes, newspaper, and brown paper bags. Sugar and flour were quite often purchased in bulk in hessian bags. There was no such thing as plastics, which meant that there was no fear of plastic bags and the like being blown around the farm from the 'tip' and being eaten by the cows, possibly resulting in their agonising death because of a blocked gut.

Sleeping arrangements in the little farm house were 'cosy'. My two elder sisters, Merle and Joan, shared a double bed in the second bedroom while Mum and Dad slept in a double bed and I in a bunk bed in the main bedroom. The main bedroom also accommodated a wardrobe and additionally served as Mum's sewing room, simply because that was the only space in the house where the Singer sewing machine would fit. When my younger sister Valmai Beth arrived, Mum and Dad moved with the times and sensibly dropped the Beth and called her Valmai. At first, she slept in the pram and later in a single bed in the second bedroom with her elder sisters. It was not until my younger brother Colin Thomas arrived six years later that a larger house was built to accommodate the then five children.

CHAPTER 2

The Early Years of Farming

D ad always had a driven work ethic, and it would be fair to say that he was a 'workaholic' who possessed a high level of intelligence and sound commonsense. Over time, he was able to add his father's and then his brother's farms to his original land holding.

My paternal grandfather died in 1938, the year prior to my birth, and he left his farm solely to Dad. I expect that this would have caused quite some friction amongst his seven siblings, and as I understand the situation, there was no requirement for Dad to pay any money to any of them. Dad and Mum undertook to look after all of Ma's needs for the remainder of her life, and it is my assumption (quite possibly wrong) that this was a verbal agreement entered into prior to Grandfather's death and one that influenced the decision in his will. Mum adored her mother-in-law and the feeling was mutual, so it was an easy undertaking for my parents to enter into and uphold. The house where Grandfather and Ma lived on their farm was approx. two kilometres from our house. This made it difficult for Dad and Mum to be in everyday contact with Ma, so Dad built her a small house about 200 metres from our home, where she lived her remaining days. It consisted of an eat-in kitchen, bedroom, bathroom, and a front veranda with an enclosed 'bedroom' at one end. The wall and roof were of galvanised iron, and I do not recall if it had any ceilings. It was freezing in winter and must have been very hot in summer. Ma was a wonderful grandmother, and even though I was not quite six when she passed away, I still have very fond memories of the many very enjoyable times that Merle, Joan, Valmai, and I had at her little home. Sometimes we all piled into her double bed in the morning after we awoke from a sleepover at her place and she told us stories. She passed away in the Mt Morgan hospital, and I recall that just before she died, Dad took us into her room one by one to say our goodbyes to her.

As sad as the event of Ma's death was in the Mt Morgan Hospital, whenever I think about the occasion it reminds me of the horror of me having to spend a week or so on two occasions in the same hospital. The first time was as a two-year-old to have my adenoids and tonsils removed. I suffered a repeat of the same operation when I was eight. Apparently, the first operation was not fully successful and they had re-grown and become infected once more. I do not have a memory of the first experience, but I vividly recall the second visit. It was terrifying—a country kid, being away from home for the first time and in a hospital room on my own, having to suffer the indignity of an enema and that terrible chloroform mask (which was used in those days) with its nauseating after-effects. I still remember Dad's little port (suitcase), which contained my few possessions, being placed up on the shelf above my hospital bed.

A few years after Grandfather's death, Uncle Les sold his dairy farm to Dad. This farm adjoined both Dad's and Grandfather's farm. When the areas of all three farms were amalgamated, Dad owned a combined total of approx. 140 hectares (350 acres) of mostly fairly good quality dairying country. Uncle Les's farm contained a reasonable portion of forest country not terribly well suited to dairying, and I think he possibly found it difficult to maintain a family of six children while they were there. He moved his family to a dairy farm in better dairying country near Gympie. We were all very sorry to see Uncle Les, Auntie Beryl, and our cousins leave Struck Oil as we kids had all lived very closely together the whole of our lives up to that point in time.

Dad always worked extremely hard and fast and expected all those around him to do likewise. He was a teetotaller, scrupulously honest, of the highest integrity, forthright, and did not suffer fools gladly. He set about the task of converting his rather dilapidated dairy farm asset into a highly productive and profitable enterprise and used every hour of daylight plus many hours of the night, seven days per week, fifty-two weeks per year, year in year out without a break, to achieve his goal. Mum recalls that the farm he purchased from Mrs Morgan was very run-down and the improvements on the other two farms that they eventually acquired were similarly in relatively poor state of repair. The dairy shed, milking bails, and cow yard fences were falling down, and there were no milking machines or reticulated water for the cows to drink from troughs at the yards or for washing milking equipment. There was no cattle dip despite the fact that ticks were an ever-present menace to cattle throughout Queensland and had a severe adverse effect on milk production if left uncontrolled. Cultivation for growing crops was virtually non-existent and pastures were generally of inferior quality consisting mainly of native grasses, which lacked nutrition in drought conditions. The dairy herd was sub-standard and fences were generally in poor repair—a daunting undertaking and not one for the faint-hearted.

Firstly, Dad set about improving the dairy herd by gradually introducing highly productive, quality jersey cows and heifers, which he purchased, as he could afford them, from Alf Ohl of

Kokotungo near Dululu (south-west of Mt Morgan). Alf was a frequent winner of dairy cattle prizes at the Rockhampton Agricultural Show, where he regularly exhibited his stud dairy cattle. In later years when we were living in Rockhampton, I used to spend a lot of time helping Alf at the showground when the show was in progress. I even got to lead one of his champion heifers in the grand parade one year when I was about fourteen. As often happens when cattle get into an open area such as a show arena after having been tied up in stalls for days on end, they play up and want to frolic about. This heifer played up no end and attempted to drag me around the ring. Fortunately, my previous experience with dairy cattle enabled me to keep her fairly well under control, and despite my embarrassment at her behaviour in front of thousands of people, I was able to prevent her from upsetting the grand parade too badly.

In their initial years on the farm, Dad and Mum commenced milking by hand at 2 a.m., and then when that was finished, Dad separated the cream from the milk by use of a hand-driven separator. He then took the cream to Moongan railway siding, where it was collected and taken to Rockhampton by train to be made into butter. As the milk production capacity of the dairy herd improved, Dad commenced a fresh milk run in Mt Morgan. When milking was finished, he had breakfast, then did the milk run and returned home about 11 a.m., when Mum would wash all the pint and quart pots, billies, and milk cans ready for the afternoon milking session. After lunch, Dad again rounded up the cows (on foot) for the second milking session of the day, then again separated all the milk. The cream was held until the following day, and the separated milk was fed to the pigs. Mum again had the task of washing all the milking utensils. When the afternoon milking session was finished, Dad took his afternoon tea, axe, and mattock and chopped down trees and grubbed out roots for the beginning of cultivation paddocks. He did this until almost dark when he again rounded up the cows, put them into the night paddock, then went home for an evening meal and an early night with milking due to commence again at 2 a.m.

As milk production and quality continued to improve, Dad came to an arrangement to sell the milk run and supply fresh milk to a chap named Horace (Horrie) Gregson, who would then deliver it to homes and shops in Mt Morgan. Gregson collected the milk at about 7 a.m. (365 days per year) and again early afternoon each day. The early morning collection meant that Dad and Mum had the luxury of now starting milking at about 3 a.m. every morning in order to finish the milking of about thirty-five cows by hand on time. The only lights in the bails were a couple of hurricane lamps and in winter time temperatures were quite often below freezing.

In 1937, when my sister Merle was a toddler and Mum was six months pregnant with Joan, Struck Oil experienced a very severe drought. Dad had not as yet been able to provide and store hay for drought conditions and had to move the cows on agistment to a property at Boongary about thirty kilometres away from Struck Oil. He set up temporary milking bails on that property and they lived in a tent nearby. After a couple of weeks, they received torrential rain and were flooded out. The owner of the property lived in Rockhampton and graciously allowed them to move into his house for the remainder of their stay, which was about a further two months. Each Sunday afternoon, they took a drive back to Struck Oil to see that everything was okay at the farm. It was during one of these visits that Dad's father called to see them and suffered a heart attack and died before they could get him to hospital. As time passed, because of Joan's imminent birth, Mum went to stay with Dad's brother Vic and his wife Gladys in Mt Morgan as it was considered to be too risky for her to stay at the isolated Boongary property. When Joan arrived a few weeks later, the grass on the farm had recovered from the drought and grown sufficiently to allow Dad to take the cattle home.

When Merle was the only baby, Mum got by with having Merle in a pram at the bails while she milked the cows. When Joan arrived eighteen months later, she needed the pram and there was a real problem as to what to do with Merle while the milking was in progress. Mum told me that the only way they could cope was to leave Joan in the pram and Merle in the cot sleeping at the house until she arrived back from milking. Quite often she arrived at the house to the sound of two crying babies, and at times, due to the stress this caused, she joined in the crying session. When I arrived eighteen months later again, Eileen O'Brien, a neighbour's fifteen-year-old daughter (a younger sister of Jacky who worked for Dad from time to time), was hired to look after all three of us. She rode her bike about three kilometres around the dirt road to our place and worked from about 6.30 a.m. to about 3 p.m. daily. I have faint but very good recollections of Eileen's care of us. She still lives in Mt Morgan and is now about ninety years of age, and she and Mum kept in touch at Xmas up until 2014.

Chapter 3

Hard Work for Us All

From the age of about four or five, we three older kids were expected to contribute to the workings of the farm. When not at school, we were all involved in rounding up the cows in the paddocks and bringing them to the yards for milking and doing other tasks around the milking shed and farm.

Dad was a hard taskmaster, and there was no room for us kids to play when there was work to be done. He had got it tough as a kid and I guess he saw no reason to go easy on us. Although he no doubt loved us dearly, he found it hard to show his affection and insisted that we be brought up strictly. Winters in Struck Oil often brought temperatures below freezing, and I was considered a sissy if I wanted to wear shoes to round up the cows at 5 a.m. when the frost was thick on the grass. Torches were not allowed either, so we had to walk the paddock in the dark in winter, stir the cows from their sleeping place, and then stand momentarily where the cows had been to warm our feet a little. Similarly, there would be warm water available from the wood-fired steriliser at the dairy when milking commenced, but we were not allowed to use it and had to use freezing water to wash the cows' udders before the milking started.

The stories from these times are many. One such story revolves round two missing cows. About 5 a.m. one early weekend morning, Joan and I had been assigned the usual job of bringing the cows to the dairy from the night paddock. When we got them to the yards and counted them, there were two cows missing. All the cows had names, and we knew that Yella and Big Red (named in keeping with the colour of their coats) had disappeared. They were a pair of misfits that Dad had bought from a chap named Sammy Richards of Bouldercombe, a district situated between Struck Oil and Rockhampton. Sammy was an old chap who lived as a hermit in a hut with a few dogs, chooks, and cows and Dad purchased the cows just to help the poor old fellow to exist. Joan and I went back up the paddock with Peter, our cattle dog, to locate the missing cows. Peter disappeared into a patch of lantana growing amongst big rocks, and the next thing, he came running straight to us with his tail between his legs and a big dingo right behind him. I don't know who got the biggest fright—the dog, the dingo, or us. On very many occasions, we had listened to the eerie howling of the dingoes at night-time, but neither Joan nor I had ever seen a dingo up close before then, nor had the dog, and I think all three of us thought we were about to be eaten. I screamed at the dingo, more in fright than anything else, and it took off into the long grass—it had been so fixated on the dog up until that point that I do not think it had seen us. It quickly disappeared down into the paddock and we did likewise back to the yards. Dad later went to investigate and found the two missing cows in the small patch of scrub where the dingo had chased after the dog. Big Red had calved during the night and the dingo had been trying to get at the calf. With the help of Yella, she had been able to fend off the dingo and protect the calf.

These two cows were the source of other adventures in my life. At the age of about eight or nine, I rode my pony to Bouldercombe with Dad the day he went to Sammy Richard's place to bring home

Yella and Big Red and was all excited about the big horseback trip. My pony, Bonny, had not been ridden for a while, and when I got on her that morning she behaved very uncharacteristically and started to buck. She soon dislodged me from the saddle and ran away, dragging me along with my foot caught in the stirrup iron. Fortunately, Dad was nearby on his horse and was able to stop Bonny before any real damage was done. The main thing that was hurt was my pride as the whole family was looking on. Dad jumped on my pony and gave her a rough time up and down the paddock and took the misbehaviour out of her. She was very docile after that.

The route to Bouldercombe was past the old house where Dad grew up, across the Dee River, then about three kilometres along a very infrequently used gravel road to the top of a spur of the Dee Range, a part of the Great Dividing Range, and another kilometre or so down the Range on a single file track to Sammy's shanty. The intent was to drive these two cows back up the track to the top of the Range from where we could drive them along the road to the gate into our place. The cows were a pair of 'scrubbers' and had other ideas. They soon left the track and headed straight up the very steep side of the mountain range. Dad took off on foot after them as the terrain was too steep to ride a horse up and yelled over his shoulder to me to get the horses to the top of the range and meet him there. There was no possibility of the two horses walking side by side on the track. As my horse was at the rear, I tied her reins to the stirrup iron of the saddle of Dad's horse. When I tried to get Dad's horse to move forward, she would stop as soon as the reins of my pony pulled on the stirrup of Dad's saddle and my pony refused to follow. It didn't matter what I tried; neither horse would cooperate in a follow-the-leader type move. I was just about frantic by the time Dad came back looking for me. I knew he would be annoyed and really exhausted from what he had just been through, and I was right. He gave me a tongue lashing and then we mounted our horses and got to the top of the mountain range as quickly as possible and eventually caught up with the two cows, which were still trotting along the road that Dad had shepherded them on to. Luckily, they had kept to the road as there were no fences in this extensive Crown Land forest and they could have disappeared in any direction. We got them both home without further mishap, but they were always trouble in the bails, weren't very productive milkers, and I imagine Dad often wondered why he ever entered into the exercise of 'being good to Sammy'.

I have often wondered how Dad knew the country around the top of the Dee Range and the track down to Bouldercombe so well, and it wasn't until some sixty years later that I learnt the secret from one of my brothers-in-law. After I had been transferred away from home, Graham McMillan, who married my sister Valmai, used to sit on the front veranda of our house (then in Rockhampton) and listen to Dad relating stories of his youth. It seems that on occasions, Dad and some of his sisters and brothers used to either take their horses or walk along the very same track to and from Bouldercombe while attending dances on moonlight nights. I recall that the track down the mountain was rough going, and one wonders how the women's shoes stood up to the stony path and how their dresses fared against the bushes and grasses intruding across the track. Perhaps the track was more often used in Dad's youth and therefore more orderly.

World War II began earlier in the year that I was born and it had a big effect on Dad's ability to get things done on the farm. He was not able to enlist because his role as a farmer was classified as an essential service. However, his young brother Sydney Edward (Syd) enlisted at the age of twenty-three years in the 2/15 Infantry Battalion in Rockhampton on 13 June 1940 and sadly was killed in action at Tobruk, Libya, on 29 June 1941. A history of his war service is in Appendix III; also included in Appendix IV is a copy of Lieutenant Christie's report on the activities of his patrol on the night that Syd was killed. In Appendix V is my best endeavour to decipher a crumbling air letter that Ma received from Lieutenant Christie after Syd's death. Mum recalls Syd as being a wonderful young man and said that Ma never got over the loss. Dad never talked to me about Syd's death, but we always had a large framed photograph of him dressed in his army uniform and looking very handsome hanging in pride of place in the house. Apparently, he and Syd were very close and Dad missed him greatly.

Dad became a member of the Volunteer Defence Corps (VDC) and undertook regular night training in Mt Morgan. Blackout restrictions applied and vehicles had to be driven at night with hooded lights. Dad's father was amongst the first in the Struck Oil district to own a modern Ford utility, and Dad eventually acquired it from his parents. Like all other vehicles, it had to have a white strip about five centimetres wide painted around the mudguards to make it more visible to other drivers at night. Fortunately, there were few cars on the roads in those days and gravel roads were so rough that only slow speeds were possible.

As the war in the South Pacific intensified, the Australian Government called for all aluminium utensils to be handed in to help the war effort, so off went all our saucepans and anything else made of aluminium. The thrust of the Japanese southwards into the West Pacific gathered pace with the fall of Malaya (now Malaysia) and Singapore, the invasion of Papua New Guinea (PNG), which commenced with landings on the north coast of that country, and then the historic bombing of Pearl Harbour on 8 December 1941, the day my wife was born. It was only two months after Pearl Harbour on 19 February 1942 that the same Japanese force attacked Darwin with 188 aircraft, resulting in huge damage because of very heavy bombing and strafing by machine guns. The damage to shipping in Darwin harbour was said to be more extensive than that which occurred at Pearl Harbour as was the loss of life and damage to buildings and military installations. No allied planes were lost as there were none there; the bulk of the Australian Air Force was in combat in North Africa. Air attacks on towns such as Townsville and Mossman in Queensland and Broome, Port Hedland, and Exmouth in Western Australia, soon followed. In total, the Japanese carried out ninety-seven air raids on Australia.

In PNG, the Japanese were quickly heading towards Port Moresby via the Kokoda Track and Australia's freedom was severely threatened. Almost none of these happenings were known to the Australian public at the time as the Government placed a 'blackout' on publication of this type of bad news, supposedly in the interests of not alarming the public. It is interesting to find that even today very few Australians know the real facts of that era and do not understand just how close we all came to being under the control of the Emperor of Japan. Dad and Mum devised a plan that should the Japanese land on Australian soil they would shoot all the animals on the farm and move inland to Biloela, where Dad's sister Doris and her husband Uncle Toby Henry lived. Dad would no doubt have then enlisted in the army. A large store of tinned food was kept on hand in the storeroom of the slab hut for such an emergency. I recall that after the War had ended, Mum gradually made use of the stored tinned foods. One can of tinned peas that she used had obviously passed its safe use by date (no such thing on labels in those days), and we all ended up with a dose of food poisoning. We kids had to stay home from school for a day because we were so sick with vomiting, stomach pains, and chronic diarrhoea. My teacher failed to accept that as a reasonable excuse for being absent and assumed I was telling a lie and I got the cane. School was very different then!

American troops were stationed near Rockhampton in the latter half of the war years and carried out training exercises in surrounding areas. I vividly recall, at the age of about five, seeing a platoon of soldiers marching up the road to the dairy in the early afternoon heat as we kids stood in the bails with Dad and Mum when they were milking the cows. I had heard a lot of talk about the 'Japs' and the fact that they were 'coming' and was petrified that they had arrived and that we were all about to be killed. In actual fact, the soldiers were Americans on an exercise and they were fascinated to see cows being milked by hand; most were seeing cows milked for the first time in their lives. Dad was also separating milk at the time, and the separated milk was going directly to the pigs via a pipeline while the cream was pouring into a cream can of about twenty litres capacity. We kids were amazed to see these soldiers drinking mug after mug of separated milk, which we kids termed 'pig feed'. Today, almost the same separated milk is sold in cartons in supermarkets as healthy food at amazingly expensive prices. The platoon eventually marched off, but one soldier soon returned with a very embarrassed red face as he had forgotten to take his rifle with him.

The memory of the day peace was declared (14th August 1945) and the war had ended remains clear in my mind. We were at school in Mt Morgan and a formation of fighter aircraft flew over the primary school. There was great elation everywhere, and that night our family joined the celebrations in town. There were people decked out in fancy dress and there were lots of lights, fireworks, dancing in the street, noise, music, and laughter. We virtually never ever went out at night because of the early morning milking, and although there was joy and excitement everywhere, I recall it as a quite frightening experience for me.

The rationing of food, clothing, petrol, and many other products was introduced by the Federal Government early in the war years, and for many food products, these restrictions continued for long after the war had ended. This was primarily due to the need for Australian food to be diverted to Britain in order to feed its devastated and hungry population. Food rationing was not fully lifted until 1950. Penalties for breaching rationing laws were severe, and there were no limits placed on the fines or prison terms that could be imposed. In order to obtain fuel for the farm utility, Dad had to present his petrol coupons, and once they were used, there was no more fuel to be had until the next issue of coupons in a month's time. Food-wise, we were definitely luckier than most as we produced our own milk, cream, butter, eggs, and chickens. Also, there was a ready supply of many types of vegetables and fruits available from Neils' next door, without having to produce ration coupons. I remember that rice, which had to be imported back then, was not available at all for some years after the war and the same applied to many other imported goods. Due to the financially damaging effect of the war on our economy, Australia simply could not afford to pay for many desirable imports.

In 1946, Central Queensland was hit very badly by a prolonged drought. The dairy cattle suffered terribly from both lack of feed in the paddocks and sufficient water to fully quench their thirst. Dad and Mum worked like Trojans, making lucerne chaff from the stack of hay in the hay shed. In order to make chaff, Dad had to first fork the hay down from the top of the stack, then put it through the chaff-cutter, a difficult and quite dangerous job (many people have lost their fingers and/or arms in this process). With Mum's assistance, large hessian chaff bags were then filled with chaff and finally that had to be fed to the cows day after day, when the milking sessions had finished. The most worrying thing was the shortage of water, both at the house and for the stock. In the early afternoon, Horrie Gregson, the milkman, used to bring back the morning's milk cans filled with water from the Mt Morgan town water system, and this was used to wash and sterilise the milking equipment. Water for the cattle was available from only one well about two kilometres from the dairy and the water level in the well was so low that the pump was unable to lift the water from the bottom of the well into the nearby water trough from which the cows drank. Dad stood on the huge timbers surrounding the top of the well each day and hauled the water out by hand in twenty-litre bucketfuls on the end of a rope until sufficient water had been poured into the nearby trough to almost satisfy the thirst of all the cows. This was unbelievably back-breaking work, but it had to be done in addition to taking care of all the extra difficulties that presented themselves at this critical time. No more water was available to the cows until he repeated the exercise the next day, and the next, and the next. Despite all their hard work, some cows did not survive and the supply of milk was severely depleted. As a consequence, income would have reduced while costs must have increased markedly. I cannot imagine a more depressing or demanding experience for my parents to have to endure.

After this horrifying drought experience, Dad decided to improve the water supply situation so as not to be caught by drought like that again. He hired a man who saw himself as expert in water divining, and they searched the entire property in an endeavour to find a better underground water source. Their efforts were fruitless, other than the indications of a possible small supply near the front gate of the property. It was determined that the indications of water availability there were not sufficiently strong to warrant the cost of sinking a test bore in the hope of finding water, and the decision was made to improve the small flow that we already had in the existing well. Dad first had to bail all the water from the well (and repeatedly do so throughout the duration of the work), then proceed to deepen the well by hammering a steel drill bit with a heavy-headed hammer time and time and time again until a hole about thirty centimetres deep was cut into the solid blue metal rock at the bottom of the well. He was assisted by Uncle Vic, who was then a miner in Mt Morgan. Once a number of holes had been successfully drilled in the rock, these were filled with dynamite with a fuse attached. We kids were sent about a hundred metres away for safety sake. The fuse was lit by Dad at the bottom of the well, and he then scrambled up the ladder out of the well, pulled the ladder up behind him, and ran for cover. Next came a huge explosion and large chunks of rock were hurled into the air, and on occasions some landed in close proximity. It was a thrilling time for us kids, but the work was dangerous and extremely hard for Dad and Uncle Vic. After the explosive charge had gone off and the smoke and dust had cleared from the well, it was down the well again for either Dad or Uncle Vic to shovel the loose rock into buckets which were then winched to the surface by the other and disposed of before drilling could again commence. After lowering the depth of the well more than a metre, a marginally better water supply was obtained, but still it was barely adequate for the needs of the farm in dry weather.

It was another year or so before non-galvanised steel water pipe (black polythene pipe had not yet been invented) was available due to shortage of steel after the war. Dad was then able to run a five-centimetre diameter pipeline from the well to the dairy. He equipped the well with a windmill in addition to the petrol engine and erected a holding tank on top of a hill halfway to the dairy. This allowed the water to be pumped to the holding tank as the wind blew and be stored and reticulated to the dairy as required. A trough was erected in the yards where the cows were able to drink as much water as they desired during each milking session, and water was readily available to the dairy for cleaning and sterilising purposes. Additionally, water was available for garden use at the house, but very sparingly.

In addition to all the other work he and Mum did, Dad was continually working at clearing some paddocks of all trees, stumps, and logs in preparation for cultivation. He first felled the trees with an axe (there were no chainsaws), then dug out the smaller stumps and their roots by hand with a mattock. Larger stumps were either blasted out with dynamite or burnt out after they dried by stacking lots of timber around them and setting fire to them. The remaining fallen trees and stumps were pulled into stacks with the aid of a draught horse and then burnt when dry. Once this was done, he could commence ploughing the land, walking behind a horse-drawn plough, a tractor not being affordable until later. When the initial ploughing was completed and the remaining tree roots that had been ripped to the surface were picked up, stacked, and burnt, the sewing of the crop by way of hand broadcast could begin. Lucerne was the main crop, and this meant walking up and down the paddock and time and time again broadcasting the lucerne seed by hand as evenly as possible. Later came the mowing of the mature lucerne sitting on a horse-drawn mower, followed by raking the crop into rows sitting on a horse-drawn rake, then raking the rows into stooks by hand with a pitchfork (long wooden handle with three steel prongs), then loading the stooks on to a horse-drawn dray by hand with the aid of the pitchfork, and lastly packing the hay into the hay shed by hand, again with the pitchfork. Later Dad found it more convenient to use the Ford utility to cart the hay to the shed if the cultivation paddock was not too steep. One day I was perched right up on top of a high load on the back of the utility. As Dad ascended a short but rather steep incline near the hay shed, the load tipped off backwards and I landed under it on the gravel road. Dad moved fast to find and extract me, and it was one of the few times that I noted an expression of concern on his face for my well-being. I was not hurt other than for a bit of gravel rash and some bruising, but it was not a fun experience. Thereafter, I sat in the front seat with Dad rather than up on top of the load.

We had five big Clydesdale draught horses that Dad used for ploughing, mowing lucerne, and carting wood and all other produce grown on the property. They were named Boulder, Nugget, Silver, Taffy, and Don. The latter two draught horses were purchased from a Mrs Kirkpatrick, who lived in the Dalma district, west of Rockhampton. Dad drove them home over a distance of about fifty kilometres un-roped, while riding his horse and keeping Taffy and Don in front of him—quite some feat. They did not settle well and soon escaped and headed for their old home. At first, Dad had a very difficult job finding them and then getting them back again, but they stayed after that. He also had two riding horses: Lucy, a fine-looking bay racehorse type, and Fairy, who was a very good, solid, silvery chestnut stock horse. It was often the job for us kids to round up the horses into the yards when Dad wanted to use them for farm work. They were cunning and knew when we commenced driving them towards the yards that work was on the programme for some of them, so they used to give us the run around the paddock. We would be on foot, so it wasn't too difficult to outrun us, but we learnt to outwit them and eventually we would get them into the laneway that led to the yards. Even then at times, they would attempt a breakaway by galloping flat out back down the narrow lane directly at us in the hope that we would get out of the way. Although we were frightened by the sight of these huge horses thundering towards us, we were more frightened of the tongue-lashing we would get from Dad if we didn't have the horses in the yard on time, so we had to call their bluff and shout and wave our arms in front of them to turn them around. We generally won the contest. Sometimes we lost our nerve and had to duck under the fence out of the way and then proceed to do another round of the paddock.

CHAPTER 4

Modernising the Farm

—————◦►●◄◦—————

I t was not only the land that was being continually improved. Both the farm buildings and the herd underwent constant upgrading.

The rebuilding of the cow yards, dairy shed, and milking bails was a major undertaking. All the post holes for the cow yards had to be dug by hand and all round bush timbers sawn by hand and dressed with adzes (an axe-like tool with the blade at right angles to the handle) and axes. The milking shed frame was constructed using milled timbers, but again the structures of the milking bails were made from round timbers. The floor of the bails was concreted as was a large covered apron area where a small number of cows at a time were brought from the main yard and held in preparation for their milking. Dad also repaired and replaced boundary and internal paddock fencing. This required him to first of all clear, by hand, the fence line of all trees, undergrowth, dead timber, and stumps. He then had to select and fell those trees that were suitable for strainer posts (stout posts which were able to withstand the strain of the tensioned fence wires) and intermediate fence posts, remove the bark from the trunk, a difficult task accomplished with the skilful use of the back of the axe head, and cut the tree trunk into suitable fence post lengths with a hand-powered crosscut saw. He then had to haul the logs to the fencing site by draught horse and split each piece of log lengthwise into three intermediate fence posts by using steel wedges strategically placed and hammered into the log with the back of an axe. Next was the task of digging the post holes, all of which were done by hand with a crow bar and shovel, whether the ground was soft, dry and hard or a lot of rocks were encountered. The posts were then lifted by hand and stood upright in the holes, lined up in a perfectly straight line, the holes back-filled with dirt and rammed tight with the head of the crowbar so that the post stood firmly in place. Each post then had holes, usually four, bored through it at varying heights with a hand brace and bit so that four barbed wires could be dragged from post to post and threaded through each hole until the end of the fence line was reached, then strained up tight and tied off to complete a stock-proof barrier. Kilometres of new fencing were erected in this back-breaking manner in between milking sessions, in addition to all the other improvement work Dad was carrying out. He was in his mid-thirties about this time, apparently in the prime of his life, and seemed to thrive on endless work. However, it was to catch up with him in the not too distant future.

At the beginning of 1945, Dad and Mum decided to have their first holiday break away from the farm since they had been married nine years previously. He was beginning to show signs of suffering from overwork and it was on doctor's orders that he took the break. They found people to care for the farm and milk the cows and took us all to Yeppoon, a seaside town near Rockhampton, for two months. This was the first time any of us kids had seen the sea and it was a great thrill. Ma was with us, and I recall that she took us kids to the pictures at the Regent Theatre one Saturday afternoon to see a movie about pirates. I had only ever been to the movies once or twice before that in Mt Morgan. We sat down near the front to get a good view and I was terrified by the sword-fighting and bloodcurdling action of the pirates. I couldn't get out of the theatre quickly enough.

The school year commenced while we were in Yeppoon, and that was where I started school for a few weeks. Merle and Joan went to the Yeppoon State School also for the short time that we were there. I was almost run over by a car on the way home from my first day at school—a country kid not used to having to look both ways before making a move, and the car stopped just in time. When we got back to the farm, there were big problems. It was a good season and the cows were producing large quantities of milk. Hand milking was an extremely testing job for people who were not used to milking cows, and the people looking after the farm had taken short cuts and had not fully stripped all the milk from the cows each time they milked. This resulted in the cows giving less and less milk daily and of course reflected very adversely in the income cheque from milk sales. Needless to say, we never went on another holiday before Dad sold the farm some six years later.

It was good farming practice when pregnant cows were getting closer to calving that they were dried off (gradually stop milking them) and spelled in what we called the 'dry' paddock for a month or so before the calf was born. There were always in between six to ten cows in this group. Dad kept a record of each cow's calving date by noting when the bull was in action, and he used to visit the dry paddock regularly to check progress in calving. Any cow that had calved was brought back to the yards, together with her calf, to rejoin the milking herd. Often it was very difficult to find the calf as it was natural for the mother to hide the newborn when she went feeding. Some cows were so protective of their calves that we had to be very careful of those with horns so as not to be charged and knocked down and gored. Dad did not have sufficient country to rear his own replacement heifers for the milking herd, so the calves quickly became a liability. After a few days, the new mother would be ready to return to the milking herd again and Dad would despatch the calf. If we kids were around and saw him get the axe and his pocket knife, we hid behind a big butcher's block in the dairy so that we could not see the action. We would cover our ears, but we could still hear the thud as the back of the axe crushed the calf's skull. It was then our job to drag the dead calf down the paddock to an old mine shaft where it was left for the dingoes to feed on.

As part of his strategy to have a purely Jersey dairy herd, Dad bought a good quality young Jersey bull from Alf Ohl and put him with the dry cows until he was old enough to work, i.e. to commence serving cows. We called this very good-looking young bull Jupiter. When I was about nine, Dad and I were in the dry paddock one day trying to find a new calf, which, by the mother's behaviour, had obviously been born very recently. Each of us was looking in different areas of the paddock amongst the long grass. I saw Jupiter purposefully heading my way and took no notice until he started to bellow and show all the signs of aggressive intent to charge at me. It was clear that he did not welcome intruders in what he now saw as his territory. There were no trees nearby that I could climb, but there was a standing dead tree with a very large trunk, behind which I quickly got. He was persistent, but I was able to keep ducking out of his way around the tree, while at the same time calling for Dad to help me. Eventually, Dad heard me and came to the rescue. The bull was going to have a go at Dad too, but one good whack from a big stick was enough to encourage him to do otherwise.

Later, when Jupiter was running with the dairy herd, we kids kept a very close eye on him when we were rounding up the cows. His anger seemed to increase as he matured, and he charged Dad in the yard one day. Fortunately, Mum saw what was happening from where she was standing in the bails. She yelled to Dad, who turned around to his left to see what she was screaming for and the bull just missed him on the right side. Jupiter wanted to carry on with the fight, so Dad went out to the woodheap, got a large and solid tree branch about five centimetres thick and two metres long, and confronted the bull. Jupiter charged again, and Dad knocked him down with the log of wood across the head. If it had not been for Mum, Dad would have shot him there and then. He didn't attempt his tricks again on Dad but was always a surly and untrustworthy animal, and we kids took great care to ensure that we had the dog with us when we were in the open paddocks with him and the cows. We knew that if he charged us we would be able to sool the dog on to him and get to safety while the dog worried him.

For some unknown reason, Jupiter hated Mum more than he seemed to hate most people. In winter, as the mornings warmed a little Mum would discard a jumper or coat and hang it over the rails of the yard, out of the way. If he saw her jumper or coat hanging there and could get near it, he would paw the ground and roar in anger. Before Dad bought Jupiter, we had a large Illawarra breed bull called Major. He was generally of good temperament but used to get edgy on occasions and particularly in wet weather. One stormy evening, Merle, Joan, and I were bringing the cows in and he decided to take to us. Luckily, we were able to dive under a nearby barbed-wire fence, through which he didn't follow us. Major and a neighbour's bull used to fight through the boundary fence on occasions, and Dad used to get furious as they would rip out panels of fencing that he then would have to replace. If the job was left to the neighbour's, it would never have been done; also, Dad didn't want their bull messing with our cows.

Initially, Merle and Joan started school at the Struck Oil State School, which had opened in 1905. However, it was closed at the end of the 1944 school year, and after that the kids in the district

47

were transported daily by bus to Mt Morgan. This is thought to have been one of the first school bus services in Queensland. We had to leave home about 7 a.m., say hello and goodbye to Dad and Mum as we walked past the milking shed, and continue walking about three kilometres across country to meet the school bus. I never wore shoes to primary school, but the girls did. We all walked barefoot until our track crossed the Dee River which also ran through the western part of our property. Here the girls washed their feet in the water, dried them on some old towels kept there for the purpose, and put on socks and shoes. In winter time, our feet used to absolutely burn from the cold of the frosty grass, and we held sugar bags in front of us as we walked along the track to prevent the dew on the long grass overhanging the track from wetting our clothes. In summer, we had to do the same thing to stop the sticky ergot grass seed from the paspalum grass sticking to our clothes and legs.

The school bus driver was a chap named Ernie Clanfield. He lived in Mt Morgan and had a day job at the mine. He had a dreadful habit of repeatedly sniffing and jerking in his seat as he drove the bus, and we kids used to mock him terribly. Occasionally, he would threaten to put us all off the bus for misbehaviour. He collected us each afternoon from school about 4.15 p.m. after his shift at the mine ended and we got to our 'home' stop about 5 p.m. It was our job to round up the cows after we got home, count them, and put them into the night paddock. In winter, Dad used to graze the cows in a paddock where we could round them up on the way home from the school bus. Even so, we used to have difficulty getting an accurate count as the cows milled around in the yard in the rapidly fading winter light. Occasionally, we had to go back searching for a missing cow or two, and eventually we would get home in the dark. There was one cow named Alice that specialised in hiding along tracks through small clumps of lantana, which Dad was yet to clear. I recall us all being very frightened when we had to go back and search these areas as darkness was falling. If we saw Alice before she saw us, we would sneak up on her and try to frighten her badly in the hope that she would in future desist from her sneaky habit, but it was to no avail.

It was around 1946 that Dad was able to afford to install milking machines. They were an enormous time and labour saver and took a lot of the hard manual work out of the milking process. It allowed Dad and Mum to commence milking at about 5 a.m., which made a great improvement to both their lives. The next improvement was the construction of a spray dip and associated yards for treating the cows against the adverse impact of the cattle tick. The cows hated going through the race of sprays that thoroughly wet them with a DDT spray, and it was not good to be around the dip on dipping day. The cows literally had to be forced up the race into the sprays, and it was very stressful for all concerned. However, there was little alternative as not spraying against the cattle tick would result in the cows being virtually covered in ticks, all of which would busily suck their blood until the ticks were bloated and then fell off. They then proceeded to lay a large quantity of eggs and so the cycle began again with their hatchlings crawling up grass stems and clinging to the next cow that passed by. In the meantime, if left untreated each animal continually lost more blood, which resulted in loss of condition and a fall in milk production; in very severe cases, it could result in the death of the beast.

During the dipping process, Dad would become completely soaked with the DDT spray, and it is only while writing this story that I have begun to wonder whether it could have been the effects of this deadly carcinogenic chemical (not known to be so then) that might have been responsible or even partly responsible for his death by cancer in later years. Another contributing factor to Dad's death could have been that at Mum's instigation and to her now great embarrassment, Dad became a cigarette smoker from

49

the age of about twenty-five years until he gave the habit up in his early forties.

The cattle dip was constructed from long-lasting ironbark bush timbers. Dad especially selected the trees, from which the posts and rails were to be cut, from a property about five kilometres away. The construction was a major task as the posts were about four metres long, thirty-five centimetres in diameter, and really heavy to work with. Post holes about 1.25 metres deep had to be dug by hand, many of which were into almost solid rock, and these huge posts hauled into an upright position by manpower alone. All the precise sawing and very skilful adzing to fit the rails into slots in the posts had to be done by hand; hundreds of holes then had to be bored through the timbers with a hand brace and bit so the rails could be tied into place securely with heavy-duty plain fencing wire. A recent photograph shows the now derelict race portion of the dip still standing drunkenly in place, some sixty plus years after its initial construction.

The hay barn was a very old, large shed with a frame of round timbers, upright split round timber slab walls, and an iron roof, mostly two storeys high, with a single-storey skillion roofed area attached on the southern side where drays, sulkies, horse and other equipment was stored. The building also housed areas for a garage for the utility, a workshop, and an area for making chaff. The chaff-cutter was driven through a series of belts and pulleys by one of the oldest single piston petrol engines that one could imagine. It was cantankerous and repeatedly refused to start. It was used infrequently, and although it had few moving parts it often caused Dad grief and he would have to dismantle it before he could get it started and commence the job he was about to undertake.

The same engine was used to drive the big circular saw when Dad cut dead tree limbs into blocks for firewood. The circular saw was a particularly dangerous piece of equipment. It was set in a moveable saw bench; the logs of timber were placed across the bench, and the bench gradually moved forward until the saw blade engaged the timber when, if all went well, there was a clean cut and the operator moved on to the next cut. However, pieces of wood often flew off in all directions and eye injuries were common because of this sort of work as no protective goggles were worn (no OH&S legislation in those days). At times, the timber being cut had knots in it. When a knot hit the saw blade, lack of concentration sometimes led to the timber twisting rapidly and dragging the operator's hand or arm into the saw blade with drastic results. Fortunately, Dad never suffered any severe injuries from this work. We kids were required to stand back at a safe distance to watch the process. The high-pitched noise of the blade cutting the wood was almost unbearable, but earmuffs were not in vogue then. The circular saw blade was about seventy-five centimetres in diameter with about twenty-five centimetres of this protruding above the bench top. It contained something like one hundred teeth, all of which had to be individually sharpened with a file from time to time, and like everything else in those days, there was no possibility of calling in the saw doctor because there wasn't sufficient money to pay such a specialist—the work had to be done by the farmer himself who became proficient in all these types of chores.

The branches and logs to be cut up for firewood were collected from around the paddocks in a heavy-duty horse-drawn dray with sides about forty centimetres high. One day, we kids were in the dray with Dad, and I was kneeling on the floor at the front. A wheel hit a stump that was hidden by the long grass and the dray shot in the air, and I flipped over the front of the dray and down between the horse's rump and the dray, bumping one of his rear legs as I fell. Fortunately it was Nugget, a fairly placid old horse, who was pulling the dray, and as I hit the ground he kicked me in the middle of the back and I flew out backwards from under the dray. He didn't have time to put a lot of power into the kick, but I still had an imprint of his hoof on my back and considered myself very lucky that all was well and that a wheel of the heavy dray had not run over me.

It was by no means all work and no play on the farm. Dad and Mum could not afford a lot of toys for us, but we kids had great times together and used our imaginations to create lots of enjoyment for ourselves. The big hay barn was one source of great fun. We spent hours playing and hiding in the two large stacks of loose hay, jumping from one stack to the other, finding previously unknown hens' nests in the hay with eggs in them, all the time on the alert for snakes. I almost believe that all snakes must have originated in Struck Oil. There were so many very large ones, mostly of the deadly poisonous black, king brown (same species as the Taipan), and tiger varieties, but there were also plenty of non-venomous brown tree snakes and carpet pythons. Thankfully, we did not come across the poisonous varieties too often in the barn, but the carpet pythons used to live in the ridge capping of the roof and it was not unusual to see two or three of them at a time curled up there. The hay used to attract mice and rats, and they were easy pickings for the carpet pythons. Dad used to sometimes show these pythons to visitors by getting one on the pitchfork. When it crawled up the handle near to his hand, he would reverse the fork and the snake would then crawl back over its own body towards him. We kids weren't really frightened of the pythons, and it used to give us great pleasure watching the stricken looks on our visitors' faces as they watched the snakes.

Mum kept a canary in a cage which she faithfully covered with a cloth each night to protect it from mosquitoes, the cold in winter, and also snakes. One morning when she uncovered the cage after she came back from milking, the canary had disappeared, and in its place was a small carpet python, unable to get out because of the bulge in its belly. Dad despatched the snake, and when us kids learnt of the disaster we took to the snake and cut it open in the hope that we might save our canary, but to no avail. Mum lost at least one other canary to a butcher bird. They used to fly at the cage when it was hung in the open and frighten the canary so much that it fluttered against the cage wires where the butcher bird pecked it and pulled it through the wire bars.

Dad had only one uncle on his father's side of the family who lived relatively close to Struck Oil and whom we kids knew quite well. He lived in nearby Rockhampton, and when Uncle Tom passed away, Dad brought home his few possessions, one of which was his old bicycle. At the time, none of us kids could ride a bike, let alone a full-sized man's bike. However, we all soon learnt to ride and had many squabbles as to whose turn it was to ride along the cow tracks to get the cows while the others had to walk. Needless to say, there were many punctures which Dad had to find time to fix. It was around this same time we got our pony named Bonny. She had lived in a yard in Mt Morgan where she was teased by the kids walking past on their way to and from school. She learnt how to retaliate and tried her biting tricks on us frequently. We had to be particularly careful as we attempted to put the bridle over her head. One morning, she almost took a piece of flesh from my ribs when she grabbed hold of me.

We mostly rode bareback as we had no children-sized saddles on the farm and Dad's saddle was too heavy for us to lift down off the peg to put on Bonny. If Dad was available to put the saddle on for us, the stirrups were too long, so we then used to ride with our feet in the stirrup leathers above the stirrup irons rather than in the stirrups. Bonny would occasionally turn her head and endeavour to nip our toes (we were always barefoot) but became a bit wary of doing this after I hit her in the nose with the stirrup iron a few times. It was always a problem to get on her without a saddle, and we had to find a stump, fence post, or log in order to be able to mount. If I had to get off to open a gate, I would then have to lead her through the gateway, close the gate, and climb the gate post to jump on again. If I fell off in the paddock, which I did on occasions, I would have to walk until I found a suitable mounting point. Bonny was very quiet and fortunately would calmly stand by and wait for me after she tipped me off.

Fun and hard work went hand in hand during these early years spent on the farm. However, it was the work ethic that I learnt from Dad at this time that was to stay with me for the rest of my life.

CHAPTER 5

Family Expansion and a New House

T hings began to get really crowded in our little house when my younger brother Colin was born on 5 March 1947. When he outgrew the pram, his cot also had to go in the main bedroom with Dad and Mum. I guess this is what sparked them into deciding to build a new home beside the old one in 1948.

The low-set new house was about four times the size of the old one and contained three bedrooms, a large enclosed sleep-out, large eat-in kitchen, bathroom, lounge, dining room plus open verandas along portion of the west-facing front of the house and along part of the northern side. The laundry was downstairs at the rear, still with a wood-fired copper boiler and an outside toilet which was now located down the back. The entire interior was lined and ceiled with tongue and groove timber except for the sleep-out where Colin and I used to sleep in a double bed. The house was set up with all new furniture and it was heavenly in comparison with the old one. However, there was still no electricity, running water, septic, or telephone. The old house had to be demolished, partly to make way for the new one, and during the construction phase we all shifted into Ma's tiny house. We were used to living in fairly cramped conditions, but we five kids must have been a handful for Mum and Dad to cope with in such a confined space. When I reflect on the occasion, life at that time must have been very trying for my parents. It was at this time that Dad once gave me a severe thrashing for not getting the kindling for the wood stove when Mum had asked me a number of times to do so. I probably got further hidings from Dad later on, but they would not have been for not having collected the kindling for the fire.

Colin had plenty of nursemaids amongst us older kids, and we treated him as a plaything to some degree. We used to take him for walks up the paddock in the old pram and were told by Mum to be careful so that the pram did not tip over due to the rough surface. Unbeknown to our parents or to Colin, as he was too young to comprehend what was happening to him, he had some fast and rough times in that pram and landed in the grass on a few occasions when we tipped the pram upside down. Today, he suffers terribly with neck problems, but I doubt that it is as a consequence of our sometimes rough treatment. We also had a little billycart that we used to sit Colin in and rush him around the yard and through under the awning of the storeroom, past the washtubs. On one such occasion, we didn't realise that a big brown snake had its eye on us from the rafters of the washing area awning, and once as we rushed past there was a 'plop' behind us and on looking back to see where the noise came from we saw this big snake on the ground. It must have missed the cart and Colin by centimetres and could have resulted in the death of one of us had it timed its dive better.

This 'snake' episode reminds me of the occasion when Merle, Joan, and I were vying for the position of being the best collector and eater of the delicious fruit off the big loquat tree that stood at the front of the new house. It was quite easy to climb and we often played in the tree. On this occasion, I led the charge up the tree to get some fruit that I had spied, and as I got well up a branch and looked up I found myself eyeballing a brown tree snake. Although I knew the snake was not venomous, I didn't like the idea of being bitten, so I beat a hasty retreat out of the tree almost taking the girls with me. On another occasion, we were picking loquats with the aid of a steel-pronged garden rake. The rake got out of control when I was reaching for a loquat and hit Merle in the head as it fell, cutting her scalp open. She still wears the scar to this day.

A possum somehow found its way into the soffit of the un-ceiled sleep-out of the new house and made it his home. Mum could not fathom why her tomatoes were disappearing in the garden and fruit in a bowl on the kitchen table was being eaten at night. Eventually, the culprit was found. Dad put on a very sturdy and long leather glove and reached into the soffit to get hold of the possum, but it bit him through the glove. Eventually, he got it into a sugar bag and we took it a couple of miles away and released it up a large gum tree that had some likely looking nesting holes in it. Another possum made his home in a disused milk quart pot (approx. 1.25 litres capacity) which stood on a high shelf in the dairy. The pot was without its lid, and he would squeeze himself into the pot and put his bushy tail over his head and eyes and sleep there all day while the milking was under way and people were passing back and forth just beneath him. Dad would reach up and get the quart pot down to show visitors the little furry bundle. The possum wouldn't move a muscle despite the noise the visitors were making as they stroked his lovely soft tail over and over again.

Dad and Mum arranged for Mr and Mrs Bill Ross to look after us kids while Mum was in hospital having Colin. On the morning that Dad went into Mt Morgan to bring Mum and Colin home from the hospital, we kids were playing in the front yard of the old house, and I stood on a broken bottle and badly cut the ball of my foot and up in between my toes. Mrs Morgan, the previous owner of the farm, had used 750 ml glass soft drink or beer bottles and turned them upside down, half buried in the ground as an ornamental garden edge. Some of these had broken over the years and one of them caused the damage. I recently read that bottles were similarly used in the deep south of America many years ago for the same decorative purpose. Really, it was a very dangerous way of creating a garden edge.

At the time, it had been wet, and as usual, we had been at the dairy earlier that morning doing our allotted jobs, one of which was bringing the cows into the bails from the boggy and mucky cow yard. I still had cow manure and mud all over my feet when Mrs Ross wrapped a sheet around the badly bleeding foot and bundled me into their very old Ford utility, and Mr Ross headed for the Mt Morgan hospital. Fortunately, we met Mum and Dad on the way, so Dad took me to hospital while Mum and Colin went home with Mr Ross. The nurses had a difficult job getting the dried mud off my foot in an attempt to clean it up so that the doctor could stitch it. Dad was embarrassed and Mum was horrified when she found out. I was deeply embarrassed also, but the ether the nurses were using to get rid of the mud was getting into the wound and magnifying the pain to such an extent that I lost interest in the state of the cleanliness of my feet.

The doctor administered a local anaesthetic and began stitching me up, and that was when I first learnt that local anaesthetics do not work very effectively on me. At places, I could clearly feel the needle being threaded through the flesh and protested loudly, but the doctor didn't hesitate in what he was doing. I couldn't walk on the foot and was not given crutches so had to hop everywhere. A few days later, I was hopping through a doorway at home and unintentionally kicked the door frame with the injured foot. It hurt terribly, but I did not know at the time that I had busted all the stitches. It was too late to re-stitch the wound when I next went back to the hospital for a progress check, and the wound took a long time to heal as a consequence. The scar is plainly evident to this day.

It was Christmas 1947, just prior to shifting into the new house, when we woke up to find that in addition to Santa calling during the night, we had a large carpet python that had taken up position in the ridge capping immediately above the refrigerator and meals preparation area in the kitchen. Mum dug in her heels and said determinedly that she would not commence the preparation of Xmas lunch until Dad got rid of the snake. The snake was as determined to stay for Xmas as Mum was to see it out of the house. It did not want to leave its position no matter what Dad attempted. In the end, and seeing that we were soon to demolish the old house, Dad shot the snake with his 0.22 m rifle, the bullet going out through the weatherboard wall. As the snake fell, it clung to the ridge beam with its prehensile tail and dribbled blood and 'whatever' down the front of the refrigerator. Eventually, everything was cleaned up and we all calmly enjoyed our Xmas lunch of roast chicken.

The mention of Dad shooting the snake brings to mind how we got our chicken for Xmas lunch. Our chooks used to run free-range and camp in a big umbrella tree each night safe from foxes and the like. They used to lay eggs mostly in the barn but sometimes went off on their own and reappeared a few weeks later with a batch of chickens. Occasionally, at night there was ruckus when the dog chased a native cat (spotted quoll) that was attempting to make a meal of a hen sitting on her nest of eggs. Sadly, I have to say that I saw Dad despatch a few native cats, which in those days were seen as vermin but are now fully protected animals. The chooks and roosters were fairly easy to catch before we acquired an Indian Game rooster. Chickens fathered by him grew into very wary and fast birds that were almost impossible to catch. We would try luring them with grain and other tasty morsels, but they continually evaded capture. In the end, Dad got the rifle and despatched the young rooster we had selected with a well-aimed bullet to the head, and so Xmas dinner was assured. A number of roosters met with this fate over the years.

Our refrigerator was a model that operated by burning kerosene fuel. Filling the kerosene reservoir each weekend and ensuring that the wick was kept in good order was another of my less liked jobs. Because we had access to as much milk and cream as we could use, we kids frequently made ice cream and milk ice block, both of which were sometimes laced with fruit salad made from fruit obtained from our neighbours. The refrigerator wick frequently burnt in an uneven manner, which resulted both in a smoking fridge and a less efficient freezing operation. When this happened, the flame had to be extinguished and the wick trimmed in order that operating efficiency was restored and the fridge became cold enough again to set our ice cream and ice blocks.

It was March 1949 when a major cyclone hit Central Queensland, and we were not spared from its ferocity at Struck Oil. Torrential rain had been falling for two days and the wind speed was increasing rapidly. A young white cedar tree about four metres tall grew on the northern side of the new house and early in the morning the strong winds blew it over, but it held tenaciously to the ground by its very substantial tap root. The wind direction changed frequently, and each time it did so, the tree was picked up and slammed down in the new direction of the wind. Our substantial new house was considered safe from the winds, but our neighbour's very old house was quite flimsy and Dad spent some time that day helping Bob and Matt Neil tie down the veranda roof of their house to the house-stumps with doubled lengths of very strong No. 8 plain fencing wire. At around 7 p.m. that evening, Mum was putting Colin, who was about two years old, to bed in the sleep-out when we all heard her scream. We ran out to find that half the entire house roof was missing. It was raining torrentially and the water was already beginning to pour through the ceilings into most of the rooms in the house. The kitchen was the only fully dry area. Fortunately it was large, and there was a rush to get as much of the new furnishings, bedding, and clothes into that room before the water that was leaking through the new timber ceilings stained everything with sap marks. We couldn't remain in the house as it was quite probable that the remainder of the roof would be blown off as the cyclonic winds continued. It was too dangerous to attempt to take shelter in the hay shed or Jacky's shed because they too could be demolished by the fierce winds and also because of the possibility of encountering snakes. There was no telephone to enquire of the Neils if their house was still standing, so Dad decided that we should walk down to their place. The Neils' house and outbuildings were in an area more protected from the winds than our house, and they also had a substantial packing shed that would afford protection if the house had been damaged. The winds were blowing at over 100 miles per hour (180 kilometres per hour), and we were actually blown backwards at times as we tried to walk into the wind. It was pitch-dark and the driving rain stung any exposed parts. The only light we had with us was a very aptly named hurricane lamp, and to its credit, it did not blow out in the wind nor did the hot glass crack as the rain hit it in torrents.

It was a relief to find that Bob Neil's house was still standing, and we were able to stay for a few nights with them. Their old house swayed on its stumps as it was battered by the severe wind gusts. A hole cut in an external weatherboard wall allowed for a pipe and tap to protrude into the kitchen from an outside tank perched on a high stand. Either the house or the tank or both would move so much that the tap disappeared outside the wall at times. It was quite scary to watch. By morning, the wind had eased a little and we were able to survey the damage to our house. Half of the roof remained, but the other half had been ripped off in one single piece, swirled some 200 metres up the paddock and plunged to the ground. One of the roof timber rafters was driven into the ground about 1.5 metres. The large eat-in kitchen still remained the only dry room. All the new polished furniture was water-marked and timber-stained from the water that came through the ceilings before it could be shifted to the kitchen. No other farm buildings were badly damaged, but the milk cans and separator parts had been blown from their bench into the cow yard and some parts of the separator were buried in the mud. Fortunately, we were able to recover all lost separator pieces in due course; one missing part of the many pieces would have rendered the machine ineffective.

The cows were driven into the far corner of their paddock by the pelting rain and fierce wind. They simply would not walk to the yards with the rain and wind stinging their eyes and had to be left un-milked for two days. The farm was situated about 100 kilometres inland from the coast, as the crow flies, yet we found a number of sea gulls and other sea birds sheltering in our paddocks where they had been blown by the ferocity of the cyclonic winds. The damage to the new house and its contents was a major blow for Dad and Mum, to say nothing of the work it took to clean up the mess. When the rain finally stopped after a couple more days, the floor coverings had to be lifted and the place dried out in order to get it functional again. It was also a very high priority to clean up the mess at the dairy and get the cows milked as soon as possible. It must have been excruciatingly painful for the cows particularly because they were used to being milked twice a day. Their udders were virtually bursting and milk was flowing freely from their teats as they walked to the yards and stood patiently, waiting to be milked.

The new house had been unable to keep the rain out during the cyclone, yet it was substantially built. It is still standing where Dad and Mum built it sixty-five years ago.

CHAPTER 6

Always Work to Be Done

Dad's inherent drive always required him to improve the farm despite the workload it added to his already exhausting days. From time to time, if there was a particularly large project in hand, Dad employed itinerant labourers or his brother Vic if he was out of work due to a temporary closure of the Mt Morgan mine. Uncle Vic was amongst those employed when Dad decided to fell the scrub on a virgin block of land of about eight hectares (20 acres), which I think he bought from our neighbour Bob Neil. This scrub block was quite rough and was heavily timbered by jungle-type growth with lots of very large trees and dense undergrowth of vines. There were also lots of large rocks in places, and it was relatively steep in one part where a gully ran through it. The men were employed to help get the job done, and Dad joined them between milking sessions on this back-breaking work. He would finish milking around 7 a.m., have breakfast, walk the two kilometres to the scrub block, chop scrub until lunchtime, walk home, have lunch, round up and milk the cows with Mum's assistance, and return to the scrub cutting until dusk. He would then walk home, clean up, have dinner, and fall into bed only to get up the next morning at 4.30 a.m. to start all over again. Dad couldn't afford a bulldozer, so the trees had to be chopped down with either an axe or a cross-cut saw. It was exceedingly hard and very dangerous work which extended over a period of a few months.

Eventually, the scrub was felled without too many serious axe cuts or other major injuries. The timber and vines were allowed to dry out for many months, and then on a day when the climate and winds were right for Dad to safely do so, he set fire to the lot. The resulting fire was enormous—so much so that we could see the smoke billowing from it from the school yard in Mt Morgan some fourteen kilometres (8.5 miles) away. It was an extremely hot fire and all but the biggest logs were burnt completely to ash and only large tree stumps were left standing partially burnt.

Dad decided to plant corn in the very fertile ash left from the fire, harvest the crop, and then sow the area with Rhodes grass to form another paddock of quality feed for the cows. Because of the tree stumps that remained and the many large rocks and logs in various parts of the paddock, the only way to plant the corn seeds was on foot using a hand-held seed planter. This ingenious contraption was about waist high with a handle at the top. It had a long thin box as the body of the implement, in which about three kilos of corn seed was placed. At the bottom, there was a set of steel jaws, which opened and ejected a few seeds whenever the planter's jaws were thrust into the soil. Dad and Uncle Vic walked backwards and forwards for many days among the stumps, rocks, and logs, planting corn across the entire eight hectares. Not satisfied with his efforts on this block alone, and using the old steel-wheeled Fordson tractor he had recently acquired, Dad ploughed about a further six hectares of cultivation paddocks and planted corn there also— again by hand. On this occasion, seasonal conditions favoured him and the entire crop was of excellent quality. The wallabies gave the young corn a hard time in some fringe parts of the scrub block, but the overall outcome was amazing. The problems that then had to be faced were harvesting, carting, husking, and shelling (removing the outside cover from the cob and then separating the corn grains from the cob), bagging, and selling the corn. With the quantity of corn to be handled, it was clear that the husking and shelling job could not be done by hand.

Dad somehow learnt of the availability of a mechanical husker and sheller, purchased it, and brought it home only to find that the wooden frame was entirely eaten out by termites and had to be completely rebuilt before any production could commence. I recall that this was a very exacting and difficult task and I expect that Dad lost quite a lot of sleep over it. The machine was quite a large contraption approx. 6 metres long by about 1.5 metres wide by approx. 1.5 metres high. The process was that the corn cobs were fed into a hopper by hand at one end where they passed into the machine. The machine first removed the outer husk covering, and the grains of corn were next removed from the cob and funnelled out into sack bags of approx. 50 kg capacity. The husks and the empty cobs came out the other end of the machine on a conveyor belt. The machine was driven by way of a system of belts and pulleys connected to the same cantankerous old engine that drove the chaff cutter and the circular saw. Although the machine did all the tedious work, at least three people were required to keep the process going—one to feed the hopper, another to fill the sack bags with the corn grains, sew up the bags as they filled, and stack them, and the third to get rid of the ever mounting husks and cobs, which quickly threatened to submerge the site if not frequently removed. The latter task fell to us kids, and it is fair to say that the shine of the corn shelling project soon wore off for all of us.

Before any husking and shelling could take place, the corn had to be harvested and all of this had to be done by hand. The ripe cobs of bright yellow corn were picked from the stalk of the plants by hand and then loaded into sack bags which were tied at the top.

Gathering the full sacks from the cultivated paddocks was a major task in itself but achievable due to the fact that the Ford utility could be used to cart the bags to the work site. However, the scrub block was a very different proposition. The only way that the bags of cobs could be collected was by the use of the heavy-duty horse-drawn dray. Boulder, the big black Clydesdale, was the only horse strong enough to be able to haul the fully laden dray up and down the rough terrain and in and out between the logs, stumps, and rocks. He did this for days on end and on the last day of the carting became lame because of a bruised hoof. Eventually, all of the corn was shelled and the grain bagged and ready for sale. Dad sold it to Rowe's Department and Produce Store in Mt Morgan, and Mum tells me that they did very well financially from the venture.

I have mentioned previously that rounding up the cows each evening to bring them to the yards, count them, and then turn them out into the night paddock was an everyday-of-the-year job. In summer time Merle, Joan and I were home from school early enough to be able to get the cows before dark. Sometimes we rode our horses, and when the cows were feeding in paddocks on Dad's old family farm, we used to feast on fruit when it was in season as we searched the paddocks for the cows. There was an old unkempt mango orchard located on this property that had many varieties of mango trees, most of which still produced fruit. While we were picking and eating the mangoes, my pony Bonny would be picking up mangoes from the ground with her teeth, chewing them, and discarding the seeds. The cows liked mangoes also but ate them seed and all. Later, in the cow yard when lying down chewing their cud and waiting their turn to be milked, they would regurgitate the seeds and spit them out in little stacks in front of them. The old farm also had some old orange, mandarin, and loquat trees that we also used to feast on.

Neighbouring Dad's parents' old farm was a farm owned by a family whom, for reasons unknown to us, neither Mum nor Dad liked. I recall one day we were rounding up the cows from the paddock right next to their house when a severe thunderstorm broke and started showering us with heavy rain and lots of huge hail. There was no way that we were prepared to go to our neighbour for cover, so we pushed the cows towards home while we were being bombarded by the hail and rain and scared by each terrific thunder clap.

Another difficult time was when we were rounding up the cows at around midday in very hot weather. The only water available to the thirsty cows, before they got back to the yards, was from an old disused well in the bed of Turkey creek which ran through Grandpa's old farm. This well was usually totally dry, but it must have been soon after good rain as the water level was right to the top of the well at the time. A group of cows was gathered around the well drinking when another bossy cow with long sharp horns poked a cow named Alma from behind and forced her forward into the well. There was no way that she could get out by herself and we kids could not help her. Alma was a big red and white cow and one of our best milkers. All we could do was run as fast as possible the 1.5 kilometres or so home to alert Dad. He got ropes and raced over to the well in the utility, but it was too late—Alma had drowned. It was impossible to haul her carcass out of the well, so she stayed there and gradually rotted away. Not only did the foul smell almost make us sick for months afterwards, as we passed by regularly, but the well was no longer a drinking source for the cows, which was a real blessing to us—no more drowning. We thought the easy solution would be to put a fence around the well. However, Dad pointed out that the fence would be washed away each time it rained and the creek flooded, hence the reason for no fence. I guess a solution would have been to fill in the hole, but I expect he had many more urgent priorities to attend to.

Recalling Alma's death brings back memories of a disaster we kids caused with Dad's dairy herd. Dad liked the horse races and very infrequently went to the races in Rockhampton on a Saturday afternoon. On this particular day, he entrusted us kids to mind the cows in the lucerne patch and to make sure that we got them out by the specified time. Lucerne is a wonderful feed for milking cows, but too much can cause bloat, a build-up of gas in the gut, and can quickly cause death. He even left his precious fob watch with us to ensure that we knew what the time was and when the cows had to be removed. Needless to say, we got involved in other activities, and by the time we thought of the cows again, it was well past the allotted time. We hurriedly got the cows out of the lucerne patch and thought no more of it until we went to round them up that evening. As we walked up the paddock, we came across dead cow after dead cow. We were horrified as to what we were going to tell Dad but had to confess, and we raced home to tell him the bad news. He had the correct instrument to deal with bloat—a sharp, pointed, hollow needle-like knife which, when inserted through the hide on the cow's side into the gut, allowed the gas to escape and saved the animal's life in most instances. About half a dozen valuable cows died and we were not at all popular.

As mentioned previously, some of our neighbours attempted to dairy on forest country, some of which would hardly keep a bandicoot alive in the best of times. Also, they made no long-term provision for water security and often their cattle were starving and thirsty. Somehow, these animals knew that the grass was actually greener over the other side of our fence and spent a lot of time breaking through fences, and some even learnt how to walk across the planks where the car tyres crossed the cattle grid at the front entry to the property. It was not unusual to go down to the yards and find a half dozen or so of our neighbour's cattle watering at the trough. A frequent unwelcome visitor was Mr Daniel's bull. He was a scruffy ill-bred type, ginger and white in colour, and we used to call him Gingermeggs. It didn't seem to matter how many times we turned him out of our place, he returned again and again. The Daniels lived about four kilometres along the gravel road on the way to Mt Morgan. As well as being the owners of Gingermeggs and some other free-ranging cows, they had a lot of free-range chooks. When our chooks were not producing well, Mum used to get me to ride the bike down to their place and buy a few dozen eggs each weekend. Although the ride was pretty strenuous over a hilly and stony dirt road, I didn't mind too much as the Daniels had incubators and I quite often got to see lots of chickens hatching. I recall that one day we were talking, and in all innocence I started criticising the Daniel's bull in the way I had heard Dad do so on many occasions. There was a deathly silence from Mr and Mrs Daniels, and I suddenly woke up to my mistake and I must have gone the colour of a beetroot. Mum and Dad were embarrassed when I told them, but I don't think it did too much damage to the relationship, which I think was virtually non-existent anyway.

CHAPTER 7

I Become a Milk Delivery Boy

———————⟶✦⟵———————

I n the 1940s, there was no such thing as supermarkets with a dazzling array of different brands, types, and flavours of milk products on their refrigerated shelves. Nor did many homes have a refrigerator. Most had an ice chest only and purchased a block of ice from the ice delivery man a few times weekly in summer. People had to rely on the delivery of fresh milk to the home daily, and a milk run was a serious and quite profitable business.

At the time, the local milk run from the farm was owned and operated by Tom Kilpatrick, a likeable former jockey. It was not until the late 1950s that the first pasteurised milk became available in glass bottles sealed with a waterproof cardboard lid that the crows soon learnt to pick holes in while the bottles stood on the front steps after delivery. Milk in bottles then became available at the local corner store, and the slow demise of the milkman began. Up until then, Tom Kilpatrick needed assistance in the delivery of the milk and employed a couple of boys to assist with a lot of the running back and forth to homes. From time to time, he found it difficult to employ boys that he could rely on, and on one of these occasions when he was short of a worker, Dad volunteered me to assist. I was about nine at the time, and it meant leaving home about 7 a.m. in the milk truck with Tom and delivering milk until 9 a.m. when I was dropped at the school gate. It was a fairly demanding job for a nine-year-old. Often I was required to carry a couple of gallons (nine litres) of milk in large billies, delivering it in pint or quart lots to various homes around an entire town block and then meeting up with Tom again at a given point. I was expected to run mostly, and for seven days per week, including five hours on each of Saturdays and Sundays, I was paid the sum of ten shillings ($1) or roughly five cents per hour. Talk about slave labour! I got to school each day smelling of milk, barefoot and filthy. I didn't realise it at the time, but I must have been seen as one of the urchins in the class, arriving at school smelling of milk, probably with clothing and hair looking untidy and with dirty feet and legs. I found the job quite tiring and at times went to sleep in class, and I got the cane on one occasion because of it. It was not then the 'done' thing to tell one's parents of these happenings—grin and bear it was the order of the day.

A number of items of interest from my milk boy days remain with me. One family that I delivered milk to had a daughter in my class at school. She had about ten siblings, all looking as unkempt as her. The house was a very old and dilapidated Queenslander on high stumps, and I had to run up the front steps and pour the milk into whatever utensil they might have left for me. Frequently, there wasn't anything to put the milk in and I had to yell at the top of my voice to be heard over the ruckus going on inside. Whatever jug or saucepan was eventually produced invariably had the cream from the previous day's milk still encrusted on the inside.

The real skill at this place was escaping being bitten by their fox terrier dog. It sat on the top of the back steps and could see me out front through a hallway that ran right through the centre of the house. As soon as I turned to leave, it ran down the back steps and came after me straight through under the house. If I hurried as fast as I could, there was just enough time to slam the gate as the dog arrived. A number of customers used to be really generous and leave a piece of fruit or cake for me beside their milk jug. At times, others never left any money to pay for the milk, and when I called out for the money they claimed someone must have stolen it. Surprisingly, it was always the same ones who offended—their kids were probably the culprits if in fact they had put the money out. Suffice to say, I did not get rich delivering milk and I'm not sure what skills I learnt from it other than how to jump off the running board of the moving vehicle, holding two heavy billies of milk in one hand and the pint pot measure in the other, without spilling a drop of milk or falling flat on my face.

One day, Tom Kilpatrick unintentionally ran over a snake on the way to the farm. He couldn't see it on the road in his rear vision mirror after he had passed over it, and after he got to the farm, Dad and he searched for it under the vehicle and under the engine bonnet without success. Some vehicles in those days had a lever under the dashboard, which opened a flap in the bonnet immediately in front of the windscreen to allow additional air flow (no such thing as air conditioning then). Tom opened this flap a few days later, and to his horror the snake appeared through this vent. Fortunately, it was outside the cabin of the vehicle and Tom was safe.

A few years later, after the farm was sold and we were living temporarily in Yeppoon, Dad agreed to give Tom Kilpatrick a holiday break for six weeks during the Xmas school holidays and undertook to do the milk run for him. We lived in the Kilpatrick's house in Mt Morgan while they were away. Naturally, I was volunteered to be one of the milk boys. We would go to our old farm to collect the milk at 6 a.m. and worked until lunchtime every day of the week. I cannot recall whether I enjoyed the experience on that occasion, but I vividly recall Dad handing me a £10 ($20) note as my pay at the end of the six weeks, which meant the hourly rate had now increased to about eight cents. However, at the time I was elated. I had never seen a £10 note before and it really looked good, so I put it straight into my bank account.

During the six weeks' stay in Mt Morgan, there was a lot of very heavy rain which not only made the milk delivery job miserable on occasions but also presented great difficulty in getting to and from the farm to collect the milk. When we left the bitumen road at the turn-off to Struck Oil, there were six creek crossings that flooded in heavy rains. Three of these were the Dee River winding around in an 'S' fashion and the other three creeks were tributaries of the Dee River. The road into the farm was also very boggy, and Dad had to overcome a number of very difficult slipping and slithering occasions to reach the dairy. When the afternoon's milk was collected from the farm, it was then taken back to town and stored overnight at the ice works to keep it chilled, there being no such thing as on-farm refrigeration.

On one occasion, it rained heavily while we were at the farm and the creeks were running high on the way back into town. We got through the first five crossings without too much trouble, but it was a different situation when we came to the very last, which was one of the Dee River crossings. The flood water was roaring over the cement crossing and looked very menacing. Dad stopped the vehicle and surveyed the scene. He waded into the water to gauge the flow rate and determined that the relatively new Austin A40 utility would make it through because the weight of the load of milk on board would assist in holding it down. I was told to stand on a ledge at the rear of the utility and hold on to the milk box, a purpose-built box on the back of the utility to cover the milk cans. I was instructed that should the vehicle be washed off the crossing, I was to grab on to one of the many small Melaleuca trees in the centre of the raging torrent and hold on until rescued. Away we went, me thinking what a great adventure it was and not for one moment considering the possibility of drowning as I had not as yet learnt to swim. Dad had a lot of past experience of driving through flooded creeks, so I had full confidence in him getting us across safely, and if not, rescuing me from the flood waters. The vehicle started to float momentarily when we reached centre stream and were hit by the full force of the flood water. We were gradually being swept closer to the edge of the crossing, and there was no possibility of turning back. Fortunately we made it, but I know Dad was a bit shaken by the experience. When I think about it now, I realise how dangerous a situation we were in. However, at the time I found it to be very exciting.

Chapter 8

Farm Life Comes to an End

J ust as Dad and Mum were beginning to reap the rewards of all their years of hard labour, Dad's health took a downturn. He made the decision to sell the family farm.

The farm was performing very well financially by 1949. The herd then consisted of excellent quality highly productive jersey cows, milk prices were sound, the paddocks were clean of re-growth, lantana, and the like, cultivation was well managed, and facilities were modern and well maintained. Still, there was no electricity, reticulated water in the house, septic, or telephone. The only seriously worrying issue was the paucity of water for the cattle in drought seasons and a lack of water for irrigation at almost any time. Despite many attempts to find alternative water sources on the property, no worthwhile supply had yet been located.

In 1950, Dad became ill with heart problems. The family doctor diagnosed the problem as 'heart strain' and told my parents that unless they left the farm, so that Dad could have twelve months of recuperation, he would be carried off the farm in a coffin within six months. I am not aware if there was a recommendation of a referral to a heart specialist in Rockhampton. If there was, I don't believe it was followed up. It seems that Mum was keen for them to lease the farm, and a local family was very interested to do so. However, Dad did not believe that anyone would operate the farm to his standards, and that was probably so; hence, the decision was made to sell. In retrospect, his decision was probably the right one as I doubt that anyone else would have been prepared to work as hard and as conscientiously as my father did, and more particularly so when they did not own the property. Had he leased the farm and been forced to watch the probable gradual deterioration of the production capacity of the cows and the lack of maintenance of the paddocks and cultivation areas, he would have been highly stressed and his health would probably have continued to deteriorate.

Although it was a good time to sell in terms of the seasons and business profitability, the forced timing was disastrous and heart-breaking for my parents. War time Government price controls were still in force and the sale price was dictated by bureaucrats rather than market forces. The latter method of valuation would have based the sale price on the current and ongoing potential profitability of the farm whereas the bureaucrats dictated an unrealistically low price without even inspecting the property and its improvements. Because of these price controls, I understand that Dad and Mum sold the farm for about £5,500 ($11,000), including cattle, horses, plant, machinery, tools, and all the household furniture—a sum that was about half of what the business was really worth. It seems that the purchaser and his family did the bare necessities, made a good living, and then sold a run-down property some ten to fifteen years later at a substantial profit when price controls had been lifted.

The next purchasers were a couple neither of whom was experienced in dairying, although the wife had worked with beef cattle and was very confident of her own abilities. They struggled on for many years, and then gave up dairying. He got a job off the farm and they went into raising beef cattle. I went back to Mt Morgan in 1995 to attend a fifty years' reunion of the class that commenced primary school in 1945. While I was in Mt Morgan, I took the opportunity to revisit the old farm. It was so disappointing to see the state of disrepair that it had been allowed to sink into. Fortunately, Dad was not there to see what had happened to all the improvements he had worked so hard to implement. The only part of the farm that was maintained was the house. The bails, cattle dip, yards, fences were all dreadful. There were trees up to 10 metres or more high in paddocks that were once prime lucerne paddocks. The pastures had been allowed to revert to native grasses, and the young beef cattle on the property were an undernourished lot of mixed breeds. I think Dad would have wanted to shoot the lot on sight.

A man named David Jones owned the farm in 2003. He is a part-time grazier, raising Santa Gertrudis cattle while both he and his wife are employed at the Capricornia University in Rockhampton. A few years ago, he sent me a few photos of the property as it is now, and really there are no useable improvements left, except for the house. He did mention that a good alternative water supply is now available and was found not far from the entry to the property. I recall my dad divining for water in that area but not getting sufficiently strong indications to make it worthwhile entering into the costs of sinking a test bore. Hindsight tells us that he should have tried the location. My cousin Tom Chatterton recently made a nostalgic visit to Struck Oil as part of his 80th birthday celebrations and was surprised to find that a number of small rural residential housing lots have been subdivided from the farm blocks and homes erected thereon.

When the day finally came for us all to depart the farm, the Ford utility tray was loaded halfway up to the cabin roof and well above its sides. Mum and Dad were in the front with Colin and Valmai while Merle, Joan, and I were perched on top of the load in a manner that would be seen as totally illegal today. Dad was driving very slowly and carefully, but we got lots of surprised looks from people in cars when they drove up behind us. I recall feeling quite uncomfortable as we went around some of the bends in the road. Yeppoon is about forty kilometres from Rockhampton, so we had about eighty kilometres to travel from the farm to Yeppoon. It was a really exciting adventure for us kids from our vantage point up on top of the load. I guess Mum and Dad were feeling very sad about leaving their beloved property, but we three older children were delighted to be getting away from the work about the farm. Dad returned to the farm the next day to get another load of gear, but two utility loads of personal belongings, five children, and approximately $11,000 in sale proceeds plus other savings were the sum total of what my parents left the property with after their twenty years of unbelievably hard labour.

Dad had arranged to lease a furnished house for a year in Cliff Street, Yeppoon. The lady who owned the house must have freaked when Dad told her there were five children, but Mum tells me she let him have the house because of the manner in which he presented himself and the immaculate state of his clothing for which Mum was responsible. After we left this house about a year later, the owner was full of praise at the excellent state in which it was left. Generally we kids had a great time in Yeppoon. We had electricity and couldn't stop turning the lights on and off for a few days. We also had hot and cold water on tap; the phone was down the hill at the phone box. The toilet was still outside but only about ten metres from the back door and there was an outside light for night use. Dad must have been delighted that there was a 'dunny' man and a garbage man to take over these distasteful jobs. There were movie matinees on Saturday afternoons, and we used to pay our sixpence (five cents) entry fee and would have three pence to spend on an ice-cream. We learnt to swim and often I used to go for a swim with my new friends after school. They had lived by the sea all their lives and could swim well whereas I could not swim at all when we arrived in Yeppoon.

78

The move to Yeppoon meant that all of us (except Colin who was three or four years old) had to start at a new school. Merle was in high school, and there being no State High School in Yeppoon in those days, she had to go by train daily to Rockhampton with a number of other local students. As traumatic as the change of schools was, I recall settling into school reasonably well and making friends quite quickly. My teacher was a strict disciplinarian and a sadist to boot. He usually carried a piece of pine wood around in class. It was about forty centimetres long, four centimetres wide, and two centimetres thick. His sadistic trick was to crack one down the middle of the back with the stick and then ask you what you were up to. If he didn't have the stick with him, he would grab you by the ear and start lifting until he almost pulled your ear off. It didn't help if one stood up on the seat to ease the hurt as he simply lifted the ear higher.

Although we kids may have enjoyed our time in Yeppoon, Dad certainly didn't and I guess this means that Mum was quite unhappy at times also. Dad really missed the farm and on top of that his health was not good and he had to endure the stress of having to keep a large family with no money coming in—there was no such thing as unemployment benefits then. He longed to get back on the land and at one time wanted to purchase a beef cattle property. Mum had had enough of the hard life, and with a young family growing up and needing to be educated, she was not interested.

Dad met a chap named Jimmy Ganter, who had a beef cattle property of sorts at Byfield, which is about forty kilometres north of Yeppoon near the coast. Dad used to love going with Jimmy to help him muster and dip the cattle. I got to go with them sometimes and I loved the experience also. The country was quite tropical and the drive to the property was through lots of rainforests with Byfield ferns, which are indigenous to this small area, growing in profusion. This fern looks somewhat like a bracken but is much more appealing and is sought after by florists. I recall that on one trip to Byfield, Dad took his prized 0.22 calibre rifle to show me how he could shoot and give me a few tips. We put a small tin on top of a broken off sapling and took shots at it. Dad was about forty-one years of age and like most people at that age his eyesight was not as sharp as it used to be as a youngster. Although he did not let on to me, I think he was quite chuffed to think that I hit the tin each shot whereas he had quite a few misses.

During our stay at Yeppoon, Mum and Dad decided to travel to Mt Mee near Caboolture in Queensland to see Uncle Les and Auntie Beryl and their family. They had shifted there from Gympie after they left Struck Oil and were dairying and growing bananas. A few days before we left on the trip, Dad sold the Ford utility and bought a big old Dodge sedan. We kids felt like royalty to actually be able to ride inside the vehicle. The Bruce Highway, the State's number one highway, in those days was mostly a terrible unsealed gravel road and I recall that the corrugations near Miriam Vale almost shook the car and us to pieces. When we got on to the bitumen surface in Miriam Vale, Dad noticed a clicking noise coming from the rear axle of the Dodge. The local garage couldn't diagnose what the problem might be or tell how serious it was without dismantling the rear axle, so Dad put Mum and us kids on the train to Bundaberg, where we were met by Mum's sister Aunt Jean and her husband Uncle Bill Gear. They escorted us to their cane farm at Fairymead outside Bundaberg. We had a fun few days there getting to know our cousins Ken, Eric, and Janice—also, visiting the local Fairymead sugar mill and seeing the huge fires as the sugar cane trash was being burnt the night prior to hand harvesting commencing the following day. Uncle Bill was a cane cutter, and it must have been one of the hardest jobs ever. Harvesting was all manual labour then right down to the lifting of each stalk of cane on to the cane train. He was another one whose health suffered as a consequence of excessive work and died at a relatively young age.

Dad eventually arrived from Miriam Vale with the Dodge in good shape again, and off we went to Mt Mee. Uncle Les and Auntie Beryl's house was quite small and could not accommodate four adults and ten children. Jean, their eldest, was away working in the Commonwealth Bank, and this relieved the pressure a little. Fortunately, there was a disused little cottage on the property, and Bob, Tom, Ray, and I slept there each night. I do not recall where Enid, May, Merle, Joan, Valmai, and Colin slept, but I do seem to remember some of them sleeping under the kitchen table. The Mt Mee district is situated on the Great Dividing Range and is quite elevated with steep, hilly areas and lovely views. It was no mean feat for Uncle Les and his family members to walk up and down the hills to get the cows. Because of the altitude, it was very cold at night and we Central Queenslanders were totally unprepared for it. I had a great time with Bob, Tom, and Ray. We went shooting flock pigeons in the huge fig trees in the scrub, fishing for Jew fish in the little streams, and generally getting to know each other again after being separated for about six or seven years. I recall that Dad had advised Uncle Les on dairy cattle when he went to Gympie, and as a consequence he had purchased some Jersey heifers from Alf Ohl at Dululu where Dad used to get his cattle. I think I am right in saying that Uncle Les had taken some of these cattle to Mt Mee, but they had not acclimatised well and he had moved into a more suitable breed of Holsteins.

Although this was a happy period in the lives of us children, it was difficult for my parents. Dad was not at all well and unable to work and Mum worried for him. Additionally, there were seven to feed, and this was taking a heavy toll on finances. For the benefit of our schooling and work opportunities for Dad, it seemed that Rockhampton would be the place to settle, and after twelve months in Yeppoon we moved.

Chapter 9

The Move to Rockhampton

———————

Mum and Dad purchased quite a nice house in Eldon Street, North Rockhampton, and it was this house that was to be my home until I was transferred away from Rockhampton due to my work some four to five years later. The house exterior was clad in asbestos-cement sheeting called fibro and the roof was of corrugated fibro. Nothing was known of the dangers of asbestos in those days, and a big percentage of post-war housing in Australia was then constructed from these materials. The house was on high wooden stumps and was battened in underneath. It consisted of an eat-in kitchen/dining room, bathroom, lounge, two bedrooms, an enclosed sleep-out, open front porch, and toilet (sewered) at the top of the rear steps. The car was parked underneath by way of driving up the side of the house, turning in the backyard, and driving under. The property had a reasonable sized yard and backed on to Ryan Park. The park was largely undeveloped at that time but for a shed and a number of swings, see-saws, and hurdy-gurdies, and it was a popular play area for the local kids.

Dad got a job at Hinz Timber Yards in 1952 at £15 per week and worked with Les Dodd, who lived about five doors down Eldon Street. It was heavy work, and although he was still not well, he used to comment quite often about how reluctant some of his co-workers were to put in a good day's effort. Eventually, due to an economic slump, Dad's job at the timber yard petered out and he was out of work. Unemployment benefits were either still not available to families then or Dad was too proud to apply; whatever the situation, again there was no money coming into a household with five growing children. The financial strain must have been unbelievably difficult. Fortunately, Mum was very good at managing within a budget, and it is fair to say that we never went hungry, but luxuries were few and far between. Eventually Dad got a job through Bill Howard, who was an old Mt Morgan friend, as fitter's assistant at Central Queensland Meat Export Company Pty. Ltd in a suburb known as Lakes Creek. The meat works were then owned by the very wealthy aristocratic Vesty family of the United Kingdom and later by one of Kerry Packer's companies. The pay wasn't great, but Mum and Dad managed to feed, dress, and educate all of us—needless to say they never had any holiday breaks and few social outings.

One of Dad's hobbies was reading. Usually on Saturday mornings, one of us kids was sent into the city on our bicycle to the library to change his three books. We selected what we thought looked okay, and he read it without complaint. There must have been some odd material chosen in the random choice process that I think we all used. His other hobby was listening to the races on Saturday afternoon, frequently having a bet on the horses with his local SP bookmaker. He went to the races very infrequently. I found it to be better for my health and probably Dad's to be out of the house when the races were on, as the noise we kids made interfered with his ability to hear the wireless—still no such thing as TV in the very early 1950s.

Mum had no social life whatsoever. She was so busy looking after the family and spoiling Dad that she had no time for herself. She went into the city by bus about once a week to shop, and that was the extent of it. Occasionally on weekends, we went to Yeppoon on Sunday afternoon for a swim, but such outings were infrequent. Mum did her weekly grocery shopping at Laurie Vaughan's corner store about five or six houses up Eldon Street—we kids took the order up and Laurie delivered it on to the kitchen table later that day. Fruit and vegetable purchases were predominantly from a wonderful old Chinese man whom we called Charlie. I have no idea of his real first name or his family name. He came around in his horse and cart weekly and had a great variety of good-quality fruit and vegetables at reasonable prices. The horse was also very old and slept while Charlie attended to customers. Charlie treated his horse with great care, and it was never required to walk fast. In fact, if it walked any slower it would have gone to sleep again. Milk was delivered by the milkman on to the front steps in pint bottles (568 ml), and it was the job for us kids to ride our bikes daily to the bakery and butcher shop about 750 metres away on Berserker Street. The *Morning Bulletin* paper was delivered on to the front lawn daily by the paper boy on his bicycle.

When we arrived in Rockhampton, the State Primary School where Joan, Valmai, and I were enrolled was located about one kilometre away in Berserker Street. Merle went to Rockhampton High School in the city by bus. Colin was still only about five years old at this time. We either walked to school or rode our bikes. I still had the old bike that we got when Uncle Tom died. It was battered and bent a bit, but it got me there faster than walking. My teacher for the first year and a half was about the worst teacher I had in all my school days. I guess I can't blame it all on to him as I was far from the model student and gave my parents a lot of pain and possibly some to my teachers also. I really hated school, and although I did not lack intelligence, I found it difficult to remember what I had studied. I was very poor at reading, and in later years I found that I had a touch of dyslexia, which I unfortunately passed on to our youngest son, Andrew. I was not a particularly troublesome student in class and I was always in the top quartile when it came to exams, but my reports always said something like: 'If John was prepared to apply himself to his studies, he could do much better'. I frequently hear my grandchildren talking about how much they love school these days and how interesting it is and wish I could have experienced teachers who were capable of finding my 'on' button in the manner that seems to be almost universal in today's classrooms.

Fortunately for me, my teacher for the last year at primary school was probably the best I had in all my school years. Bernie Mahoney was a small, energetic man who commanded respect and had the knack of finding the 'on' switch for each pupil. Due to teacher shortages at the time, he was required to teach two year eight classes of about seventy students at once. They were in adjoining rooms with an open inter-connecting door between. He applied himself with great zeal and stood for no-nonsense in the class. He conducted remedial English classes after school for a number of pupils, and I am thankful to him to this day for the interest he took in me. This led me to achieve very satisfactory marks in the final examination for the year, which allowed me access to secondary school.

While Dad was working at the timber yard, Arthur and Lorice McGuire, a newly-wed couple, moved into the house next door to us in Eldon Street. He was always tinkering with and fixing cars under his house at night and at weekends, and I spent a lot of time helping him when I should have been doing homework. Arthur was also an 'A' grade table tennis player and played in the Rockhampton competition. This led to Dad getting the appropriate timber from Hinz Sawmill where he was working and making us a great table tennis table, which was located under the house. The posts on which the house stood got in the way at times, but it did not stop us having a lot of fun and becoming good players. Arthur used to come over and coach us and eventually talked us into fielding a team in the Rockhampton competition. We called ourselves the Eldons after our street name, and the team consisted of Dad, Merle, Joan, Valmai, Les Dodd, Dad's workmate from down the street, and me. The team was quite successful, and I did quite well in the 'C' grade singles championships a few times although I never got to win it.

I joined the Ninth Rockhampton Scout Troup at the instigation of Alan Sherlock when I was about twelve and soon became a patrol leader. Alan was in Joan's class, a grade above me at school, and he was always the dux of his class and the school sporting champion. He later became a very successful pharmacist and for a few terms was a Liberal politician in Queensland. The Scout troop had four patrols, each of about eight boys, and the competition between patrols was intense. We had a lot of very good times, both at weekly Friday night meetings and at the various camps that we attended. We had a couple of weekend camps each year where we had to organise all our tents, ropes, shovels, cooking utensils, etc. and carry them to the camp site on our bicycles, then erect the heavy canvas tents in a professional way so that they were not blown down in a storm or didn't flood in the rain. The Rockhampton District had a major competition camp for the four days of Easter each year when all troops competed against each other for the Rudd Cup. Judging of the winning troop revolved around the quality, tidiness, and innovation displayed at each camp site as well as the leadership demonstrated by the patrol leaders. I recall how elated we all were when our troop won the cup in 1954. I firmly believe that it was this early entry into a leadership-type role that stood me in good stead in my future career.

I began playing tennis at primary school, liked the game, and became captain of one of the school teams. We played in the school competition, and I enjoyed the challenge of visiting another school each Friday afternoon with my team mates to try to win for Berserker Street State School. Later in my travels around the countryside with my work, tennis was to provide me with an easy means of quickly getting to know people in the community and making new friends.

I made some good friends during that relatively brief period that I attended Berserker Street State School, and many of them went on to Rockhampton State High School with me in January 1954. Lester Barnett was a particularly good friend of mine at Berserker Street School, and we spent a lot of time together on weekends and after school. Lester was very much like me in that he also disliked school. He was always at the bottom of the class and did not go on to secondary school. He was a great bird fancier even at that very young age and had a big aviary of all kinds of birds from parrots to numerous varieties of cockatoos, finches, quails, budgerigars, canaries, pigeons, cockatiels, and others. He purchased, bred, sold, and swapped birds and cared for them entirely by himself. We used to go trapping finches using bird traps that he made. We would ride our bikes for miles out into the bush and place the traps amongst lantana with a finch in the trap as a 'lure' for the wild finches. The 'bait' finch also became an attraction for snakes on occasions, and a few times we had to rescue the trap and finch from interested snakes.

My friend Lester and I formed a friendship with Laurie Hegarty, who lived about five doors from Lester's place. He was about the same age as us and went to a Catholic school. He was an only child and had all the latest toys, the best bike, and also had a 0.22 calibre rifle. We used to do a lot of shooting of birds in the paddocks outside the suburban areas of North Rockhampton and followed our safety procedures closely. As a consequence, we never had an incident that might have resulted in an injury or worse. This brings to mind an experiment we carried out one day, which almost caused a very embarrassing outcome. We had decided that we would see what would happen if we placed a penny bunger fire cracker down the outer metal casing of a bicycle pump, pulled the wick of the bunger through the hole in the bottom of the casing where the flexible coupling screwed in, tamped down some wadding on top of the bunger, and then inserted a marble. The bicycle pump casing was placed against a rock with another big rock on top of it to hold it steady. The mouth of the pump casing was aimed at the galvanised iron back wall of Laurie's father's garage. The fuse was lit and we ran for cover. There was an enormous 'boom' and a lot of smoke from the explosion. We had expected that the marble might put a slight dent in the heavy gauge galvanised iron, but when the smoke cleared, to our horror, we saw that the marble had gone right through the galvanised iron at a level that appeared as though it must have shattered the windscreen of Mr Hegarty's very expensive Jaguar car. In fear and trepidation, we ran around to the front of the garage and quickly saw to our great relief that the car was undamaged. Luck was on our side as the marble had hit the top edge of a timber cross-piece that the galvanised iron was nailed to, and this had deflected it upwards over the top of the car and out through the open front of the garage.

For some unknown reason, Dad decided that he was fit enough to ride to work at Lakes Creek rather than drive the car, so he bought himself a new bicycle, of which I was very envious. I was not at all surprised when he decided against continuing to ride after the first day. Lester and I had ridden our bikes to Lakes Creek and back on many occasions; it was probably a five kilometre ride each way and in the main slightly uphill on the way home. If the breeze was against you on the way home, it became a very exhausting ride even for young and fit lads like us. Dad could hardly walk when he got home on that first day and was grey from heart strain. He drove the car again the next day, and so the new bike stood under the house. I was not allowed to use it until I had passed my scholarship exams and gained entry to Rockhampton High School at the end of that year.

I surprised my parents by getting quite a respectable pass in the State Scholarship examination at the end of 1953. I was then fourteen years of age and commenced an academic course at Rockhampton State High School at the beginning of 1954. The subjects included in the course were English, Maths A, Maths B, Geography, Physics, Chemistry, Latin, and French. Personally, at that stage of my life, I would have preferred to do the industrial course, which included subjects such as woodwork, metalwork, and technical drawing rather than Latin and French. However, Dad and Mum felt otherwise and I bowed to their wisdom.

It was around the time I started at high school that I began doing a Sunday paper run for Keith Golding at his North Rockhampton news agency in order to earn some pocket money; there was no such handout from home simply because it was unaffordable. Although it was more than sixty years ago, when I look back on it now I realise that it was a poorly paid job, but at the time I was happy to have a job where one could earn a little pocket money; such opportunities were few and far between. I started work about 5 a.m. on Sunday morning, rain, hail, floods, or sunshine. I used my own old bicycle, carried a heavy load of papers on the handle bars in a specially made sack in all weather, rode about ten kilometres in the process, finished work about midday, and was paid ten shillings, the equivalent of $1 or about fourteen cents per hour. I did this for about two years before I gave it up.

I joined the army cadets in high school, which meant I went to school one day per week dressed in army uniform comprising a slouch hat, broad-legged khaki shorts, khaki shirt, webbing belt, a highly polished brass belt buckle, army boots, long khaki socks, and puttees. Most of us were still gangling young kids at that stage and looked a hoot in the 'Bombay bloomers' type shorts with our skinny legs. Our instructor, Sergeant Major Jones, was a permanent army officer. After school, we had drill and other instruction at Army Regimental Headquarters, and occasionally we got to fire the World War II 0.303 Lee Enfield rifles at the rifle range. I had previously had a lot of experience with a 0.22 calibre rifle, but those 0.303s really packed a punch and one was easily injured if the rifle was not held appropriately.

I was promoted to Corporal after the first year, and in the middle of my second year in high school, I was selected to go to a sergeant's training course at Greenbank Army Camp outside Brisbane. At that stage, I was still uncertain as to whether I would go on for another two years at school and complete the Senior Certificate, which allowed entry to university. Mum and Dad wanted me to do so, but I had doubts because of the difficulty I had with studies. However, I liked the idea of doing the sergeant's course and the trip to Greenbank also interested me, so I accepted the offer. A group of kids from various Rockhampton schools was on the train on the way to Greenbank when, about fifty kilometres south of Rockhampton, the water tender on the front of the Garratt steam engine came off the rails, parted them, and speared down between them, causing the train to crash to an extremely abrupt halt. Our kitbags and rifles which were in the racks above our heads came crashing down upon us, and our carriage ended up twisted across the tracks with the toilet at one end torn off. Fortunately, we were able to put the old-style wooden framed windows down and jump out. No one was killed, but the driver and fireman were badly injured and a number of kids had nasty cuts and abrasions because of being thrown about and/or hit by flying rifles and kitbags. Luckily, the main road was only about 250 metres away from the train line at that particular place, and the wounded were treated by ambulance while the rest of us were taken back home by coach. Those of us who were not injured and who were allowed by our parents to attempt the travel again set out for Brisbane and Greenbank on another train the following day. A diversion had been built around the crash site, but the water tender was still buried between the tracks and the engine had followed it halfway under. I recall some anxious moments on that trip to Greenbank whenever the brakes of the train were applied abruptly—was it another crash commencing?

Although my good mate Lester Barnett did not go on to secondary school, he and I stayed close friends and we still saw a lot of each other on weekends. Lester got a job as a builder's labourer and went on to run his own building business in due course. He was still very much into birds (the feathered variety) and had extended his aviary and range of birds. He had become quite successful and expert in breeding various species and made good money from their sale. We joined a tennis team at Victoria Park tennis centre across the other side of town and used to ride our bikes there and play in a competition each weekend, then go to the movies occasionally on Saturday nights.

Those years living in Rockhampton were good years, that is, if I could leave school out of the equation. It was not until I left home that I learnt the real value of a peaceful, secure, and stable family life which we all enjoyed at home. Although my parents were not well off financially, there was always adequate and well-cooked food available; we all ate our meals together, my parents rarely raised their voices at one another, and they were always home with us. Luxuries were few and far between, but we were afforded the opportunity of a good education and it was a warm feeling to be part of a respected family.

Chapter 10
The Wide World of Work

Although Dad and Mum were keen for me to continue my education, they could see that I did not have my heart in school work and they were no doubt fed up with nagging me to get on and do my homework and study. They agreed that I could leave school at the end of year 10 and enter the workforce. The next question of course was: 'What work am I going to do?' I had ideas that I might like to be a carpenter, although the academic slant of my secondary education had diminished my chances there. I certainly knew that I didn't have any intentions of doing what Dad had warned me on many occasions of what might become of me if I didn't study—a garbage man or worse. Merle had joined the Commonwealth Bank a few years earlier, and it was suggested that I might like a bank job. I doubted that the Commonwealth Bank would employ me in the same office as my sister, and at sixteen I was not really looking forward to moving from Rockhampton. I had no knowledge that there were such institutions then as private banks whose shares were held by the public. This gave me additional options for a job in my home town. Dad and Mum banked at Australia & New Zealand Banking Group Ltd (ANZ), so it was agreed that I should apply there and, as an additional safeguard, also apply at the Bank of New South Wales (Wales). I saw the accountant at the ANZ Bank first, and although he gave me a good hearing, I felt very uncomfortable throughout the interview because of the habit he had of saying after every response I gave to his questions: 'So that's the story'. I felt that he doubted my word, and I still remember that negative occasion to this day. Ben Hall, the accountant at the 'Wales' was, on the contrary, a very personable fellow who made me feel completely at home. The outcome was that I was offered a position at both banks and had no difficulty selecting the Wales. So on 12 December 1955, I entered the workforce as Postage Clerk at the Bank of New South Wales, Rockhampton, on the annual salary of £350 or the equivalent of $13-46 per week. Superannuation at the rate of 7½ per cent of my gross salary and income tax were then deducted, leaving me to receive approx. $11-00 per week. After paying board at home, there wasn't very much spending power in the $5-00 per week that I had left in my pocket.

I was instructed to report at 9 a.m. to commence work on my first day at the Wales, so I dutifully ensured that I was at the front door about 8.50 a.m. I began to get worried when no one else turned up for work by 9 a.m. until a chap about thirty years of age came along, stopped, looked me up and down, and said, 'You must be the new recruit.' When I told him that I was, he said, 'Well, don't bloody well stand there doing nothing. Get inside and do some work.' I responded that the door was locked! He then said, 'Of course it is. The bank doesn't open until 10 a.m. Get around to the back gate and enter that way like everyone else.' I wondered what I had struck. He turned out to be Kevin Hinchen, one of the greatest wags that I met in my entire career in the bank, who was forever playing tricks on people in the office. He was very helpful to me, but I always had to be on my guard with him as one never knew what to expect next.

I had been in the bank about nine months when I was told to relieve the ledger keeper/junior at the Mt Larcom branch. No one was given the option to refuse in that era, and to do so would mean the end of one's career. Mt Larcom was about 100 kilometres south of Rockhampton on the road to Gladstone. I had no knowledge whatsoever of hand-posted ledgers, or any other ledgers for that matter, as my job at Rockhampton branch was virtually only dealing with the mountain of mail that came into and went out of the branch daily, mainly from all over Central Queensland. In that era, due to the lack of other forms of communication together with poor rural roads, much business was conducted by way of the postal service. The Mt Larcom job was a steep learning curve and thankfully the manager, Eric Morris, was a very patient and helpful person.

I roomed at Mrs Condon's pub, the only hotel in town, for the first week and ate there together with Noel Yarrow, the second officer from the Wales, who lived in staff quarters, a room and bathroom behind the bank's office, and a chap from the Commercial Banking Company of Sydney. When I say that I roomed at the hotel, I had a stretcher on the front veranda separated from the footpath by a barrier of lattice and a curtain. It was quite an experience to find chooks wandering in and out through the dining room and leaving their 'trade marks' on the floor. The meals were fairly good country style cooking, but Mrs Condon used to get upset at the quantity of food that we young fellows ate—all her children were daughters and she didn't quite understand the appetites of growing young men. I recall one morning asking one of her little daughters to go get some more butter and hearing Mrs Condon in the kitchen saying, 'Those bloody bank boys eat all my butter.'

I was able to move to the staff quarters to sleep for the last two weeks and nearly froze to death at night. It was the middle of winter, and the second officer had first call on the available blankets. The supply was insufficient for the two of us, and I had to use the mats off the floor to stop shivering. They were full of dust, the cleaning responsibility being left to the second officer, and I spent each night sneezing a lot. Showering was the funniest ordeal that I ever encountered in all my years of moving around in my banking career. In order to have a shower, one was first required to chop the chips out at the woodheap, light the chip heater with paper and chips, stand in the old tin bath that stood on iron legs, and in order to ensure one didn't freeze or scald, use a hand pump to pump precisely the right amount of water at any one time from the exterior rainwater tank into the chip heater. The procedure involved, while pumping with one hand, soaping up with the other and washing off, turning around and pumping with the other hand, soaping up, washing off, all the time keeping the chip heater burning at just the right heat. Fluctuations in the degree of heat put out by the flame in the heater meant that the water temperature in the shower could rapidly change from cold to scalding unless the pump action was well coordinated. All good experience for a young banker, I was told!

Part of my job at the Wales in Rockhampton was to deliver the daily bills of lading to various warehouses and stores around the town and collect payment on behalf of suppliers for the goods that had been delivered, mainly by boat. Because I had to use my own bike for these deliveries, I was paid a bike allowance of £1 ($2) per week. I learnt later that it was the only such allowance paid throughout the whole of the bank. I enjoyed getting out and delivering the bills around town, and because I missed the morning tea break at work, I didn't feel guilty about stopping for a milkshake each day, which I paid for out of my bike allowance. One drawback in this part of my job was the need to go out in all types of weather. It was almost impossible to keep the bottoms of my long trousers dry in really heavy rain. Shorts were then not allowed as part of business dress. On occasions, I got back to the office looking very much the worse due to the weather.

The manager of Rockhampton branch was a very stern man named Mervyn Parrott. As the branch junior, I was told by him that it was my responsibility to be at work at 8.30 a.m. in order to be able to get the mail from the post office and have it sorted prior to him and the other staff commencing work at 9 a.m. Any mail addressed to the manager personally had to be on his desk by 9 a.m. with the smallest envelope at the top and the rest arranged in pyramid fashion according to their size. There was one exception to this rule, and that was the daily envelope from the State head office in Brisbane which had to be placed neatly on top of the pile. Also before 9 a.m., I had to finish changing the manager's and the clients' ink blotters, cleaning and refilling the black and red inkwells, and inserting new nibs in the pens on his desk and the writing desks in the public space. Quite often, the clients' blotting paper did not have an ink mark on it from the previous day and I could not see the point of wasting good blotting paper, so I left them unchanged. On one such morning, Mr Parrott spied a very small speck of ink on the customer's blotter that I had not noticed, and he tore strips off me. Also, there was a buzzer arrangement, whereby he pressed the button under his desk and it buzzed under my desk. I was expected to be beside his desk before the buzzer stopped sounding, and if not, the outcome was quite unpleasant. He ruled the office with an iron fist, and if he stood at the door of his office, surveying what was happening in the office, a wave of quiet descended across the office as people became aware of his presence.

On the same day that I started work, another junior named David McCarthy commenced work at the branch. One of our joint jobs was to assist in packaging and wrapping large bundles of bank notes that were then despatched through the post to various branches around Central Queensland. It was quite a feat to learn how to neatly tie a parcel of notes wrapped in thick strong brown paper with one piece of strong string that encircled the parcel three times length-wise and three times breadth-wise. There could be only one final knot, and at all points where the string crossed, there had to be a knot tied so that the string could not be manipulated and slipped from the parcel. The final knot was then covered in a blob of molten wax and the bank's seal imprinted on it.

It was then our job to carry the packages valued at many tens of thousands of pounds to the post office to despatch them by registered post. One of us carried the suitcase with the bundles of cash in it while the other carried a concealed small silver revolver and acted as escort. The revolver was loaded with live ammunition, and I do not know how anyone was not hurt through mishandling of the weapon. When one thinks back on this time, it was really ignorant of the bank to require firearms to be carried by inexperienced young people. The citizens of Rockhampton, innocently walking down the footpath near us, never knew how dangerous their situation was with us in charge of a revolver with six bullets in the chamber.

Around the time that I commenced work, a young lady also joined the bank as a typist. She was the daughter of a judge and her brother worked at the local branch of the Commercial Bank of Australia. She was quite an attractive young girl, and towards the end of my first year at work, she became my first date when I invited her to a dance at the Town Hall. I dutifully rode my bike right across town to meet her parents before we rode our bikes to the dance and I escorted her back home.

At the time of the Xmas school holidays in 1956, after I had been working for twelve months, I was told to report to Yeppoon branch, which is a seaside resort near Rockhampton, to lend support for six weeks during the busy Xmas holiday period. There wasn't really a lot for me to do, but I learnt some new tasks and spent a lot of time cleaning a badly rusted Smith and Western 0.32 calibre revolver. Had anyone attempted to shoot with it prior to the clean-up, the gun would have exploded as the barrel was almost completely filled with rust and mud because a hornet had built its nest there.

While in Yeppoon, I boarded at Mrs Clayton's boarding house with Des O'Neill, who was teller at the Wales. It was while I was at Yeppoon branch that I learnt of my first transfer. Des and I were having a swim in the surf one weekend when we met some of the staff from Rockhampton branch. They had heard that I was transferred, but no one from the branch had bothered to contact Yeppoon branch to inform me. They thought the transfer was to a place called Cooroy, but no one had ever heard of it and we had no idea where it was. I found out the following Monday morning that the news of the transfer as Ledger Keeper/Junior was in fact true and that Cooroy was situated between Nambour and Gympie and inland from Noosa on the Bruce Highway about 100 kilometres north of Brisbane.

I had enjoyed my first year in the bank, and although I had no wish to leave home at this early age, I never once thought of declining the transfer, which would have resulted in my forced resignation from the bank.

Maternal Great Grandparents Jane (nee Hardgrave)
& Alexander Cunningham

Maternal Great Grandfather Alexander Cunningham

Maternal Great Grandfather William Taylor Camplin

Paternal Great Grandmother Ann Chatterton (nee Wilson)

Paternal Grandfather (Private) Robert Chatterton in
WW1 - 2nd Light Horse Regiment uniform - 1915

Aunt May Chatterton, Paternal Grandmother Minnie
Chatterton (nee Sutton), Aunt Olive Chatterton - c1935

Maternal Grandparents Charles Edward (Ted) &
Elizabeth Jane Camplin (nee Cunningham)

Aunts Jean & Val, Uncle Hall, Grandfather Ted, Mum (6yrs)
& Aunt Beryl Camplin - Branyan, Bundaberg - 1921

Father John Thomas (Jack) Chatterton (24 yrs) - 4th
from left back row - Struck Oil Cricket Team - 1934

Uncle Hall Camplin, Aunt May Chatterton,
Dad and Mum's wedding - 25 Jan 1936

Father John Thomas (Jack) Chatterton - 1956

Mother Mavis Chatterton (nee Camplin) and Me -
Rockhampton Agricultural Show - 1940

Me, Main Street, Mt Morgan, Queensland -1941

Chatterton family - Dad 38, Me 8, Valmai (seated) 6,
Merle 11, Colin 1, Joan 9, Mum 33 - March 1948

Chatterton family - Colin, Dad, Me, Merle,
Joan, Mum, Valmai - August 1963

Chatterton family - Merle, Joan, Me, Valmai, Colin
and Mum (80th birthday) - March 1995

Great Aunt May Cunningham

Great Aunt May Cunningham & Mum

Aunt Doris Rose (Dolly) Chatterton

Uncle Don and Aunt May Kruse (nee Chatterton)

Aunt Olive Chatterton - 1935

Matt Neil (neighbour), Uncle Don & Aunt May Kruse
(nee Chatterton), Mum & Uncle Les Chatterton

Neil's house (neighbours) - Struck Oil - 1988

Uncle Sydney Edward (Syd) Chatterton - 18yrs

Grandmother Minnie Chatterton (nee Sutton), Dad, Uncle Syd &
Aunt Edith Bonney (nee Chatterton) - prior to Syd's embarkation

Uncle Syd Chatterton - killed in action -
Tobruk, Libya - 29 June,1941

Cousins Eric & Ken, Uncle Bill, Cousin Janice
& Aunt Jean Gear (nee Camplin)

Uncle Bill, Cousin Geoffrey & Aunt Val McDonald (nee Camplin)

Uncle Hall Camplin

Aunts Val & Beryl, Uncle Hall, Aunt Jean &
Mavis (Mum) Camplin - c 1923

Mavis Camplin in basketball costume

Cousins Tom, Jean & Bob, sister Joan, Me, sister
Merle, cousins Ray & Enid Chatterton - c 1943

Cousins Doris, William (Bill), Phyllis, Ruth & Gladys Chatterton

Mum & Aunt Edith Bonney (nee Chatterton) - 2 Nov 1997

'New' farm house - Struck Oil - built 1948 - image 1988

Me - 17.5 yrs - December 1956

Val Bennett - 17.5 yrs - May 1959

Me & Val Bennett - June 1961

Me & Val Chatterton (nee Bennett) - 29 September, 1962

Valerie Bennett - in self-made debutante dress - 1957

Keith, Valerie, Alan & Mary Bennett (seated) -June 1961

Mother-in-law Mary Bennett, Val in going away
outfit, Me & Mum - 29 September 1962

Father-in-law Jack Bennett - 1954

Brothers-in-law Alan & Keith Bennett, Val Chatterton (nee
Bennett), mother-in-law Mary Bennett (90th birthday) - July 2000

Sister & brother-in-law Dorothy (nee Heironymus) & Alan Bennett

Brother-in-law Keith Bennet, mother-in-law Mary Bennett (80th birthday) & Annette Bennett - Keith's wife (nee Outridge) - July 1990

Son Paul (aged 2 yrs) with Sister Korst - Mater
Children's Hospital, Brisbane - April 1967

Son Mark, Val with baby Andrew, son Paul & daughter Lisa -
passport photo prior to transfer to England - May 1973

CHAPTER 11

The Tour Begins

——————⟩⦿⟨——————

At home, there was great consternation—no one had expected that I might be transferred away so soon after joining the bank. I must say that I was a bit uneasy about it myself, but I felt that the move would be a real adventure. So in January 1957, at the tender age of seventeen years two months, I set out on a journey the likes of which I could never have imagined. It would take me around the world, allow me to meet a wonderful wife and my life partner, to travel widely both within Australia and overseas, to meet many interesting people some of whom became lifelong friends, to experience the joys of having four children, and to suffer the ongoing heart-break of the loss of two of them. Moreover, I was to accomplish career highlights that exceeded my wildest dreams.

There was much weeping from Mum and my sisters as the train departed Rockhampton station for Cooroy and on to Brisbane. I was met at Cooroy station by the second officer of the branch at about one o'clock in the morning and shown to a room in Jack Flannery's Railway Hotel. The next day I was shifted to Mrs Dobe's boarding house. It was an old house where I had a room at the back, off the kitchen. Bob Webb, who was a school teacher at the local

State School, had a room at the front as did Maurice Herrington, a timber mill worker. Mrs Dobe was a widowed shearer's cook about sixty years of age, and although the meals were not fancy, they were wholesome and there was plenty of food. She was a fanatical card player and tried to get me to play crib at every opportunity. As a consequence, I became quite a good crib player. She was an early riser and had most of her housework done by the time I had to get up to commence work at 9 a.m. She gave me breakfast in bed every morning, mainly so she could keep on with her chores, but I enjoyed it all the same. The bathroom was downstairs under the house, and it had a chip heater with a bath but no shower. Water was supplied from a tank and was always in relatively short supply. We were able to bathe daily but were regularly reminded to use as little water as possible. There was a shower under the enclosed tank stand, but that only got used in the summer months as there was no hot water connected to it, and then only if good rains had fallen and the tank was near full.

The manager at Cooroy was a highly eccentric First World War veteran named Edwin Wallys Kellaway. A severe war injury to the jaw meant his false teeth fitted poorly and they almost rattled out of his mouth when he got wound up, which was often. He was a highly negative individual who raved on ceaselessly about the poor quality of all things Australian made. He never answered correspondence from the head office until they threatened to sack him. He always called me Mr err . . . err . . . err . . . err . . . Chatterton and had trouble recalling my name even after almost two years, but he refused to use my Christian name. Under no circumstances would the pompous old blighter stoop to call me John, and this riled me no end. When he called out to me from in his office, on principle, I refused to answer until he mentioned my name and at times he would shorten the 'err . . . err . . . err' and roar, 'You, you stupid bugger, come in here'. After going into his office, he would ask me to get him an envelope or some other mundane thing. What a lovely introduction to what my future in the bank might be like! After spending two years with him and his lazy second officer with whom I often clashed quite heatedly, I knew that there wasn't a lot that anyone could throw at me in my later career that I could not handle.

I joined the tennis club and the Rugby League Football Club and soon got to know quite a few young people around town. There were frequent dances on Friday and Saturday nights, both in Cooroy and at nearby towns or farming districts, and there was a change of movies at the Memorial Hall at least weekly. I had a good social life and enjoyed the type of work I was doing despite having to cope with the two officers I worked with. I became friendly with a young lady and kept company with her for about six months, although there really wasn't a great deal of spark in the relationship. I knew virtually everyone in town and most of our customers quite well. Clive Hawkins was a dairy and banana farmer customer, and one day when he was in the bank, he asked me if I would partner his daughter Glenda to the forthcoming debutante ball. I knew Glenda and she was a nice girl, but she did not really interest me; yet I felt I couldn't really refuse her father's request. I arranged for Jack Daly, the local tailor, to make me my first suit, at great expense to my very limited budget, and attended the rehearsals where I met a young lady who really did set the sparks flying. On the night of the ball, I did the 'escorting Glenda thing' appropriately until the presentations were over, and then I spent most of the rest of the night dancing with Valerie Bennett, the same young lady who is now my darling wife and soul mate of fifty plus years. I felt a little embarrassed the next time I saw Glenda and her father but only a little bit, as I had my sights firmly set elsewhere. Clive attempted to keep me interested by bringing me bananas, but it didn't work.

At the time, Val was not long out of high school and was working as a shop assistant and bookkeeper at Harry Spring's pharmacy.

I passed the shop twice each day at set times on my way to The English, Scottish & Australian Bank to do the exchange of cheques between the two banks. She used to pretend that she didn't look out for me and used to blush in embarrassment when I caught her looking, as I guess I did too. I sometimes caught up with her when walking home from work and got to know her better. I plucked up the courage to ask her to go to the movies with me and she said 'yes', but I would have to ask her mother for permission. I fronted up and got the third degree. It wasn't too bad and I was given permission provided we came straight home. To Val's embarrassment, her mother always waited up for us to get home and always had a cup of tea prepared together with a freshly baked cream sponge cake. She was a great cook and I enjoyed her great biscuits and cakes but could have done without them at the time. I was often invited for meals with the family and generally got on well but only as long as I agreed with Mrs Bennett's opinion and wishes. I could appreciate her protectiveness of Val, whose father had tragically died from a heart attack about two years previously, and I carefully respected the proper care of her only daughter. I also respected the fact that Val's mum had the sole responsibility of caring for her and her siblings. Her elder brother, Alan, was apprenticed as a pharmacist at Harry Spring's pharmacy. Keith, her younger brother, was then in his final year of secondary school at Nambour High and later went on to successfully undertake an engineering degree at Queensland University.

Although Val's mother always treated me very well and was quite generous to me, the relationship was never easy. When I was transferred from Cooroy, I think she felt relieved that my friendship with Val would evaporate and with it would go the possibility of losing her daughter from Cooroy.

Val learnt the piano for many years, and when I met her she was at an advanced stage with her studies. She drove to Pomona, a small town about 10 kilometres distant, on Thursdays in Harry Spring's jeep and worked in his Pomona pharmacy and did the books of account while she was there. She also had a music lesson at the convent during her lunch hour. On Saturdays, after the Cooroy pharmacy closed about midday, she again travelled to Pomona for another lesson, this time by train. She was taught by Mother Bernadette, who had told Val that her family name was Kitty Hayman and before she entered the convent she was a school teacher. Val took me to meet her at the convent on one occasion, and it turned out that she taught my dad at Horse Creek, Mt Morgan when he was a youngster. She was a lovely lady and Val was very fond of her.

During the latter part of my stay at Cooroy, I was requested to report to Kingaroy branch to relieve the ledger keeper for three weeks. The only option that I had to be able to get there was by train to Gympie, then another train to Kingaroy. However, the difficulty with this arrangement was that there was a wait of about five hours at Gympie before the Kingaroy train arrived. I felt I was going to freeze to death on the Gympie railway station that night as I waited for the train that arrived about 1 a.m. Ernie Yelland, the manager at Kingaroy, was another war veteran who had been gassed in Europe and had a very deep-seated chesty cough and a terrible pallor about him. This didn't stop him from chain-smoking, and he used to sit at his desk with a tailor-made cigarette always in his mouth. He coughed repeatedly and never knocked the ash off his cigarette into an ashtray. The ash would hang down from the tip of the cigarette and eventually fall on to his desk or lap. At that time, I was a smoker, and despite the fact that I didn't have a repetitive hacking cough, all my attempts to do what he was able to unconsciously achieve in having the ash dangling downwards always ended in failure.

I was transferred from Cooroy in early 1959 to the position of Ledger Examiner at Chinchilla. This was about six months after meeting Val, and in that time we had become very close friends. We parted very sadly as I left town, neither knowing where the future would take us. Chinchilla is situated on the Darling Downs of South-Western Queensland between Dalby and Miles. The surrounding country is flat, and in winter it is windy and very cold. Accommodation for single males was scarce, and I first stayed at a boarding house with two other lads named Rodney Smith and Graham Ives. Rodney worked as the junior at the Wales and Graham was the accountant at Slessor's Garage, a large local car dealership. The boarding house was owned by a dishonest old woman of about seventy years of age, who charged £5 per week for board plus an additional 5/- if one had an electric shaver. This was more than 75 per cent of my entire net salary and meant that living options otherwise were very frugal indeed. She washed and ironed only three work shirts per week and after that one had to pay 1/- per shirt to iron them oneself with a pots iron heated up on the top of the wood stove.

There was no reticulated hot water, and one had to fill the twenty-litre bucket and put it on the woodstove on arriving home from work if one wanted a bath. Meals were so bad and skimpy that Mum used to send me fruit cakes and jam for snacks, and sometimes we were still so hungry after having dinner that we went down to the cafe for another meal. The old woman used to steal the cake out of my room to feed it to her friends for morning tea while we were at work, and then when I tackled her about it she would swear black and blue that she had not touched a crumb. It used to be hard to sit at the table with her mature-aged son, who also lived there and who would often be eating a juicy steak with cooked vegetables for dinner while we were served up half a sausage with our vegetables. She felt no embarrassment when we objected. We used to walk home for lunch each day and buy the bread for her on the way. She always gave us yesterday's bread as she said we ate too much of her bread if it was fresh. Quite often, the lights would go out at about 9 p.m. as a consequence of her turning them off at the power board to save electricity. We were expected to go to bed. Needless to say, we were anxious to move although we had to put up with the conditions for nine months because of the difficulty of finding another place.

Eventually, we advertised for alternative accommodation and got only one reply. It was from a middle-aged married couple named Stan and Jo Bishop. They had one very young son named Tony and offered to take two of us in at £5 per week each. One of us would have to sleep in a double bed with another young chap Graham Kartz from the National Bank. We were so desperate to move that Rodney and I decided to take the plunge. I drew the short straw and had to sleep in the double bed with Graham. Rodney had to sleep in the 'junk' room on a bunk bed, but it turned out to be much better than what we had been suffering. Jo and Stan were really friendly and we were treated like their own kids. Her cooking was atrocious, but there was plenty of it. We were served up fried steak almost every night with tinned beans and mashed potato together with some watery gravy over it. I tried to teach her how to make good gravy, but she couldn't grasp the process. Sweets consisted of tinned pears and ice-cream every night; hence, the reason I haven't eaten tinned pears since. Jo was also a procrastinator extraordinaire and at times damped down our shirts before ironing and then forgot about them for days; the result was that all the shirts ended up with mildew spots on them, which were almost impossible to remove in those days. Stan was the president of the local Rugby League Football Club, and I soon became treasurer. I also got involved in a tennis club and used to play a lot of social tennis with a group from work. Flo Hutton, one of my workmates, was an excellent young player and a district champion. She had a tennis court at home and was always looking for someone to practice with. She used to beat us every time.

There was no easy way to get from Chinchilla to Cooroy to see Val, and I did not have a car nor could I possibly afford to buy one let alone cover the running expenses. I had to somehow get to Brisbane and then catch a train to Cooroy. Banks used to open on Saturday mornings in those days, so I could not leave Chinchilla until about 12 noon on a Saturday. I learnt that a young local pharmacist often went to the Gold Coast for the weekend and left at Saturday lunchtime after his shop closed. I used to hitch a ride with him about once each six weeks. He drove a modern utility at breakneck speed, dropped me on the western outskirts of Brisbane, and collected me there again on Sunday night. I then hitched a ride to the train terminus at Roma Street in Brisbane and got to Cooroy about 8.30 p.m. on Saturday night. I had to catch the train back to Brisbane about 4.30 p.m. on Sunday afternoon, and the short time that Val and I had together seemed to simply fly. My pharmacist friend would be so tired on occasions as a consequence of his escapades at Surfers' Paradise the previous night that he would go to sleep at the wheel before we got halfway to Chinchilla. I would then take over the driving even though I did not have a license at the time. I did this mad scramble for the two years that I was at Chinchilla. Otherwise, Val and I saw each other only during annual holidays. We used to write to each other a few times a week, and I occasionally felt that I could afford to ring Val, as the cost of long distance calls (then known as trunk calls) was exorbitant and generally beyond my budget.

The manager at Chinchilla was Bill Atkinson, and he and his wife Dade lived in the bank's residence, which was both beside the bank on the ground floor (entry, dining room, eat-in kitchen, bathroom, and maid's room) and above the bank (bedrooms, lounge, bathroom). Dade was a large and very outspoken woman, but she had a heart of gold and was very good to young bank officers like me. The Western Downs can be bitterly cold in winter, and on the first really cold morning, I was told that it was part of my job to light the office fire when I got to work and to keep it burning all day. I saw the woodheap down the backyard, so I proceeded to get an armful of wood and some chips. As I was about to enter the back door of the bank, this raucous female voice bellowed from the kitchen, 'Where did you get that bloody wood?' I almost dropped the lot in fright and turned to explain that I got it from the woodheap. I was immediately told in no uncertain terms, 'Take the bloody wood back to where you got it from and get the bloody wood from outside the back fence because bloody Bill is too bloody lazy to throw the wood over the fence for me and I'm not going to let you have my bloody wood.' I did as she said without question, and eventually I got the fire started, but it smoked terribly. In my scouting years, I had lit many fires under all sorts of circumstances, but I had not had previous experience in setting a fire in a fireplace. I was quite embarrassed at this initial attempt. Apparently, Dade smelt the smoke in the residence, and she came barging into the office (before opening hours luckily) wanting to know, 'Were you ever a bloody Boy Scout and how bloody useless could one be?' In a few minutes, she had the fire burning beautifully, and after that she lit the fire every morning before we all arrived at work. Her generosity far outweighed her loudness. She never missed putting on afternoon tea for every staff member's birthday and for Xmas and Easter.

I had my first experience, and I think the only one, of being mentioned unfavourably in a report to the bank while I was Ledger Examiner at Chinchilla. An audit of the branch had been conducted by Jack Fisher, who was a very tall, stern man and a stickler for the rules. He reported very favourably on my ledgers' section but criticised me for not following the procedure set out in the Book of Rules for identifying 'stopped cheques'. The fact that I had never paid one and actually identified several via the use of my own more efficient process did not carry any weight with him. In Fisher's view, the 'rules are the rules' and that was all there was to it. I was very disappointed, but Mr Atkinson strongly supported me and told me not to worry. It then happened that the bank required Jack Fisher to relieve Mr Atkinson for six weeks immediately after the audit was completed. While the boss was on leave, my relationship with Jack Fisher mellowed. Eventually, we got to talk about the rules governing the identification of 'stopped cheques'. He finally accepted the process which I had instituted and agreed that the rules should be modified and that he would take it up with the bank. Whether he did or not, I do not know.

My next transfer was in 1960 to Teller/General Hand at Mt Gravatt in Brisbane, and it was with some trepidation that this country boy arrived in the big city to work for the first time. By then, my sister Merle had married her childhood sweetheart Brian Dwyer and they owned a house at Salisbury in Brisbane. I was very grateful to them for asking me to board with them, but the daily travel was a problem—a fifteen to twenty minute walk to the tram and an hour's tram ride to Mt Gravatt, changing trams at Woolloongabba on the way there, then the reverse in the afternoon. The ride in an open tram in the middle of winter convinced me that I should buy a car. This meant that I no longer had to travel to Cooroy by train, which I was doing each weekend, and the trip to and from work was reduced to approx. fifteen minutes. I had little available cash, and the Austin A40 that I purchased turned out to have been 'prettied up' for the sale. It was very well worn and I was required to spend a considerable sum on it to keep it on the road, although some years later I was able to sell the car for a reasonable profit.

Mt Gravatt branch was quite busy on the front counter, and when I balanced my cash one afternoon I found to my horror that I was £100 short. The bank's policy then was that tellers had to cover shortages from their own pockets, but surpluses had to be declared and were eventually paid by the bank into the Buckland Fund. This fund was set up by a former director and chairman of the board,

Sir Thomas Buckland, and its objects were to provide support to the widows and children of bank officers and retired bank officers in financial difficulties. The size of the loss at the time was equivalent to many weeks' net pay, and needless to say, I had a very uncomfortable time until I located the error the next day. It arose because the manager, Guy Hamlyn-Harris, had a habit of coming into my teller's box and talking to the customer as I dealt with their banking needs. This had distracted me sufficiently on this occasion for me to make the error, and fortunately when I determined where the error might be, the woman concerned immediately agreed that she had banked only one lot of £100 whereas there were two separate deposits for her for the same amount in the bank's books for that day. Guy Hamlyn-Harris never got into my teller's box from then on while a customer was at my counter.

My promotions then followed in quick succession. I had been at Mt Gravatt for only nine months when I was moved to Teller 'C' Townsville and then six months later to Teller 'B' Mt Isa and another nine months later to Teller 'A' Annerley in Brisbane. On hearing of my transfer to Townsville in 1960, I visualised a place in the tropical north, but I was quite mistaken. Townsville is a dry and relatively unattractive area whereas one hundred kilometres or so further north there are true tropical conditions. I was told before I left Brisbane that I was allowed two days to drive to Townsville, so I decided to stay at home in Rockhampton on the first night and then go the rest of the way the following day. All went well until I was about seventy-five kilometres north of Rockhampton early on the second morning when a large truck travelling in the opposite direction flung up a rock that shattered the windscreen of the Austin A40. The most likely place to be able to get a replacement windscreen was Mackay about two hundred kilometres further north, so I had to press on. Slivers of glass from the shattered windscreen began to hit me in the face, so I put my sunglasses on to protect my eyes. Finally, I had to stop and knock out the entire shattered glass, lots of which ended up in the car. A substantial portion of the nation's number one highway, the Bruce Highway, was still unsealed then, and to add to the dust that flooded the car every time a vehicle passed, it rained. So here was I driving along with my raincoat on and the sun visor down to keep the rain out of my eyes and to stop all the insects hitting me in the face. When I got to Mackay, I think I had collected all the insects along the way in the back seat of the Austin A40 and I was absolutely covered in dust.

I called on my friend Don Flatman, who was previously with me at Mt Gravatt branch, to get assistance, and he did not recognise me, I was in such a state. I was able to clean up a bit in the branch staff washroom and then find a replacement windscreen. The only one available in town was from a wreck. It was a little scratched, but I had no option. It was duly installed and I headed north again late in the afternoon. I was driving in the dark when all of a sudden I noticed that there were eyes all around me and realised that I was in the midst of a herd of cattle that were calmly walking along the sides of the road. I got as far as Bowen that evening, and the publican there was a bit suspicious about giving me a room. When I told him why I was in such a mess, he relented but asked that I go easy on the water usage as they had only tank supply. I had no option but to use more water than I wanted to in order to get the red dust out of my hair and off my body.

The next morning I set off for Townsville early as I had figured that I could still be there by 9 a.m. to commence work on time. I pushed the poor old Austin A40 along more rapidly than it liked to go and was able to knock on the front door of the bank at 9 a.m., only to be told that I was not expected until the following day. The person who opened the door was a very short, rotund chap about fifty years of age with a crew cut, toothbrush moustache, and a few bottom front teeth missing. He looked a little like a Sumo wrestler, and I immediately classified him as the cleaner. It came as a real surprise shortly afterwards to note that he was in fact Teller 'A'. My job was as Teller 'C', and in between our teller's cages was Teller 'B' Stuart Whitehead, who was about forty-five years of age. Teller 'A' Tammy Miller was the boss of his domain. He ran the teller line of five tellers very well, was an accurate and fast worker, did as little as he could possibly get away with, had his own regular customers with whom he joked and talked, and usually went home at about 4.30 p.m. without being questioned by the accountant who was the boss of the office staff. Tammy rolled his own cigarettes, smoked continuously while serving customers, and very rarely took the cigarette from his mouth. When he did so, he stuck it to the counter edge by way of the wet and sticky end that he had taken from his mouth. He had only one tie, which he took off as soon as the doors were closed at 3 p.m. in the afternoon and hung it over the back of his teller's cage ready for the next day. On one occasion, the tie got caught in his teller's cage door when he closed it on the way home. Next morning, it had a big kink in it, but Tammy put it on, gave it a tug, and it was business as usual, kink and all. In summer, and before air conditioning was installed in the office, Tammy kept a hand towel draped over his teller's cage door. Every so often, he stopped counting cash, took off his glasses, stuck his cigarette to the counter, undid the buttons on his shirt front, and wiped his chest, armpits and face in full view of the customers. Despite all this, Tammy was universally very well liked by customers and staff and no manager was prepared to take him on.

While living in Townsville I boarded with Des O'Neill at his invitation. I had first met Des in Yeppoon in 1956, and he was now married to Pat, who was a ledger machinist at Rockhampton when I was there. They had a very young son Shane and as a young married couple needed the extra money that I paid in board. A number of the young staff in Townsville played squash regularly and I became a very keen player. They also occasionally took a boat to Magnetic Island for the day on weekends. The island was virtually undeveloped at that time and featured only two very small 'resorts', where fairly basic holiday accommodation was available. One of these was called Arcadia Bay and had the remains of a shark net, which the American military stretched across the bay when they were there during the war years. Really, the only parts of the net that remained intact were the two thick steel ropes that originally supported the top and bottom of the net, and there was no longer any shark protection whatsoever. It was great fun to walk out along these old ropes, jump off, and then swim to shore. I thought I was to become shark food one day when I looked down after I had dived in from off the wire rope. The water was crystal clear, and as I looked down, I saw this giant black shape beneath me. I immediately swam as fast as I could until I eventually realised that the shape beneath me was my own shadow being cast on the sandy bottom through the clear water by the sun above. The trip across to Magnetic took only about forty minutes by a small boat, but at times the wind blew up in the afternoon and seasickness was always a possibility on the way home.

John Jackson, a staff member about my age, was a very keen fisherman and often went out to the Great Barrier Reef on fishing trips. On one such occasion, he gave Des and me a beautiful big Red Emperor that he had caught and we looked forward to many tasty fish dinners. Within about twenty-four hours of the first meal, we were all in agony from pain in every muscle of the body. Little did we know that at certain times of the year, Red Emperor become poisonous to eat and we had ciguatera poisoning. We kept on eating the fish until Pat sought advice from her doctor and found the cause of our pains. The only way I could relieve the pain in my legs was to lie on the bed with my legs up the wall. I expect this reduced the pressure of blood in the legs and thus had the effect of easing the pain. I have always been a bit hesitant about eating Red Emperor ever since that experience.

For a short period of time in Townsville, I was given the Agency Officer's job. This involved me and another chap going to a very busy agency in suburban Rising Sun with a large sum of cash carried in a leather bag similar to those held by bookmakers. We went in the Austin A40 and, on the way, followed the long-established routine of calling at a large private bus operator's depot and collecting his deposit from the previous day's bus runs. He used to fill my petrol tank for free in return for me picking up the deposit, which consisted mainly of 2/-pieces, all wrapped, and lots of other coins, all of which weighed the little Austin down quite noticeably. My assistant was one of the young strongman types, who always had to demonstrate his athleticism. One day we were unloading trays and trays of wrapped coins from my car outside the front doors of the branch in Flinders Street, the main street of Townsville. He had about four of these very heavy trays in his hands and tripped on the gutter. Rolled coins went everywhere down the footpath and into the gutter. People walking down the street helped recover the loot, and despite lots of the rolls spilling their contents all over the place, we did not lose one coin.

The manager of Townsville branch was a little fat guy with a moustache, named Roy Taysom. He was unanimously disliked by the staff because of his rude attitude to all and sundry. One knew he was in a good mood if he grunted in response to your greeting when he entered the premises in the morning; otherwise the response was stony silence. As a teller, it was my responsibility to efficiently receive customers' deposits, cash their cheques as there were no ATMs in those days, and deal competently with their sundry enquiries. When cashing cheques, it was my additional responsibility to assess the customer's bona fides before cashing the cheque and if in doubt refer the cheque to the Ledger Department for prior approval. Customer pressure was fairly constant, and I prided myself on my overall abilities as a teller. One day, I cashed a £5 cheque for a known client. It turned out that he had only about £2/10/- in his account, and Mr Taysom dishonoured the cheque with the answer 'refer to drawer' and left me with the responsibility of getting the money refunded from the customer or else paying the full amount myself. I was vehemently opposed to this decision and maintained that the cheque should have been debited to the client's account and the small residual debt written off in due course if the client did not cover the amount in the near future. My reasoning for taking this stance was that I had not at all been negligent in my duties, and as a consequence the risk involved in the transaction should reside with the bank and not the teller. I refused to pay the amount and lodged the cheque with the bills clerk with the instructions that he should refer the cheque to the Ledger Department daily, together with his other bills for collection, in the hope that the client had deposited funds. In the meantime, I wrote to the client in an endeavour to have him cover the small amount outstanding. The situation was left unresolved when I departed on transfer to Mt Isa in 1961.

During the nine months that I was in Townsville, I saw Val only twice, once when I went south on holidays and on another occasion when she spent a week in Townsville and stayed at Des and Pat's place before I went to Mt Isa.

In 1961, Mt Isa was growing rapidly and had a population of about 12,000 (now about 25,000), most of whom were single male immigrants from about thirty different countries. It was a really rough mining town, where the miners worked hard, earned huge money, drank and gambled hard, and fought frequently. The smart ones saved their money and within twelve months had sufficient funds to put a sizeable deposit on a home down south. The bank provided excellent quarters for its single male staff. There were twelve of us accommodated in non-air-conditioned single rooms. The bank supplied the sheets and towels and paid for their washing and the cleaning of the premises. Although I was not quite twenty-two years old at the time and far from being the oldest or senior most at the quarters, the branch manager, Doug Miller-Morrison, told me upon my arrival that I was to take over the management of the quarters, which included resolving the issue of a mess fund debt of about £250. Even though I had just arrived, I was told that I was to assume responsibility for my share of the debt and get the situation under control quickly. I soon found that the 'wonderful' cook, whom the boys had hired and all raved about, was also feeding her family from the mess funds, hence the reason for their inability to make ends meet. She accepted my invitation to move out gracefully, and with close control over the new cook, we quickly got the mess fund back into the black.

Although Mt Isa is very isolated, extremely hot and very dusty in summer, very cold at night in winter, and a long, long way from Cooroy, and anywhere else of interest for that matter, I recall my relatively short stay in the 'Isa' with a degree of fondness. It was the most unusual banking experience one could come across in Australia and certainly the only place where I have seen the bank manager frogmarch a client out of his office and through the front doors. He held him by one hand on the back of his shirt collar and the other on the seat of the pants and tossed him out on to the street. It was a bit like a return of the Wild West days! Also, the experience of living with a group of young fellows really broadens one's perspective on the behaviour, both good and bad, of other human beings. I saw the best and worst of behaviour from so-called civilised young bank officers, and it became very obvious that some would have a very short career in the bank. I made some long-lasting friendships there, and over fifty years later Bruce Alexander and I are still close friends. Bruce and Wendy and Val and I have socialised together regularly during the intervening years whenever we were in the same vicinity. They now live in retirement in the Hunter Valley of New South Wales and we occasionally spend nights at each other's places.

Social life was fairly limited in Mt Isa, and isolation was a real
issue for most of us to deal with. Cloncurry was the nearest town
of any size, but it had no attraction and one had to be a masochist
to put one's car to the test of tackling the unbelievably bad road.
An alternative was to visit Camooweal out near the Northern
Territory border. The road was all sealed, but very narrow and road
trains were a constant danger. Camooweal has a large aboriginal
population and little else of note other than its millions of flies.
Joseph Freckington owned the general store and banked with us
at Mt Isa. I recall we went there on one occasion and bought some
ham sandwiches for lunch. We had great difficulty eating them
without devouring a number of flies at the same time—and that
happened when we were seated inside the store. Three of us were
engaged to girls in faraway places and trying to save money on our
frugal wages. We mostly spent our time by visiting the free open
air movies provided by the Mount Isa Mines two nights per week,
swimming at the mine's dam, watching local sport, playing table
tennis at the quarters, and occasionally visiting one of the three
pubs. The latter activity was always a dangerous one to pursue as
many of the local miners spent their off-work hours in the pub and
any small incident would provoke a fight. It would not be correct
to describe the town as lawless; it was simply filled with many very
fit young men of different nationalities, some of whom hated each
other by dint of birth, all of them full of testosterone, and only a few
of them able to find a partner due to the extreme shortage of young
women in the town. The police had a tough job keeping order, and
as a consequence they patrolled the streets at night in pairs.

On one occasion, a few of us decided to have a game of golf to fill
in time and relieve the boredom. It was Boxing Day 1961 and the
course was officially closed because of the summer heat, but that did
not stop us. With the temperature at about 110 Fahrenheit (45 °C),
we set off and soon needed a drink of water. None of us had thought
about taking water with us. Sprinklers were in action on the course,

so we had a drink from that source whenever we felt the need. Later that night, all four of us found ourselves in the bathrooms at the staff quarters at the same time, either with severe diarrhoea, severe vomiting, or both at the same time. I was the only one fit enough to go to work the next day, but on many occasions during the day I had to excuse myself quickly from my teller's duties and run out the back. Bruce Alexander was very ill and subsequently was diagnosed with hepatitis. We later learnt that the water we had consumed was the effluent from the sewerage treatment works. Although I was never diagnosed with full-blown hepatitis, it took about six months for my system to get back to normal.

While in Mt Isa, I received a request from Roy Taysom, the manager at Townsville, via a letter to the manager at Mt Isa to pay the £5 for the cheque that I cashed, which overdrew the customer's account. If I didn't pay, he threatened to report the matter to the head office. Doug Miller-Morrison was stunned when I told him to tell Roy Taysom to go ahead and report the matter and that I would only pay if the head office said I should. I learnt later that Doug did the very same thing to his tellers. Without Taysom's knowledge, Townsville staff subsequently sent me a copy of the correspondence that he sent to the bank and the bank's response. Taysom was reprimanded for the action he proposed taking and was instructed to write the debt off. Naturally, he didn't bother to tell me the outcome officially. Subsequently, I cashed a cheque for about £13 for a known customer at Mt Isa, and it overdrew his account by that amount. The chap had been laid off by the mines due to a huge labour strike at the time and had gone to Brisbane until it was over. The cheque was dishonoured, and as usual Doug wanted me to pay up. I refused and he started to threaten me. I told him to ring the manager at Townsville to see what direction the bank had given him in dealing with such situations, and I never heard any more about the matter. Later, the offending customer returned to Mt Isa and cleared the small debt, but only after my mate Bill Hughes, the teller next to me, recognised him, extracted the money from him, and told him not to come back to the bank.

The most senior amongst all of us living at the staff quarters was the appointed Securities Clerk at the branch. He was a pain to almost all of us for various reasons and particularly so to me as the person responsible for the quarters. Because of his seniority, he seldom agreed to comply with the decisions of the group as a whole and at times went out of his way to offend people. Bruce Alexander, Ralph Chandler, Billy Hughes, and I got our own back on him in a very odorous way. We found a large 'T' bone steak buried in the iced-up freezer when we were doing an infrequent defrosting and cleaning job. The steak was well past its use-by-date, so rather than ditch it we decided it would be good punishment if we tacked it to the back of his wardrobe, which we immediately proceeded to do in his absence. The hot weather played its part quickly. The next afternoon as we arrived at the staff quarters from work in my Austin A40, we spied him crawling out from under the quarters through a small gate immediately below his room. Keeping a straight face with difficulty, we asked him what he was doing. He replied, 'It smells in my room as though there is a dead cat under the building', and we almost gave the game away then trying not to laugh. He searched around the place, without our help of course, but he never divulged whether he had found the offending 'cat' or not. Some months later, he was transferred from Mt Isa, and during the clean-up process in his room we had a look behind the wardrobe. There hung the 'dead cat' in all its glory. It had grown penicillin fur about two centimetres long all over it in all colours of the rainbow, but it had no smell left whatsoever. It was so hard and dry it could possibly have been used to sole shoes!

Val and I saw each other once only while I was in Mt Isa, and that was in early 1962 when I again took leave. We became engaged on that occasion, and I recall clearly having to ask Val's mum for permission for us to marry as Val was then only twenty-years of age. I can't say that Val's mum was thrilled, but she did agree and gave us her blessing. She also lent us her car to drive to Brisbane in order to purchase an engagement ring. I later called on the head office in Brisbane to alert them to the fact that we were to be married in the coming September. We had decided that we were going to marry and live in Mt Isa even though we couldn't see how we could survive the astronomical rental costs in the 'Isa' unless Val was able to get a well-paid clerical job at the mines. John Wilson, the chief clerk and head of staff in Queensland at the time, solved our problem immediately by telling me that the bank did not allow young male officers to marry and stay in Mt Isa because of the impossible rental housing position. The bank provided housing for its married appointed officers only. He asked me where I would like to go from Mt Isa, and I told him, 'Anywhere but Cooroy.' Val and I had discussed this issue previously, and she agreed with what I told John Wilson.

My transfer to Annerley Branch in Brisbane as Teller 'A' came through in about May 1962, and I again boarded with Merle and Brian at Salisbury. I had sold my Austin A40 in Mt Isa, and so I took the tram to work, which was only a twenty-minute ride after the walk to the terminus. I travelled to Cooroy each weekend by train, and the few months we had together before we got married enabled us to get to know each other again. I later calculated that during the four years that we were going out together before we were married, we saw each other only one day per month on average and that includes all the days that we spent at each other's homes during our holidays. We were obviously meant to be together, and there is little wonder that our relationship has stayed so strong over all these years despite the tragedies of life that have befallen us.

A funny happening at Annerley branch was that Mr Kellaway, the eccentric manager I worked with in Cooroy in 1957-58, had retired by this time and was now living nearby and banked at the branch. I recognised him as soon as he walked to the teller's counter, and he sort of half recognised me. I refused to remind him of my name and he didn't ask. After I had served him he asked to see the accountant Aubrey Wehlow. When he eventually left the branch, Aub came to me at a quiet time and laughingly recounted his conversation with Kellaway. Aub knew the history of Kellaway and of my time with him in Cooroy and had heard on the bank's very effective grapevine about his difficult and eccentric behaviour. Kellaway had asked Aub who I was. When Aub told him, he then asked what sort of an officer I was. Aub told him that I was showing great promise, and Kellaway claimed that I should be as he had trained me. We had a great laugh, and I told Aub that I could not recall one good thing that I had learnt from Kellaway but that I had learnt a lot about what not to do. He came into the branch weekly to cash a cheque or bank dividend cheques for the next eighteen months or so while I was at the branch, and despite the fact that I was always polite to him he never ever called me by name.

It was while I was at Annerley branch that I made a pivotal decision, one which I consider was positively life-changing for me and probably for Val also. I am convinced that that decision must have contributed to the stability of our marriage, our family life, and my career. After coming back from annual leave on one occasion, I found that my job was in a mess; numerous things had been left undone and some jobs had been done in a very sloppy manner. In those days, employees of all banks in Australia were paid on an age related salary scale, which was dictated by the Bank Officers' Union and clearly supported mediocrity. It meant that comparative efficiency and productivity amongst employees, when recognised, was not able to be properly rewarded. On this occasion, the fellow who relieved me was some years older and was paid significantly more due to the age-related salary scale, and yet he was unable to perform to the standard I had set for myself. I found this to be inequitable and said so to my manager, Valentine (Val) Swanwick, who was an extremely considerate and personable manager, and although he agreed with me wholeheartedly, he was not in a position to be able to do anything about it. His advice to me was to keep working hard and the rewards would flow in due course. I respected him and took his advice, but wondered when or if the 'in due course' might materialise.

This whole episode led me to carefully examine the way in which I wished to see myself living my future life. Until then, I had an inferiority complex and during my short years in the bank had seen myself simply as one of the 'run-of-the-mill' type officers. On reflection, I came to realise that in recent years my overall performance level had been consistently high and superior to most of my contemporaries, and this was confirmed in the annual staff appraisals from various managers. It also became clear to me that if, in my future life, I continued to adhere to the high ethical standards that I had inherited from my parents, treated others as I should like to be treated, believed in my own abilities and leadership qualities, saw myself as more than equal in ability to most of my contemporaries, and continued to strive to do my best at all times, then I could have respect for myself and be the type of person that I desired to be throughout the remainder of my life. I there and then made the firm decision that these would be the guiding principles in my future life. I further determined that as long as I always did what I thought was the best and fairest for all concerned and not let what I thought others might be thinking about me influence my decisions or actions, then I was on the correct road through life and could feel content with myself and my behaviour. This decision had far-reaching positive consequences for my future, and it gave me the belief in myself and strength of character, which not only has resulted in a very stable marriage and family life but also allowed me to achieve the career successes that were to follow.

Chapter 12
Val becomes a 'Wales' Wife

We married in the Church of England (now Anglican Church) in Cooroy on 29 September 1962. Incidentally, the church building was constructed by Val's late father in the 1950s after the previous old building had been destroyed in a cyclone. Val made her own dress and she looked stunning. The marriage was conducted by Reverend Neave and seemed to go on forever. I did not enjoy the reception at all until such time as the formalities were concluded and the speeches were out of the way. I was very nervous as I was not one who sought or enjoyed the spotlight. I had no previous experience at public speaking and I found the occasion very stressful. Regrettably, my dad was not well at the time and he was unable to attend our wedding. Mum's brother Hall Camplin, whom I knew quite well and really liked, thankfully stood in for Dad and accompanied Mum.

We spent our honeymoon travelling to Sydney and then to Canberra by car, which was generously loaned to us by Val's mum and her brother Alan, who jointly owned it. We had booked accommodation at Bondi Beach, which we knew to be on the south-east side of Sydney Harbour. Neither of us had been out of Queensland previously, other than Val making trips to Casino in northern New South Wales, with her family to visit Bennett relations. Being good country folk, we simply pointed the car towards the east when we got over the Sydney Harbour Bridge and duly arrived at our destination without too much drama. I recall that we decided to visit the Jenolan Caves one day, and without really knowing the distance we had to travel to get there, we set off for the Blue Mountains. We had a look at the Three Sisters, travelled on the railway down into the valley, took a ride on the Skyway, and then had a late lunch at Katoomba. We were amazed when we were told how far it still was to Jenolan, and we got there with sufficient time to visit one cave only before closing time. The day was a very memorable one, and I often think back to then as we now frequently pass through the Blue Mountains and the turn-off to Jenolan on our way back and forth to Sydney from Mudgee. It is also interesting to note that our eldest son, Paul, subsequently became a cave guide at Jenolan during his university holidays.

The visit to Canberra, the nation's capital, was an eye-opener for us young Queenslanders, even in those days. The planning and layout of the place, with no expense spared, was almost breathtaking and this reminds me of an experience I had early one morning. We were packing up our motel room in preparation for heading back towards Queensland after spending three or four days in Canberra. As usual, I had dressed in shorts and a T-shirt for the drive ahead. I stepped outside to put our gear in the car, and that experience was really breathtaking. It was 32 Fahrenheit (0° C) outside, and the air conditioning in the room had left this unsuspecting Queenslander completely unprepared for the impact of the cold. That was the first occasion where I experienced ice on the windscreen of a car and the difficulties it could present to the uninitiated.

Our first home as newly-weds was a rented flat at Annerley in Brisbane close to where I worked. My brother-in-law Brian

Dwyer had arranged it for us while we were away, and we were very thankful to him for his efforts on our behalf. The property contained about five units and they were old and infested with large cockroaches, as was much of Brisbane housing, but it was very handy for us. It was a fairly lonely existence during the day for Val as she had little to do to occupy herself and was unable to work as she was still recovering from a very severe bout of glandular fever that she had contracted a few years earlier. The lingering effects of the illness resulted in a reoccurrence of swollen glands whenever she became overtired. Fortunately, I was able to walk home for lunch and that broke up her day a little. We had been married only a few months when I woke in the very early hours of the morning with a terrible stomach pain. It got progressively worse, and eventually Val had to wake our landlord and ask him to ring for an ambulance as phones were not commonly available in units then and there was no nearby public phone. I was diagnosed with appendicitis and operated on in the small hours of that morning at the nearby Princess Alexandra Hospital. It was then the practice that one was kept in bed in hospital for about a week after the operation before being allowed to go home. I joke that my operation must have been performed by the cleaner as the large wound area has never felt right up to this day. It took a lot longer for me to get back to work than the average, despite the fact that I was young, fit, and otherwise very healthy. By then, I was twenty-three years of age and was bringing home £16 ($32) per week. We were required to pay £6/6/- (six guineas) rent and had the remaining £9/14/- ($19-40) per week to buy food, clothes, pay for electricity and so on, and save. Needless to say, despite Val being a very good manager of our small budget, the level of our savings didn't increase dramatically.

My sister Valmai had married Graham McMillan on 21 January 1963, and they had moved to Brisbane from Rockhampton and were now living in a flat about a kilometre from us at Dutton Park. On 3 August 1963, my sister Joan married Jim Chattell and they too moved to Brisbane and were living at Ascot. Our main entertainment was to visit each other and also Merle and Brian. We could not afford to do anything else and also we enjoyed each other's company. About once a month, we had a splurge and shouted ourselves to the movies at Annerley. There was no possibility of our being able to afford to visit restaurants, not that there were many of them to choose from, or even a cafe. We went to Cooroy for weekends quite often and were mostly able to get a ride there and back with Kel Waldron from the bank, who was courting a girl in Cooroy. This cut our travel costs appreciably as Kel's mini minor used little fuel, and he mostly refused to take any payment as he was going to Cooroy anyway. Val's mother had a large vegetable garden in addition to a half acre of flower gardens and lawns, which she maintained by herself with the support of Val's brothers when they were home. She very generously kept us in vegetables and some fruits also. Val's mum's house was situated on two allotments and also had a very wide nature strip at the front and another narrower one in the laneway at the rear. She was a wonderful gardener and had flower gardens of all shapes and sizes everywhere; however, there was still a lot of lawn to be mowed and it was about a three hours' job for me with the Victa mower each time we were there.

After we had been married about eighteen months, Val felt she had recovered sufficiently from the ongoing effects of glandular fever to apply for a job. She did so and got the first job she sought at a local Annerley pharmacy. No sooner had she commenced work than she was able to tell me the exciting news that she was pregnant. Around about the same time I was transferred across the city to Stafford branch as Second Officer. Also, around that time we resolved to move from the Annerley flat because of the cost and also because of the 'creepy' way the owner, who lived on site, used to sneak into our flat when we were away in Cooroy. Val suspected that he entered the flat because things seemed to be moved around. So one day as we left the flat and closed the door, I reached inside behind the door and placed a matchbox close to the door—it was pushed out of the way when we came home. And no one else had a key! Fortunately, the parents of Jim McDonald, my best man at our wedding, had a flat attached to their home at Dutton Park opposite Webster's biscuit factory and across the road from Boggo Road jail. It became vacant at that time and was offered to us at £3 per week, which was a great saving of £3/6/- ($6-60) per week or 20 per cent of my net weekly income. It is almost incomprehensible to say in the present era that this cost saving meant a lot to the state of our finances at the time, but it really did.

In 1964, I decided to give up smoking for good. I had attempted to quit a number of times previously but had failed each time. As a consequence of the 1964 Federal budget's imposition of an additional tax on cigarettes, the price of a pack of twenty Rothmans cigarettes had risen by about 10 per cent from 3/- (thirty cents) to 3/3, and this was the catalyst that I needed. I threw my cigarettes in the garbage bin before I left for work and told Val that I had given up smoking. When I arrived home that evening Val had retrieved them thinking, from past experience, that I would be smoking again. To her astonishment, I screwed up the cigarette packet and said I was not going to smoke cigarettes ever again. I almost came unstuck a few days later. A Rothmans salesman used to bank the company's sales takings at Stafford branch almost daily and I knew him well. He put a proposition to me that day that if I was prepared to leave a packet of Rothmans cigarettes opened on the counter for customers to sample he would provide me with free cigarettes. Although my mouth was watering for a smoke, I stuck to my resolution and told him that I no longer was a smoker. I am ever thankful that I made that strong-willed decision then and I have never had another cigarette since. For a few years after giving up, I had an occasional cigar when at a dinner party or similar event, knowing that I could never take to smoking such things permanently.

Our first child, Paul John, was born on 5 November 1964. He arrived at 2.45 p.m. and weighed in at 3.35 kg (7 lbs 6 oz). In those days, fathers were not welcomed at the birth and were virtually shooed away at the front door of the maternity section of the hospital. I recall driving Val to hospital in the middle of the night and going home for a good night's sleep. I was phoned at work from the hospital the next afternoon to be advised that we had a son and all had gone quite well despite the rather lengthy labour period. Naturally, we were as proud as punch, and Paul was the most beautiful baby ever born. Although we were young parents, we were quite confident in our ability to manage our way through this life-changing event. We didn't own a car at that time, and Valmai and Graham McMillan, together with their ten-month-old-son Peter, collected us from the hospital and drove us home. Val was very proud of the baby clothes she had made for Paul, and when we arrived home she dressed him in a particularly nice little nightdress, which was then very fashionable. We then laid him on our bed to sleep and a short time later went into the bedroom to check on him and to see that he was okay. Val almost fainted when she saw that her pride and joy had one hand that had turned blue as a consequence of the elastic in the sleeve of the nightdress being a little tight, cutting off the blood flow. The situation was quickly rectified by snipping the elastic with scissors while Paul slept on, oblivious to what had happened to him.

Our new landlords, the McDonalds, were wonderful to us, and when Paul arrived they absolutely doted on him. Their son and my friend Jim was their only child, and at the age of about twenty-five years, he was not married nor did he have a steady girlfriend at the time. They saw no prospects of grandchildren of their own in the future, so they focused their whole attention on Paul. Mr McDonald in particular was besotted by Paul, and eventually Val had to place a time limit on their access to Paul. The rule was that after 4 p.m. each day Mackie, as he was affectionately known to Val and me, could have access to Paul and take him for walks around the house garden for a while. This eventually grew to walks up the street, then around the entire block, Mackie pulling Paul in an ancient billycart followed by two dogs from next door. Mackie proudly showed Paul off to all and sundry, all of whom assumed Paul was his grandson, and Mackie made no effort to dissuade them from their belief.

Travel to Stafford branch was an hour's trip via bus to the city and then by tram for the balance of the journey. As Second Officer at Stafford branch, I worked directly under the supervision of the manager, Don Fraser, who was a really personable man. It was here that I was first able to observe closely the nuances of branch management and found that I had gained sufficient knowledge and experience in recent years to be able to give Don some suggestions on various matters, together with some others that he didn't really want to hear. It was while at this branch that I realised that I would be able to achieve my ambition of reaching branch management status.

In early 1965, I was transferred to the Staff Department of the Queensland head office on the corner of Queen and George Streets as Assistant to Staff Clerk. In this role, I had to interact with many of the branch managers and accountants throughout Queensland by phone, through correspondence, and sometimes face to face. I soon realised that the competition at this level was not particularly challenging and that my cherished branch management dream was not only possible but also senior branch management and possibly even chief management of a small State division might be achievable. One of my tasks was to interview all young people from Brisbane who were applying for a position in the bank. Amongst the first was a very mature and rather good-looking young lady about seventeen years of age named Dawn Meikle. She had spent the previous six months at business college and was quite confident and mature for her age. The interview went well and Dawn was accepted into the bank's staff. A few years later, she began keeping company with my friend Peter Galliott and they later married. Peter and Dawn have been close friends for some fifty years now, and Dawn later provided strong support to Val during some very tough times.

About this time in my career, I learnt of the fact that officers could borrow virtually the entire cost price of a home from the bank at concessional rates of interest, which were less than 50 percent of public rates. We decided to proceed down this path. We felt we should build a home and set about finding a suitable block of land at a reasonable price. Dad and Mum had by then shifted to Brisbane following all the family except for Colin, who remained in Rockhampton working in insurance. Dad finished work early of an afternoon and offered to supervise the construction of a house on land we had bought at Marlton Street, Holland Park West, if we contracted a builder to do the construction work. It all worked out well and we shifted into a very nice home in about mid-1966.

I was on leave and at home hanging curtains when I noticed a bank car pull up out front. My friend Don Flatman, who also now worked in the chief manager's office and lived nearby, had come in to inform me of my appointment as Review Clerk in the Loans Administration Department of the State Head Office. Not only was I excited about being the youngest ever appointed officer in the State up until that time but I had also gained a salary increase of about 30 per cent. Val Swanwick's advice to me at Annerley branch had come to pass, and I recall thinking at the time how unfair it was that I was now earning more than my father, who had been in the workforce about thirty years longer than me.

This appointment gave us the ability to purchase a car, which we had gone without since we got married some three years earlier. It meant that we could spend a little money on developing the gardens at our new home and occasionally have a treat, of which there had been few in our married life to date. Dad was a great help with the building of garden edges, car tracks, concreting the area under the house, and the like. He arrived by 6 a.m. on most Saturdays and Sundays, ready to start helping me with mixing cement, excavating an area under the house by hand, laying bricks or Besser blocks, and moving tonnes of soil by wheelbarrow. There was only one work pace with Dad, and that was full steam ahead all day long, starting at about daybreak. Although he was nearly thirty years older than me and suffered from heart problems, he could still work really hard, and initially he was able to push me hard. As I became fitter, I used to mix the cement in the motor-driven mixer and deliver it for him to level out as fast as I possibly could until he had to ask me to slow down so he could have a break for a few minutes. Although I had great respect for Dad, he and I had never been really close, I guess partly because of the way he was raised, which dictated the sort of father he became as a consequence and also because I left home at seventeen years of age. However, we got to know each other a lot better during these days of hard toil, and I know he respected me and my capabilities much better as a consequence of this period of close association and I learnt to understand him better also.

The mention of laying bricks at Holland Park West, sends a chill up my spine each time I remember an event that happened during this period. Val and I were in the front garden one Sunday afternoon admiring the brickwork I had just completed. Paul was about eighteen months old and Val had him sitting against her chest facing outwards with both of her hands coupled under his bottom. Paul gave a jump forward in excitement, and in an attempt to stop him from falling, Val unintentionally catapulted him forward and he fell, hitting his forehead on the edge of a brick. He was cut to the bone in a gash about four centimetres long and the blood flowed very freely. We were both shocked and Paul was traumatised. We didn't have a car, so we ran to our neighbours Rosemary and Graham Trevaskis, as we knew she was a nurse. She advised us to take Paul to the doctor immediately, and they drove us there in their car. We eventually ended up at the doctor's surgery, where he inserted a number of stitches in the wound while Paul understandably screamed. Val was very shocked, and all in all, I think she suffered more than Paul because of the unfortunate event. Paul has no memory of the incident but still has a faint scar to prove it happened.

Around the time that Val was expecting our second child, I was selected to go to Melbourne for a major inter-State Bank of New South Wales sports competition as a member of the bank's Queensland table tennis team during the Easter break in 1967. I was to leave for Melbourne on the Friday of Easter, so Val headed off with Paul on the Thursday afternoon to go to Cooroy with her future sister-in-law Dorothy Heironymus, who was going there to visit Val's brother Alan. At about 4 p.m. that afternoon, a chap arrived at the house where I was up on scaffolding in the process of washing down the external paintwork of the house. He asked if my name was Chatterton and told me that the car that Val was travelling in had been involved in an accident and people were badly hurt. This turned out to be the first of the very bad knocks we have experienced in our married life. One moment I had a lovely wife and wonderful little son and we were expecting another baby in four months. The next moment I was unsure as to whether I was going to be left by myself. I got to the accident scene with great difficulty because of the traffic snarl the accident had created at work knock-off time in a busy industrial area on Easter Thursday afternoon, only to be told that all the injured had been taken to hospital. No one knew which hospital, though it was thought to be the Princess Alexandra Hospital in South Brisbane. I finally located Val in the Princess Alexandra Hospital, unconscious and in a coma with bruising of the brain and lots of cuts and very severe bruising to almost every part of her body. The hospital staff couldn't, or wouldn't, tell me how seriously she was injured, whether she had any broken bones, or how the unborn baby had fared. All they wanted from me was that I sign a consent form that allowed for amputation and the like. Dorothy very fortunately was not seriously injured, but nevertheless she suffered severe bruising, abrasions, and shock and her car was a complete write-off.

Paul was two years five months old at the time, and with the help of staff at the Princess Alexandra Hospital, I eventually located him in the Mater Children's Hospital a few miles away. No one could tell me what his condition was or even whether he was alive. I was in a complete daze. Thankfully, by this time some of my family had arrived at the Princess Alexandra Hospital to give me support. I found eventually that Val was in the intensive care ward, that there were no limb fractures, and that the baby was still in place and apparently undamaged—also that the surgeons were preparing to operate to relieve the pressure on her brain. I finally got to the Mater Children's Hospital about three hours after the accident occurred and found that Paul was alive but had a broken thigh, a depressed fracture of the front of the skull immediately above the bridge of the nose, and a myriad of facial cuts as a result of being catapulted through the windscreen. I couldn't see him as he was in theatre having plastic surgery performed on his face and his leg was being put in plaster. It seemed that he would survive from what I was told.

The surgeons eventually decided against operating on Val, and I was able to see her in intensive care late that evening or very early the next morning—I am not sure which as I was operating in a fog. She was still deeply unconscious and I did not recognise her, such was the extent of the damage, bruising, and swelling to her face. She had lots of shards of windscreen glass embedded in the left side of her cheek. Apparently the bleeding from these wounds was quite profuse, and I was told that in her deeply unconscious state and with the blood running into her mouth she had almost drowned in her own blood before the ambulance arrived at the crash scene. I was also told that she had suffered a number of epileptic seizures as a consequence of the bruising to the brain and the increased pressure within the skull cavity. She remained unconscious for the next three days, and it was heartbreaking to see the anguish she suffered from the pressure on the brain and the irritability and thrashing around that it caused. During much this time, I was accompanied by Val's elder brother Alan, Val's mother, and various members of my family and I remain deeply appreciative of their support in those darkest of hours and days. Fortunately, Val suffered no more epileptic seizures once she regained consciousness. The situation with the baby seemed to be stable and her tummy area was the only part of her body that was not black and blue from bruising or had not suffered cuts. Her eyes were completely closed over because of the bruising and swelling to her face, and the nurses had to force each eye open every fifteen minutes, shine a light into the pupil, and endeavour to get Val to respond. The uncertainty of what the eventual outcome might be was torturous to endure, and it was a great relief to have her back semi-conscious on the fourth day.

I had been visiting Paul a number of times a day, and his position had settled down fairly well although he couldn't understand why his mummy was not visiting him. The nurses were wonderful to him, and he ended up with his photo in the *Brisbane Telegraph* together with Sister Connie Korst in April 1967. The plastic surgery that was performed on his face was fantastic. An eyelid that had been split, but the eyeball not marked, had been sewn together with the finest of stitching as had the very many other cuts. There were more than 100 stitches involved. The left leg was in plaster that encased almost the whole of Paul's body from the waist down to beneath his heel. A traction device was attached to the plaster under the foot of his broken leg, which was permanently elevated. The device consisted of a chord going up over an elevated pulley with a heavy weight attached to the end in order to prevent the large thigh muscles from contracting the leg and resulting in a permanent limp. As a consequence, Paul couldn't move much or turn over in bed but behaved marvellously in the circumstances.

As Val's degree of consciousness improved, she was moved from intensive care to a ward with eight or ten beds and she began to ask for Paul. Her mental state was so precarious at that stage that I had to lie to her that I had left him at home with Mum and Dad so he wouldn't disturb the other people in the ward. The move to this ward was not at all conducive to improving Val's mental state. It was noisy all the time whereas Val needed complete quiet to heal her brain injury. A young girl suffering from a drug overdose was admitted to the ward during the night and she constantly created noise. We protested to the hospital staff, and eventually Val was moved into a room with two beds. I then had to tell her what had happened to Paul. I was able to assure her that he was coming on fine, but it was a week or so later before she was in a fit enough state and I was able to obtain permission for her to be able to briefly leave hospital to visit him at the Mater Children's Hospital. Val spent a few weeks in hospital, and her mum then came to help at home. She stayed for a few weeks, and when Paul was released from hospital about a month later, my mum and dad moved into our home to assist during the week when I was at work and they went home on weekends. Val was still very unwell, and although her speech, memory, and nervous system were quite badly affected, she coped with the remainder of the pregnancy term reasonably well. It took many years for her to recover to anywhere near her old self. We both believe that a lot of her health issues today are due to that accident and the damage she suffered to her brain, nervous system, and body as a whole.

I decided to go back to work in the chief manager's office before Val came out of hospital in an endeavour to relieve my own stresses. Tom Pollitt, Chief Manager for Queensland, was very good to me and gave me permission to take off whatever time I needed and to leave work early and go to the hospitals mid-afternoon each day. If Val felt that she was well enough to be able to cope with the stress of visiting Paul in his battered state, I used to take her to see him in the evening and I would spend a few hours each afternoon with him. For one who has no drawing skills whatsoever, with lots of practice I became quite adept at drawing trains and the like. Our old friend and landlord, Mr McDonald visited Paul every morning while he was hospitalised. The plaster cast on Paul's left leg had to stay on for some weeks after he came home from hospital. His leg was set straight and the heavy cast was inflexible from the waist down to the ankle. Consequently, it was very difficult dealing with him while toileting, bathing, and feeding him and almost impossible to get him in a comfortable and safe position in the car. Happily, I am able to say that the only outwardly visible signs of Paul's injuries today are a depression just above the bridge of his nose where the skull fracture was, some scarring on his face that is noticeable when one looks carefully, and his left leg is a little shorter than the right but fortunately not noticeably so.

Naturally, we were both very anxious about the health of our as yet unborn baby and were both delighted when an apparently very healthy little girl arrived on 20 July 1967. We were blessed with a daughter Lisa Jayne and now had the pigeon pair. She was born at the Brisbane Mater Private Hospital at 10.20 a.m. and weighed 3.65 kg (6 lbs 12 oz). Despite the traumatic time Val had endured in the latter stages of the pregnancy, the birth process progressed well, and anxious checks by Val as soon as the baby was in her arms revealed that the accident had caused no apparent damage to the healthy looking bundle of joy. The adverse effects of Val's trauma were not to show themselves as a physical impairment in Lisa until later.

Val remembers:

*Our life was wonderful! We were in our first new home
with a gorgeous little son Paul (two years old) and another
baby due in July. It was now March 1967 . . .*

The next thing I recall was wondering: Where am I?

*I opened my eyes and after a while realised that I was in
hospital. My head ached terribly.*

*John came forward, kissed me, and held my hand. His
father was behind him. John told me that I had been in a car
accident. I did not remember where or when this happened.*

I remember little else of my time in Intensive Care.

*Later, I remembered Paul and also that I was pregnant.
Talking was very difficult because I could not recall words.
I was five months pregnant and had had a catheter inserted
for several days and as a consequence I needed a bedpan
fairly frequently. However, by the next time I required it,
I could not remember the word 'pan'. When I look back, I
have to smile, but it was very distressing at the time.*

*After many days, I was 'well enough' to go home. John
took me to the Mater Children's Hospital to visit Paul. I
was shocked to see his injuries but delighted to see him at
last. I tried not to cry in front of him so as to upset him,
and he was okay when I left on that first visit. The second
and subsequent visits were different and he wanted to come
home. It was very distressing leaving him. My mission now
was to endeavour to become well enough to look after Paul
when he came home and additionally to be able to manage
without help with a new baby in a few months' time. John*

was very helpful when he was at home, but he had to go to work during the day.

When Paul came home from hospital, his left leg from his waist to his toes was encased in plaster. After a few days he learnt to roll on to his tummy and to push himself forward with his right leg, dragging the plastered leg along the polished floor. This activity made him happier and relieved his boredom somewhat. The accident initially had a profound effect on Paul's mental state. At night, he often woke screaming from an awful nightmare. He sometimes made a noise like a siren and said, 'That's what the ambulance said.'

I was very grateful for the help of my mother first, then John's parents for some weeks until I was able to cope. I had a month or so being on my own during the day with Paul before our baby was due. I was far from well but had to think positively and try to stay calm to avoid stress which resulted in extremely bad headaches.

Because my gynaecologist, Dr Keith Free, assured me that it was very unlikely that my baby would have been adversely affected by the accident, due to the protective sack around it, I felt assured that all would be well at the birth.

We were delighted when our beautiful, perfect little daughter Lisa Jayne arrived.

I felt I had so much to be grateful for with a wonderful husband who loved me dearly and two gorgeous healthy children and I had to focus on moving forward positively.

Fortunately, Lisa was a very placid, happy baby who rarely cried and smiled frequently. This helped with my recovery.

Paul by now was fairly well and enjoyed his little sister but wanted her to grow bigger to play with him.

My speech and memory were slowly improving, but I had many years ahead before I became confident to speak at any length with people I knew and it was worse still with strangers.

Lisa did not walk unaided until she was about seventeen months old. She seemed rather clumsy and fell quite often. We assumed that perhaps she was quite happy crawling everywhere in her own relaxed way. As time went by, I queried Lisa's clumsiness with various doctors to no avail. Finally, when she was three years old I decided to take her to see Dr Keith Free. He examined her thoroughly and said, 'This is the little one you were carrying when you were involved in the car accident?' I agreed, and he said, 'There is something wrong', and he referred Lisa to a neurosurgeon. She was diagnosed with mild cerebral palsy as a consequence of the severe injuries I suffered in the car accident, which included five epileptic seizures that interrupted the oxygen supply to the foetus, causing permanent damage to the left side of the brain. Some ten years or so later, the diagnosis was that Lisa's right hand was smaller than her left and her right arm was four centimetres shorter than her left arm; also, she had 25 per cent loss of use in her right leg. I was told that had the accident happened in the earlier stages of my pregnancy the adverse impact on Lisa would have been far greater. John and I felt devastated that Lisa was left with this lifelong legacy as a result of my injuries.

Our aim now was to seek advice on ways to assist Lisa with her dexterity, to strengthen her right leg and arm, and to overcome a slight speech impediment so as to help her attain the utmost that she was capable of in life.

Fortunately, she was blessed with a very happy disposition and was always willing to learn such things as riding a bicycle, playing tennis, participate in dancing, playing the piano, and doing speech therapy in order to improve her coordination, balance, and confidence.

Consequently, Lisa was able to complete her Higher School Certificate exams with quite acceptable results, spend six months at a wonderful business college, and immediately afterwards start work as Receptionist/Office Assistant at a computer company. She now had her own little car and her life going forward looked very promising.

John and I felt very happy that Lisa was becoming independent. This was our primary aim in helping her as much as possible to counter the effects of her disability. She was now a beautiful, caring, confident young woman.

We were very proud of our daughter.

As Val has said, she began to notice that the right side of Lisa's body might not be developing in sync with the left. She noticed that the creases in the back of her little legs just above the knees were not quite aligned, and the following medical investigations produced the next devastating blow that we were to suffer. Val worked relentlessly over the following years to find ways of moderating the adverse effects of the disability on Lisa's life. In due course she walked with a slight limp, had a slight speech impediment, and did not have the same degree of strength in her right side limbs as those on her left side. Her dexterity was impaired a little as was her speech on occasions, and she was often a target for hurtful comments at school as a consequence. It was not until Lisa was about fifteen that Val finally located a wonderful clinical psychologist named Anna Tesoriero in Sydney, who was able to diagnose the slight disconnect between Lisa's brain function and speech action and provide an avenue for improvement. She referred Lisa to a speech therapist, who was able to achieve some improvement for Lisa. Although Lisa was mostly a bright and happy young girl and usually was able to fend off the hurt she suffered from name-calling and the like, she nevertheless felt the sting terribly, as we did.

Around the end of 1967, Dad was diagnosed with terminal cancer. He hadn't long completed the construction of a retirement home for Mum and himself in the Brisbane suburb of Salisbury. The cancer was discovered in the lymph glands of his left shoulder, and we were told that it was probably the secondary cancer, the primary probably being lung cancer from smoking for about twenty-years until he gave it up at about forty-five years of age. The effects of many soakings in DDT while dipping cows may also have been a possible cause. Treatments for cancer almost fifty years ago were very rudimentary. Dad suffered horribly from radiation burns to the oesophagus, and the left arm literally died on his body as Mum and the family looked on helplessly. Regrettably, he died on 6 May 1968 at the age of fifty-seven years. Although he was a very hard taskmaster and unable to show affection when I was a kid, we had grown quite close in later years and I missed him a lot. Mum was left to fend for herself at the relatively young age of fifty-three years but with the strong support of the family. She had never been involved in outside activities other than playing social tennis with the family, so we all urged her to join the local ladies' bowls club in order to have an outside interest. She soon became a member of the Salisbury Women's Lawn Bowls Club and over the years collected numerous badges and medals for her tournament wins. It was pleasing to see her involvement and the enjoyment and company the game brought her. In later years, Val and I used to joke that we virtually had to make an appointment in order to go to Brisbane to see her so that we did not interrupt her bowls schedule.

As regards my career progress, after about two years in the Loans Administration Department reviewing various types of loans, I was appointed to the Legal Department of the head office in Brisbane as Section Clerk. This involved me in giving low-level legal guidance to about a fifth of the branches in Queensland, and initially it was a very daunting time for me. I knew nothing about the legal process for mortgages, property transfers, guarantees, and the like. Terry Dunne, who was also a section clerk and very experienced, told me one day, 'Don't let it worry you, John. It is only when you begin to gain a good understanding of the legal field that you really begin to realise just what you don't know about it.' I am not sure that I felt any better as a consequence of hearing that, but I soon learnt from personal experience that the more I began to understand the legal process, the more daunting it became. Terry had joined the bank at the Post Office branch in Brisbane on the same day that I joined the bank at Rockhampton, and we first met a few months later at a bank training course in Brisbane in early 1956. We became very good friends over the following years.

Neither the move to Legal nor Terry's advice did a lot of good for my confidence at the time, as I felt that for some unknown reason I had been shuffled sideways into a backwater. Most of the chaps in the legal area had been there for many years and were comfortable in their surroundings. Chief Manager Tom Pollitt asked me how I was enjoying the change when I met him one day. I told him how I felt about the move and he was quite shocked. He assured me that it was a planned move which would stand me in good stead in my future career. Pollitt was an outstanding administrator and I saw him as a role model for my future career. His assurances were sound advice as I was in the legal area for only about six months and was then transferred back to Rockhampton in late 1968, the place where I had commenced working in the bank some twelve and half years previously, as the manager's assistant.

The move to Rockhampton was Val's first of many house moves at the behest of the bank. It also presented the first occasions where Val was required to attend bank functions with me and suffer the gaze and inspection of both senior officers and clients. She was on the way to becoming a 'Wales' wife. At the time, she was still suffering quite badly from her lack of memory and speech difficulties and found these occasions to be embarrassing and stressful. Over the years, she became very adept at this role and I always felt very proud of her on these occasions. She also became an excellent planner of the about twenty bank-inspired house moves we made over ensuing years.

Rockhampton branch in 1968 was a very large, predominantly rural-based business with about forty staff and managed by the notorious Leslie (Les) East. I was his assistant and worked very closely with him in all respects. When I arrived there, the branch senior staff contingent was extremely discontented. I had been warned about this before I left the head office. At about the same time as I arrived there, two other highly capable officers, my friends Don Flatman and Paul O'Brien, arrived to add some additional balance to the place. Initially, Les accused me of being a head office spy when I used to refuse to sign off on some of his returns to the head office. I told him that I was aware that the head office was reviewing him and that he could be dealt with quite severely. He disregarded my advice, and when my warning eventually became a reality, he couldn't believe why it had or even should be happening to him. His censure was a very severe warning and it got through to him. He then came around to accepting that I was on his side and we began to get on very well. He was an exceedingly hard worker and I learnt a lot from him. I attempted to teach him a few better ways to deal with staff, but I have little doubt that he continued to do his own thing after I left Rockhampton. When I was transferred back to Brisbane eighteen months later, he actually cried when he told me of my transfer and said that he would never give a good officer an outstanding report again because the bank then took them away. I saw him many years later in his retirement on the Gold Coast in Queensland when I was Chief General Manager, Australian Banking. I was the guest speaker at a Westpac retired officers' function and he claimed me like a long lost friend. I really did enjoy seeing him again.

Drought hit Central Queensland with a real vengeance in 1968-1969, and it was a very challenging time for all those whose livelihood was derived from the land. In the managerial department at Rockhampton branch, we were soon overrun by clients seeking financial assistance to see them through these difficult times. It was obvious that not every enterprise was going to be able to remain viable in a major drought. As bankers, it was our responsibility to discern the extent of the clients' difficulties, the most appropriate way in which the bank could manage the risk going forward, what could be the best option for the client, and in some more drastic cases to decline to assist further. Although Les East was a very seasoned rural banker, it became obvious to me that he had no good basis for forecasting a client's future financial position when undertaking a full cash flow forecast and review of their financial affairs. Further, it seemed some of his recommendations to the bank may not have been in the best interests of the client or the bank. This is not to say that he set out to intentionally harm a client or the bank; on the contrary, he was a very conscientious manager in this regard. As an older manager, he had received little if any formal managerial training and simply was deficient in the appropriate skills required in exceedingly difficult times. I endeavoured to explain to him a very effective and simple-to-use system of forms that the bank now had in place to assist managers and clients to assess their current financial position and future cash flow needs. He would have none of what he termed 'this newfangled stuff from head office' and insisted that his system had stood the test of time and that he would stick with it. However, he obviously took careful notice of office copies of various submissions that I was putting forward to the head office on behalf of the drought-affected clients. Although he never admitted that the bank's rural finance assessment system that I was using was obviously better than his approach, it wasn't long before he began referring what he considered to be his most difficult drought-affected clients to me for attention.

One such case involved a highly respected family from Dululu (a district south-west of Rockhampton), who were descendants of some of the original settlers in Central Queensland. They had been very successful cattle graziers over many years and owned considerable tracts of well-developed land and a substantial herd of quality Hereford cattle. This client had seen Les a few times previously during the period of this drought and had his overdraft extended to cover the cost of fodder and ongoing running expenses. However, there were no clear projections available to demonstrate where the drought costs might take the family, in a financial sense, over say the next twelve months. With the client's cooperation and that of his bookkeeping daughter, I was able to fairly quickly demonstrate that to continue as they planned could possibly run them into a very tight financial position and require them to sell land at a sacrificial price in order to provide cash flow to survive. Like many others, they were asset rich but cash flow poor at the time and were caught in the vice-like grip of this terrible natural disaster that no one was able to predict when it would end. The client had the flexibility within his affairs to be able to amend his and his family's forward cattle sales plans. He took my advice and was extremely thankful to me for the financial management education that the review process had brought to him and his daughter. I have selected this case to write about not only because it was one where I gained a lot of satisfaction from what I was able to achieve for these very nice people but also because some forty years later, on a cruise together with Val down the Vietnamese coast, a fellow cruise member came to me, introduced herself, and asked, 'Are you the banker on board the ship who used to be in the Wales at Rocky in the late 1960s?' She was the former bookkeeping daughter, and although we never met during the review process all those years previously, she clearly recalled all the additional bookwork she was required to do for her father in order to satisfy my requirements. Rather than berate me, she wanted to tell me that as a consequence of that event the financial management of the enterprise was upgraded to such an extent that she had to show a set of income/expenditure books, with cash flow forecasts, balanced to the cent, to her dad at the end of each month. It was very nice to meet her and rewarding to hear what she had to say.

By 1968, my brother Colin was the only member of our family still living in Rockhampton, my parents and three sisters all having moved to Brisbane. He was now about twenty-two and working in insurance and going steadily with Sharon Keepkie. They were married in Rockhampton on 11 October 1969 while we were there. We saw a lot of them during our stay and it was good to get to know them both—I had left home when Colin was a ten-year-old boy. He was now a young man, and in the intervening years, I had been able to spend time with him only when I was home on annual leave.

During our stay in Rockhampton, Mark was a very welcome addition to the family on 7 January 1970. We were anticipating the birth both with excitement and trepidation, the latter because of the extremely high summer temperatures in Rockhampton in January. He was born a very healthy baby at the Rockhampton General Hospital at 1.40 a.m. and weighed in at 3.29 kg (7 lbs 4 oz). This was a very trying time for Val. She was still suffering the after-effects of the dreadful car accident. The temperatures regularly exceeded 40 °C for days on end and the situation was exacerbated by very high humidity during days and nights and no air conditioning. Lisa was a toddler of two and half years and

Paul was just starting school. Val was hard-pressed to protect them and the new baby from these conditions; with the rather fragile situation of her own health, she also had to try to protect herself. We were both quite concerned for Mark's well-being and directed a fan on to the cot day and night. Val was very much relieved when I received notice of a transfer back to Brisbane.

In about May 1970, I was appointed to the prestigious position of Staff Clerk for the Queensland Division. Although the position was not of managerial status, an appointment to it signified that one was highly regarded by the head office. At that time, the bank's housing policy for staff required that when an officer was transferred from a location where he/she owned a house that was concessionally financed by the bank that house had to be sold. Hence, we had sold our Holland Park West house only eighteen months previously when we left Brisbane and now had to go through the house acquisition process again. We settled on a house in Gatton Street, Mt Gravatt, which was being sold by a builder. As is often the case with a builder's home, it had a number of unfinished aspects to it, but we saw the potential and value that we could add with a little bit of hard work. Additionally, it was a nice family home in a good high location with views. Helen and Barry Thompson were our neighbours, and they are still close friends today.

The move from Rockhampton back to Brisbane, although a disruption to our lives after such a short stay, was nevertheless welcomed by us both. For my part, the appointment as Staff Clerk for Queensland was a really plumb job, which meant that I would be working for the state manager, personnel, and have lots of direct contact with the chief manager of the division and with managers and staff throughout Queensland. I was responsible to the state manager, personnel, for the proper recruiting of new staff, the appropriate staffing of branches, and the selection for training, rewarding, and promotion of the division's personnel. The demands of the job were enormous, but it was also very fulfilling work and a great development experience for my future. Clearly, I was successful in the role as I was appointed to the position of Manager, Monto, from there and became the youngest managerial appointment in the division up to that time.

In 1971, the board of the bank in Sydney decided that a detailed review of the cost of the bank's entire administrative structure was required. One day, an impressive-looking officer in his late forties walked into my office, introduced himself as Bob White, and told me he was a senior bank executive whom the board had appointed to do an in-depth review of the bank's administrative costs. He had permission from my chief manager to spend quite a bit of time with me and was seeking my views on what I believed to be much needed changes. We spent much of the next two days talking about the bloated and frustrating administrative processes that the bank currently had in place. I went home on the first day Bob was there and said to Val that I had just met the smartest and nicest guy I had ever come across in the bank. Much efficiency was introduced throughout the bank's administrative areas as a consequence of Bob's study, and a short while later, he was appointed as Chief Manager for United Kingdom and Europe based in London. My comment to Val at the time of that appointment was along the lines that it was made as a reward for his great work on the administrative costs project. Little did I know that he was already marked as the next managing director of the Bank of New South Wales!

I reached my branch management goal with my appointment to the Monto branch in mid-1972. This was a small mixed farming community of about 1,700 people with five different banks, situated some five hours' drive north-west of Brisbane and about 160 kilometres in from the coast at Bundaberg but with no all-weather access in that direction. Access to the south was via Eidsvold to the Pacific Highway north of Gympie on a sealed but very narrow and poorly maintained road. Access to the north to Biloela some 100 kilometres away was via a mainly bad unsealed road that became impassable in wet weather. The Wales branch had three on the staff including me. The bank provided us with a very comfortable fully furnished four-bedroom house, free of rent, and for the first time in our married lives we actually saw our bank balance grow appreciably month by month as many costs were covered by the bank. We made lots of good friends in the short time that we were there, and Val still corresponds with Merriel McGuigan who, together with her husband John, was a good customer of the branch. They recently visited us in Mudgee some 41 years after we left Monto and it was great to see them again.

I began playing golf in Monto, and I still enjoy a game today although the standard has not improved at all. The golf club was only able to operate on the basis of the members being responsible for all course maintenance and clubhouse duties. I was quickly appointed the keeper of the tees, and it was my job early each Saturday morning to put the motor mower in the car boot and mow all the tees and their surrounds. Additionally, in dry weather I had to ensure that the tees were watered. I played golf both on Thursday and Saturday afternoons. Thursday was businessmen's afternoon, and it gave me the opportunity to meet and get to know that important group in a small town that was heavily overbanked. Getting to the golf club by hit-off time at 3.30 p.m. each Thursday used to present a real challenge because the bank doors didn't close for business until 3 p.m. This meant that all after-hours processing had to be finished, cash balanced, and locked away, and then we all walked out and locked the door after us in time for me to get to the course. The other two on the staff cooperated fully as they enjoyed an early afternoon also.

My first customer in this my first branch management was Gordon Hutton of Comingla Grazing Company, whose family was one of the biggest family grazing connections at the branch, and he was far from happy. The previous manager had failed to complete a long-outstanding financing transaction, which was required to allow the family to pay a rather large sum of death duties. This was a tax imposed on deceased estates at that time, and large penalties were imposed by the authorities if payment was not made by due date and the due date was within days. I was given a few days to fix the problem or the entire business was to be transferred to the Commonwealth Bank, where an alternative financing facility had already been arranged. Fortunately, I was able to draw on the knowledge I had gained in the bank's Legal Department, solve the issue quickly, and give Gordon his cheque the following day. He became a very good friend, and I used his expertise to gain a good knowledge of the local beef cattle industry.

As the branch manager, I reported to an administrative officer (regional manager) in Brisbane and was required to set down in writing my objectives for furthering the bank's business over the ensuing year. It was very clear to me that the town could do with at least one less bank, so I set my sights on the Commercial Bank of Australia Ltd (CBA) by way of influencing its better customers across to the Wales. I had actually become good friends with the CBA manager as we were both on the committee of the local swimming club and saw each other frequently at social functions, in the street, and at golf. He had on occasions asked my advice on banking issues, and I had great difficulty in keeping a straight face when he came in to see me one day to ask for my advice as to how he should go about valuing the CBA's premises across the street. I immediately guessed that the CBA Bank was intending to pull out of Monto and his head office was seeking valuations for the eventual sale of their premises. During my time at Monto, I had been successful at swinging some good CBA business my way and was quite chuffed to later learn while in London that the CBA Monto had closed its doors.

CHAPTER 13

To the Other Side of the World

I must say that the transfer to London came as a really big shock for both Val and me. Every year since the first year that I joined the bank in 1955, I had answered the question on the reverse of my staff appraisal form by indicating that I would be happy to accept a transfer to Papua New Guinea, Fiji, or New Zealand, where the bank had extensive branch networks. This was an option given to every staff member yearly on the occasion of the completion of their performance appraisal. Disappointingly, nothing ever eventuated. We had only just arrived home in Monto from five weeks' holidays, which were taken at the bank's insistence in order that I catch up on some outstanding leave. I had a few days to spare before recommencing duties and was out mowing the heavily overgrown lawns at the bank residence. Val, who was some eight months pregnant, and Mark, who was then three, were having a rest on the bed after lunch. The phone rang, and I quickly answered it in the hope that it wouldn't disturb them. Ben Neilson, the State Manager, Personnel, was on the line. After a little small talk, he wanted to know if I would be prepared to accept a transfer to London as soon as possible. He knew of Val's advanced pregnancy, and I said I would love to but I needed to discuss such a major shift with Val first. She took about two seconds to say 'yes', but she added that the bank would have to wait until the new baby was at least six weeks' old for us to travel. I conveyed this message to Ben, and he said my conditions were acceptable and that I would soon be officially advised of the move in writing. We now had to tell our respective mothers and relatives and I had to advise my staff and customers. I shall never forget the expressions on the faces of various friends and customers as I told them some nine months after we arrived in Monto that I had been transferred to London. My statement usually took a while to sink in, then the eyes would pop and the mouth would drop open and they would say in disbelief, 'London, England?'

About a month after the transfer to London was advised, Andrew was welcomed by us all at 8.20 p.m. on 7 March 1973 at the Monto Hospital, weighing in at 3.35 kg (7 lbs 6 oz). We were both concerned about the standard of medical care available in Monto, but all went well and Andrew was a healthy and contented baby. Lisa was quite sure that she was going to get a little sister this time and prior to its arrival referred to the baby as 'her', but after Andrew's arrival she thought he was gorgeous and wanted to help care for him. Val had about a week in hospital and actually asked to be kept in for another day in order to give her a bit more time to regain her strength to tackle the huge task ahead of us. Fortunately for us at the time, we had no concept of what would lie ahead of us in getting ourselves and four young children around the other side of the world to London. Had we been able to know in advance, we may not have had the fortitude to tackle this 'monster' move. However, in May 1973, we departed Monto for London with four children between the ages of eight years and six weeks.

The only advice the bank gave us about how to get to London or what to take with us was about three lines in a letter confirming my appointment and suggesting that I should contact the bank's

Travel Department in Brisbane to make the necessary travel arrangements. Fortunately, the Travel Department did a great job with the arrangements and built in rest breaks of a couple of days at both Los Angeles and New York. We had no idea as to what accommodation was to be made available to us in London and what personal effects and furniture we should take with us. I wrote to London office, seeking their help with the matter as soon as the transfer was advised, and I actually got a response on the day the packers were at our house and had already half loaded the pantechnicon. At about the same time, we received a letter of welcome from Marie and Ian Grieve, whom we had known in the Wales in Brisbane and were now also based in London, and this raised Val's spirits somewhat. We eventually had to determine for ourselves what we were taking to London and what went into storage in Brisbane; the arrival of the letter from London helped us little.

Before departure, I was required to spend two weeks in the industrial relations section of chief staff office in Sydney. This meant leaving Val to cope with the four young children. She spent the first week with her mother in Cooroy and the following week with my mother in Brisbane. I had arranged the sale of our car to the second officer at the Monto branch, and he had agreed to collect it in Brisbane when Val departed for Sydney to meet me. When she arrived in Sydney with the kids, there was no time for sightseeing as we had to re-pack and rearrange six big suitcases, some of which had to go to London by way of unaccompanied baggage. Early on the morning we were to depart, Mark came into our interconnecting hotel room to say he had a very sore throat. The glands on each side of his neck were clearly quite swollen and he was running a temperature. An urgent visit to a doctor revealed he did not have measles, mumps, or some other childhood illness, and after a shot of penicillin he was cleared to travel. He felt quite unwell and was not in good humour.

Before we were transferred to London, the bank's travel policy allowed for first-class travel for families who were transferred overseas. The deputy chief manager, London, to whom I was to report in my new role as Manager, Personnel, had been to Australia recently, and on his return he decided that it was inappropriate for Antipodeans with young families, like us, to travel in such comfort, so he immediately downgraded the staff flight policy to economy class. The trip was excruciatingly long for all of us and Mark was quite sick during the entire journey. It was so distressing for Val and me that we gave deep consideration to staying in England permanently if we were to be required to fly home in economy class.

Upon our departure from Australia, we got to Sydney International Airport with a few hours to spare only to be told, contrary to previous telephone instructions from British Airways, that unaccompanied baggage had to be booked in on the other side of the airport near the domestic terminal. I had to leave Val and the kids where they were and rush three big suitcases by taxi to the correct place. This procedure took me a good hour to arrange, and when we finally got on the plane our seating arrangements had been changed such that Val was seated with a sky cot for Andrew on the two vacant seats beside her and the other three kids and I were separated by about seven rows of seats. This was despite the fact that the Travel Department had booked and confirmed all seating arrangements and the sky cot, supposedly affixed to a bulkhead, more than two months previously. I protested very strongly to the head steward on the plane, but the British Airways staff couldn't have cared less. During the flight, they never answered a call button and almost had to be tackled to be asked to heat a bottle for Andrew. Even so, the bottle would invariably come back boiled and unpalatable for the baby.

We had a break for a few days at Disneyland and another in New York. Mark was ill the whole time, and just prior to arrival in

London the British Airways staff, with no medical knowledge, determined that he was suffering from German measles. They alerted the entire aircraft via the public address system and warned all pregnant women on board to see their doctor as soon as possible. Despite our protestations to the flight attendants that Mark was only suffering a penicillin rash from a penicillin shot he had been given by a rather heavy-handed doctor in Disneyland two days before, we were detained on the plane until a doctor came on board, examined Mark, and confirmed exactly what we had said. However, we survived this 'flight of hell', and the first policy I reinstated, with the support of Bob White, was the first-class international travel policy for Australians on bank-initiated transfers.

My role in London was very demanding. It took me a while to get my head around the approach I needed to employ in the very different cultural environment that I found myself in and the differing circumstances that I was dealing with. I found myself, at thirty-three years of age, the personnel manager of an Australian bank that had been operating in London since 1853. It had a staff of 500 who were, in the main, fairly demanding locals, and most of them were older than me. Past chief managers appeared to have almost entirely neglected the responsibilities of their position in ensuring they dealt fairly with the bank's local staff, and consequently, the mood of the division's staff was openly hostile towards management. To make matters even worse, I was reporting to the deputy chief manager who was not noted for being a competent administrator. The saving grace was that Bob White was the chief manager of the division, and he was one of the best administrators I ever encountered throughout my career.

The job required me, together with Bill McInnis, the newly appointed Industrial Manager, whom I was replacing in the personnel role, to develop staff policies, then negotiate them with a feisty in-house union, which was supported and advised by a very militant left-wing external union named the Association of Scientific, Technical and Managerial Staffs (ASTMS) led by Clive Jenkins, who was a very shrewd performer. This initial stage of policy development was then followed by obtaining final approval from Chief Staff Office in Sydney, which was not necessarily easy, and subsequently the implementation of the new policy. During Bob White's reign as Chief Manager, the process was manageable as I simply involved him when needed. Regrettably, this happened more often than I would have liked but almost nothing got done otherwise, and the mood of the staff was demanding that prompt remedial action be taken. After Bob White returned to Australia in 1974 to take up the role of Deputy Managing Director and later to become Managing Director, the board of the bank saw fit to replace him with the deputy chief manager and work became very frustrating.

When we first arrived in England, we were required to live in a very small furnished two-storey townhouse in Bromley, Kent, for about ten months until such time as the bank's house became available to us. The only clothes and belongings that we had for the six of us were those we had taken in the six suitcases when we left Australia. To say that we felt cramped after living in a large four-bedroom house with a huge yard was an understatement; however, we got used to it and felt like royalty when we moved into the bank's nicely furnished and recently renovated four-bedroom house a few blocks away. Bromley was a very nice suburb in which to live, and the beautiful English countryside was but a few kilometres from us. We went driving after an early lunch most Sundays and saw a lot of south-east England as a consequence. The kids would have preferred to stay home and watch colour TV, which was a wonderful new treat for them and us. They were really too young to enjoy the beauty of England, and no sooner were we out of the door than one or other of them would be asking: 'Are we there yet?' or 'When are we going home?'

We had no sooner arrived in London than it was suggested we should consider what summer holiday we were going to have, and it was pointed out that we should go within the next few months, as we would not wish to go on leave in a European winter. It was difficult to decide where we might go with four young children, but eventually we elected to take a motor-home tour of Scotland in September 1973. Cliff Smith, one of the English staff who was an authority on touring Scotland, drafted up an itinerary for us and away we went. It proved to be a real eye-opener for all of us and whetted our appetite for making many more trips to various parts of England to view the wonderful scenery and explore historic places. We always stopped at a caravan park, such as they were, well before dark in a location where the older kids could have a good run to release some excess energy. We never got going again the next morning until about nine thirty when breakfast was out of the way, the baby had been fed and bathed, Val had done the washing (Andrew was still in cloth nappies), and all the beds and blankets were folded away and stored under seats. At times, we must have looked like a travelling laundry, but we didn't care as everyone was enjoying the trip. The Bedford motor-home engine was severely under-powered for the size of the vehicle and its load. I used to put the accelerator to the floor down the latter part of some of the big Scottish hills to gain enough momentum so that I was at least a quarter of the way up the next hill before I had to shift down through the gears to low and grind my way slowly to the top.

As soon as we crossed the border into Scotland in the motor-home, we saw a sight that made both Val and I laugh in amazement. At the time, it was so foreign to us to see road workers in tweed jackets with ties and tweed caps; no one seemed to wear hats. However, we became accustomed to that form of tradesmen's dress as time went on. The next day on the outskirts of the city of Perth, I had an amazing experience in a small corner store. We needed butter and milk for lunch, and I asked the girl behind the counter for both of these items in my best Australian. She said something in response that I could not understand, so I repeated my request. Again, she asked me a question and again I could not understand her. Fortunately, there was another customer in the rear of the shop who could understand both of us and he interpreted my order for the shop assistant. I recall getting back in the motor-home and incredulously relaying my experience to Val; two people speaking the English language, yet neither could understand what the other was saying.

Weather-wise we were very fortunate during our Scotland tour, and when winter really did set in a few weeks after we were back home in London, we, the uninitiated from Australia, realised how much trouble we might have been in had we encountered an early winter freeze while in the Highlands. The van had no heating but lots of thick blankets, so we were all quite warm on our trip. We could have become snowbound on impassable roads in the Highlands and would have had to be rescued or even worse! In hindsight, we understood what our predicament could have been, especially as we had four young children on board, one of whom was only six months old and still recovering from a very bad bout of gastroenteritis.

The first half of our time in London was not always happy for Val. She had very few friends other than the other Australian wives who all lived suburbs away, and she was home-bound to a large degree with four young children. Additionally, Andrew had been quite seriously ill with gastroenteritis and we thought we might lose him on one occasion, due solely to the incompetence of the doctors in the British nationalised medical system. Val had previous experience with this sort of infection in infants and understood how critical it was to get proper medical attention quickly. The prescribed treatment from the local doctor was so wide of the mark that the infection continued unabated and Andrew became severely dehydrated and had to be hospitalised in order to ensure he recovered. At about the same time, I was quite unfairly devoting far too much of my time to my work and socialising with Australian bank friends after hours to the disadvantage of Val and the family. Fortunately, she gave me a 'wake-up' warning one day, which I heard very clearly, and I think my behaviour became a little more balanced although I am not sure that Val would agree entirely with this statement.

While we were in London, there were about thirty other Australian staff of the Bank of New South Wales plus their families living there. Some stayed for periods as short as one year, others for as long as five years. Most of them lived to the south of central London with the more senior staff living in bank-owned and furnished housing. We tended to socialise quite a lot amongst ourselves and had some very memorable dinner parties at each others' homes. Of the group that was there, we made very firm friends with Ian and Maree Grieve, whom we knew previously in Queensland, Dick and Anne Watson from Western Australia, Bob and Pam Newman from South Australia, and Vern and Val Brockman also from Western Australia. We all ended up in senior management positions in the bank in Sydney in due course, and over forty years later, we still all get together regularly and the group have all stayed with us from time to time at Mudgee. Regrettably, Ian died suddenly and unexpectedly in 2010 while playing golf and Anne is currently suffering severe health problems.

Although we were paid on English award salary scales and were taxed at the rate of about 50 per cent, we managed to take a number of short holidays throughout the United Kingdom and drove ourselves on three occasions around Western Europe and up to Scandinavia. We left the children at home with a babysitter and rang daily to check that all was okay. Anywhere in Western Europe is virtually a few hours' drive or flight from London. There was no such thing as salary packages for expatriate staff in those days, and we suffered fairly heavily financially. Also, there was no home leave for the duration of our three and a quarter years stay. However, despite all that, it was a great education for all of us, invaluable for my future career, and we also had a lot of fun travelling around.

While in London, the bank nominated me to attend a senior management development programme named the City of London Course. Approximately, eighty executives from various countries around the world were represented. It was a high-powered course dealing mainly with the world economy, politics, and how the financial markets of the city of London operated. I befriended a chap from South Africa and another from Southern Rhodesia (now Zimbabwe), both of whom, as I learnt later, were under almost constant surveillance by the secret service due to the British Government's opposition to the then Prime Minister of Southern Rhodesia, Ian Smith, and his country's feelings towards South Africa and apartheid. I had both of these chaps home to our place at Bromley for a meal and got to know some of their background. As I got to know the South African better and he told me how he kept his black 'monkey' slaves in line with a stock whip, I expressed my disgust and soon left him to his own devices.

Because I lived in London, I was expected to know all the nightspots and shady places for the overseas visitors to sample. With our very young family, we had not had much opportunity for night life other than attending official engagements on the bank's behalf and visiting with friends. However, I managed to find out the location of some 'interesting' places and as a consequence got to see a few of them myself. Even in the mid-1970s, it was obvious that corruption was rife in black African countries with self-rule. One City of London course attendee had ordered a Jaguar Sovereign motor vehicle to take back home with him to Nigeria, and it was clear from his boasting that his taxpayers would be footing the bill. Meeting people like him was just one of the many learning experiences one encountered from attending a session such as this.

The City of London course was one of a number of training and development opportunities afforded to me by the bank during my career. I found that the bank was always keenly aware of the need to provide training to its officers. I had been assigned to my first training course in 1956 within a few months of joining the bank. In subsequent years, I attended in-house ledger examiner and manager's assistant courses, and while I was the manager at Monto I attended a six-week management development course at 'Mahratta', the bank's senior training college at Wahroonga in Sydney. Later, on my return from London, I was invited to lecture to a group of branch managers on balance sheets, rural management, and other management issues at a similar six-week Mahratta management development course.

In the latter half of our stay in London, I had a nasty health problem with a cyst forming on my vocal chords which had to be surgically removed not long before my term was completed there. I had experienced the problem for at least six months prior to the operation, and periodic visits to the local GP on Saturday mornings for determination of a cure only resulted in medication for what was haphazardly diagnosed either as laryngitis or pharyngitis (defined as an inflammation of the pharynx), the latter of which I had never heard of previously or since. Not once did the GP look at my vocal chords despite my insisting that I felt that something was sticking in my throat on occasions when I swallowed. When I finally insisted that I be referred to a consultant (specialist), the first thing he did was look at my vocal chords. To my dismay, he found a large septic cyst that had to be removed urgently. The consultant told me after the operation that septic cysts have a habit of swelling up quickly and that I could have choked had that occurred. This was the second occasion that the British nationalised medical system had let us down severely, the doctor's shocking lack of attention for Andrew's diarrhoea being the first such instance.

The head office had expected that I would move to Sydney when my term in London was up, but I elected to return to Brisbane where I knew the weather would not irritate my throat problem, as had been the case in London. We flew home in first-class seats via Rome and Athens. The children were all that much older and they were absolutely spoiled by the JAL hostesses. Val and I enjoyed a very comfortable and untroubled return to Australia and were delighted to be back on home soil.

Chapter 14

Back to Queensland

O n my return to Brisbane in May 1976, I spent a frustrating six months on 'unattached' staff. Despite my reminding the Queensland division on a number of occasions of my impending return, the then staff manager did not have a specific job arranged for me. The majority of that six months was spent in the chief manager's office, relieving in senior administrative roles, and I also relieved a few senior branch managers in Brisbane, all of which assignments I enjoyed. Eventually, I was appointed as Manager of Alderley branch, a north-west Brisbane suburb. I found this very disappointing as I had been 'leapfrogged' in seniority by most of my contemporaries as a consequence of my term in London. It was as though being chosen for three plus years of special grooming in London counted for nought; however, I got on with the job, enjoyed the role, and made considerable progress with the business growth of the branch in the eighteen months that I was there.

When we left for London, the bank's staff housing policy had been relaxed to the extent that one was able to retain a house when transferred. On our return to Brisbane, we had been absent from our Mt Gravatt house in excess of four years and had added Andrew to our family in the meantime. The house had only three bedrooms, and with three boys and a girl, we were compelled to go house-hunting once again. We found a suitable home but ran into difficulties obtaining finance from the bank. While we were overseas, the Gatton Street house at Mt Gravatt had been rented to the one family for almost the entire four years, and they had asked to be able to stay in the home for a further six months until December 1976 for very understandable personal reasons. Despite my assurances to the bank that the house would be sold by the end of 1976 and any bridging finance repaid, Chief Staff Office in Sydney was inflexible. It required me to put my threat to leave the bank on paper before they grudgingly relented to approve the finance for us to purchase a home at Molyneaux Street, Upper Mt Gravatt. After having to wait around for six months for a job, then being put through this uncertainty, I was really serious about doing what I had indicated, and I guess that after being in London where I was responsible for making the decisions on all issues involving personnel, the perceived small-mindedness of the bureaucracy of the 'big' bank was grating on me. Our tenants were true to their word, and the house was sold within the promised time frame.

We stayed with my mum at Salisbury for about six weeks when we got back to Brisbane, pending the availability of the new house. During that time, Val elected to drive Lisa and Mark back and forward to school at Upper Mt Gravatt to overcome the need for yet another change of schools. Paul was now twelve, Lisa nine, Mark six, and Andrew three, and this was Paul's fifth school. The three older children had assimilated well into their school in Bromley, Kent, and all had acquired very proper English accents. I recall Lisa being quite definite when we arrived in London that she was not going to speak 'funny' like the locals. It didn't take much more than a few weeks before she was well under the spell of the local ways of pronunciation and began to call me 'Dardy'. We decided that Paul should go to Church of England Grammar School (Churchie) in Brisbane as it provided boarding facilities, which we might have need of at some later stage if I was transferred from Brisbane. He loved the school and achieved very well. He found he was well ahead in English studies but in arrears with regard to maths. His natural abilities allowed him to catch up quickly. Mark had the most English accent of all the kids, and his teacher Mrs Thomas thought it was fascinating, so much so that she paraded him before some of the other teachers for them to hear him speak. Of course, all of us were as white as the driven snow after living in England for over three years. Arriving back in Queensland amongst the bronzed bodies, which by then were very foreign to us, made us really obvious. We went to the Gold Coast for the day soon after our arrival back in Brisbane, and Paul was walking up the beach in swimmers without a shirt. Some young fellows passing in the opposite direction made a derogatory comment about him being a 'Pom', and Paul was mortified. It didn't take us long to get tanned.

After being repeatedly praised by my regional manager for the excellent job I was doing at Alderley, I was devastated to be appointed to Manager, Administration, in the head office in Brisbane in mid-1978 with a paltry elevation in both managerial grading and salary. This move only further exacerbated my very slow promotion relative to my peers, and I made my feelings known in a very forthright letter to State General Manager Steve McCready. Steve was noted for his stormy temper. He called me into his office and started tearing strips off me before he even said 'hello'. His ranting was along the line that I was a smart arse who, because I had been to London, felt he deserved better than others and that I needed to wait my turn. I had encountered this sort of jealousy from other sources on my return, and it was clear that he was another one who was unhappy that he had been sent to head up Papua New Guinea some time previously in his career rather than going to London. I let him exhaust himself without my saying one word; then I simply asked him if he know what the bank's Selected Training Plan (STP) called for in regard to my progress. The STP was a plan drawn up for all specially selected officers to guide their future developmental training within the bank. It was agreed with and signed off by the officer concerned, then by the State general manager, and then finally by the chief staff manager in Sydney.

Perhaps part of the reason that Mr McCready was so annoyed with me was because in my letter I referred to the fact that it seemed to me that STP in the Queensland context meant 'stem the progress'. I guess he didn't see that as particularly funny, but I wanted him to very clearly understand exactly how I felt about my career being mishandled by him and others in his office, and clearly I had made my point. He attempted to divert the discussion away from the STP, but I insisted. He had to admit that he didn't know what the bank had planned for my development—a damning admission from any general manager, whose job it was to know the development programme for each of the STP officers within his/ her division and to support its implementation. I then asked him if he knew how I had fared in terms of promotion over the past five to six years in relation to my peers, and he had to acknowledge that he didn't. I pointed out that in the five years since I was appointed to London my managerial status had moved but one grade. Further, with continuing very good appraisals, this latest 'advancement' was a rather doubtful promotion. I made the additional point that I had actually dropped a couple of years behind even those of my many peers who were not on the STP programme, whereas I believed that I possibly should have moved well ahead of the latter group. Reluctantly, he had to agree with what I had to say. He then passed the buck for these disappointing moves on to the staff manager, who was one of the people who was openly jealous of my London experience. I asked Mr McCready to get the staff manager in to explain to me his motives for the appointments I had received since returning to the Queensland Division, but he had gone on leave the day my move was announced!

I made it known to Steve McCready in very calm and quite civil terms that I was seriously considering resigning as it was my clear view that I was being deliberately held back. He asked me to consider the situation carefully before I took such an action as he knew that I had a good future in the bank. I told him he would know my intentions if I turned up to do the administration manager's job on the date I was scheduled to start, which was a few weeks away, and we parted on more agreeable terms. I calmed down a little in the following two weeks and decided to give the new job a go as its responsibilities interested me greatly. Steve McCready came to see me immediately I arrived in my new office and welcomed me aboard. I told him I might not stay long as I was still most unhappy and was considering other options. I was actually investigating the prospects of buying produce in the Brisbane Fruit and Vegetable Markets on behalf of Gold Coast clients and delivering the produce to them. Both my brother and brother-in-law were well entrenched and very successful in their market business and were more than prepared to support me during the learning process. McCready sent the staff manager, who was by then back from leave, to see me, and that was an 'interesting' conversation. Chief Staff Office in Sydney had somehow heard about my concerns, probably from McCready, although he never admitted it, and soon after I was awarded an elevation in managerial grading and a special salary increase, which eased the pain a little. I must say that it turned out to be a very enjoyable job, and working for Jack Shardlow who was Chief Manager, Administration, was a great experience.

It was during this period of our life in Brisbane that Mark and Andrew joined the Cubs at Mt Gravatt. Not long afterwards, we had a visit one evening from the Scoutmaster to say that they required the services of a parent as group leader, a non-uniform position, and unless someone volunteered to take on the job soon, the group would have to close its doors. Val and I discussed the issue, and it was agreed that I should lend a hand, so I took on the role. The promised one meeting a month became at least one meeting a week as well as numerous other working bees and camps. We had some great times with the kids, and the group flourished to such an extent that we had to commence a second Cub pack. I felt really good about my involvement and the re-energising of the group. I enjoyed a lot of fun times and received good leadership training from my days as a Scout in Rockhampton, and I was pleased to be able to give something back to the organisation. It never ceased to amaze me the number of parents who used the Cubs as a child-minding occasion. The same parents dumped their kids at the door, went off and had fun, and invariably returned late to collect their child, forcing the Cub Mistress to wait for them while her valuable evening time with her family gradually disappeared. Those same parents were almost always the first to complain and hassle the Cub Mistress. I introduced a rule that all complaints had to be referred directly to me as the group leader. It was interesting to see the reaction from these people who made frivolous complaints when I challenged them to put on a uniform and do a better leadership job. Most complaints were withdrawn instantly when this proposition was raised.

Due to the problems that I had suffered with my throat in London, I had immediately advised the bank of my immobility in regard to interstate transfers when we returned to Brisbane. This meant that I was not prepared to accept any transfers other than within Queensland, as I was not certain that the cooler weather in Sydney would agree with my throat. As a consequence of this self-imposed restriction, I could see that my future was going to be marked by moves between the administration areas in the Brisbane head office, the large branches within Brisbane and along the coast of Queensland, possibly also including Mt Isa and Toowoomba off the coast, or else I might be appointed to the Branch Inspection or Audit staff, where one is away from home very frequently and possibly for weeks at a time. A pattern of moves such as this would probably result in our children either being placed in boarding schools in Brisbane or staying with us and facing further changes of schools in their crucial years. We were not content with this possibility, so after being back in Brisbane about three and half years and finding I had not suffered any further ill effects in regard to my previous throat problem, Val and I decided that we should make ourselves mobile and accept a transfer interstate, which we understood was very likely to happen. Within a few days of notifying the lifting of my mobility restriction to the bank, I was asked to consider moving to Sydney as Assistant to Deputy Managing Director Eric Tait. After due consideration, we felt that such a move would be the best way of keeping the family intact for as long as possible and also best for schooling purposes, so I accepted the move.

Chapter 15

Sydney Here We Come

W e arrived in Sydney in May 1980 during a housing boom. Prices were high, having increased rapidly over the past few years. The bank placed us in a transit house at Greenwich on the Lower North Shore, and the search commenced for a house that we could afford to buy in an area that we preferred, such as the Upper North Shore. Paul was then fifteen and in his second last year at secondary school. Lisa was almost thirteen and also at secondary school. Mark was ten and Andrew was seven. The location of secondary schooling was the factor that dictated where we might live, so it was urgent that we sort this issue out quickly. The fact that Paul had been at 'Churchie' in Brisbane enabled us to get him into Barker College at Hornsby without difficulty. Lisa attended Hunter's Hill High School temporarily, but fortunately she was able to get into Hornsby Girls' High when we eventually shifted. Mark and Andrew commenced school at Greenwich State School, pending us becoming settled in a house, and eventually went to Waitara State School.

Val diligently searched every real estate agency up and down the North Shore for about three months before we found a house that was remotely suitable for our family needs and also within our price range. She was told on occasions by some of the more 'snobby' agents that she was attempting the impossible on the budget that we had to spend, but she persisted. The house that we eventually purchased in King Road, Wahroonga, was a very ordinary five-bedroom home, two of which were extremely small single rooms. It had a small fibreglass in-ground pool which appealed greatly to the kids. We paid $122,500 for it after having sold our Brisbane home, which was twice the size and twice as good, for $65,000 and ended up with a mortgage about three times the size we had previously. Val was forced to go to work full-time from 8.30 a.m. to 3 p.m. as a teacher's aide at Masada College Pre-School at Lindfield so that we could make ends meet. Our daunting financial experience was similar to many other promising officers who were transferred to Sydney from various states around Australia where property values were much lower.

I had to catch the bus or walk a few kilometres each day to the train at Wahroonga Station and then travel forty minutes into Wynyard Station and walk up Martin Place to the bank's head office on the corner of Macquarie Street and Martin Place. I left home about 7 a.m. and usually got home about 7 p.m. My new boss, Deputy Managing Director Eric Tait, turned out to be a brilliant banker and good to work for, when one got to know how he operated. The job was very much about assisting Eric in the management of the bank's investments in all sorts of ventures from Gove Aluminium to Old Sydney Town. My job was newly created, and Eric was unsure of what I should do when I arrived at his office door, and really I was left to sort the job out for myself. Obviously, I did it to his complete satisfaction, as he gave me glowing reports and we are still good friends to this day.

Old Sydney Town is a story in itself, and the day-to-day management of this bank investment was actually under the stewardship of Jim Keck, who was the chief staff manager and a director on the Old

Sydney Town board. I knew Jim from the London days when he had to come over and sort out some issues within that division. The majority shareholder in Old Sydney Town was the State Government of New South Wales. Previous to my involvement, the general manager of the theme park and his staff were used to very little supervision from shareholders and had been able to spend money on lavish parties and the like without question. Jim Keck had never had time to really delve deeply into the financials of the business, and I soon unearthed some of these devious happenings. We used to discuss our tactics in the chauffeur-driven bank car on the way to board meetings at Old Sydney Town, which was situated about fifty kilometres north of Sydney CBD. As I was not a director of the company and with Jim Keck's approval, I was able to make some preliminary comments in order to raise the issues I had uncovered, but the final statement was left to Jim. It was agreed that I should highlight to the other board members the discrepancies that we had identified, and then Jim would set about insisting on their correction in his low-key but very authoritative way. The Government representatives on the board were impressed and cooperative, but management were not very happy at having their lifestyle curtailed.

In addition to the experience I gained from working for Eric Tait and the knowledge acquired about the workings of the bank at the head office and board levels, I found that I was working within a few metres of Bob White's office (now the managing director) and all the chief general managers of the various business and administrative divisions of the organisation. I had interaction with all of them and their staff frequently and got to know, and to become known, by a lot of people whom I had not met previously. Some of these associations were no doubt useful to me in my later career. I was involved in numerous high-level issues in the head office, one of which was membership in 1980, soon after my arrival in Sydney, of the very secret committee that was formed to advise the bank's executive committee and the board on the prospects of a merger or takeover of another of Australia's major banks. The committee's deliberations eventually resulted in a recommendation being made to the managing director that the Wales merge with the Commercial Bank of Australia Ltd, a Melbourne-based bank. The committee's preferred target would have been the Commercial Banking Company of Sydney Ltd, but as it was also a Sydney-based bank it did not provide the financial synergies that we were seeking nor would it have been passed for approval by the Federal Treasurer. The merger eventually was consummated under the name of Westpac Banking Corporation in mid-1982. In hindsight, I now view the target bank as being a rather poor choice.

Another of my interesting projects when working for Eric Tait was to undertake the initial negotiations on behalf of the Wales when Bank of America (BOA) decided it wanted to exit the Partnership Pacific Merchant Banking arrangement. The Wales, BOA, and Bank of Tokyo (BOT) were originally equal one-third shareholders. BOT was keen to continue the relationship as was the Wales, and amongst lots of other details to be sorted out, it had to be determined who among the remaining two partners was to hold what proportion of the total shares and what purchase price they were prepared to pay for the BOA shares on its exit. Over a period of some months, we representatives of each of the three banks met regularly each week and often made good headway only to be informed at the next meeting by the BOT representative that Tokyo had vetoed his agreement. This meant that we had no option but to recommence negotiations where we had ended two meetings previously. The frustration for the BOA representative and me was extreme as was the embarrassment for the BOT delegate. On one occasion, the latter's level of embarrassment was such that he appeared to not understand English when we began the meeting, and we had to spend a deal of time quizzing him until we hit the right note. It was because Tokyo had made him lose face to such an extent that he was extremely depressed. We helped him overcome this hurdle and eventually came to an agreement on the myriad of issues except for the price BOT was willing to pay. At this stage, the negotiations were elevated to the level of our superiors, and BOT sent out from Tokyo a high-powered negotiator named Roy Takata. I was present when the final talks took place and was very impressed by the way Eric Tait dealt with the repeated equivocation of Takata. In a calm and measured manner, Eric gradually wore him down to accept the Wales' position. Having seen Takata in action, I said to Eric Tait afterwards that I felt BOT had kept Takata in reserve until they had a special negotiation such as ours to contend with, and then they let him loose. He was a very polished negotiator, but Eric got the better of him.

Some eighteen months after arriving in Eric Tait's office, he informed me that I had been appointed as Regional Manager of the second largest region out of twenty-five in the mighty New South Wales Division of Retail Banking. This meant that all of a sudden I had about thirty-five branch managers reporting to me. I was both shocked and delighted. This was a major promotion to one of the prized jobs in New South Wales Division, the heart of the bank. It brought with it a handsome salary increase and a bank-provided new vehicle. My office was located at Royal Exchange in the city together with all the other New South Wales regional managers, a fact that both surprised and concerned me. It was my strong view that a regional manager should be based in his/her territory so as to better understand the environment in which the business operated and be able to have close and frequent contact with the branch managers and their staff. All my managers were older than me, some of them more than twenty years older with a lot of branch management experience, whereas I had been master of one very small branch and one of less than medium size. I soon found that years of experience didn't count for much with regard to some of the branch managers now under my control. I also quickly learnt that New South Wales Division seemed to operate in a more bureaucratic way to that which I was used to and that some managers appeared reluctant to fully accept the responsibilities of their positions and to provide the branch leadership required to achieve superior results for both the customer and the bank. My background training in Queensland together with my drive to achieve the best possible results brought about some early clashes with a few of the old diehards who were not only older than me but also senior to me in terms of salary. The manager of the largest branch in the region and the biggest branch outside the central business district of Sydney was one such manager who was not going to suffer any nonsense from 'this young upstart who he outranked', and he told me so very clearly at the outset. A few months later, he decided that he had had enough and it was time to retire. Most of the others soon learnt that I was there to make them more successful at doing what was good for customers and the bank, and that was primarily by doing things smarter, although I must admit that some of them had to begin to buckle down and work a bit harder.

Regional management was a thoroughly enjoyable role that brought me into close and frequent contact with the three state managers for the northern, southern, and central divisions of New South Wales and their boss Alan Thomas, General Manager for New South Wales. During my time in this role, I was able to influence the relocation of rural-based regional managers to individual offices within their own regions. This proved to be a very popular decision for regional personnel, customers, and for the regional managers themselves. Business-wise it was a great success. The regional managers quickly became a senior member of their community and were often called upon for press statements or to make speeches at local functions and so forth.

In 1981, not very long after I arrived in Sydney, the bank sent me for another six-week senior management development course at the Australian Administrative Staff College at Mt Eliza, south of Melbourne. There were about sixty participants from all over South-East Asia, whose occupations ranged from politicians, unionists, academics, lawyers, accountants, industrialists, bankers, and military personnel. We were broken into syndicates of eight people, and most of our work was done in these small groups. I recall clearly that on the first afternoon, after meeting in the main hall and being advised of the membership of our various syndicates, we were despatched to our syndicate rooms to introduce ourselves to each other. All went well until a young Bangladeshi took his turn to speak. He was very good looking and superbly dressed in a brilliant white shirt, black silk tie, royal blue silk reefer jacket with darker blue silk lapels, black trousers with a black silk strip down the outside seam of each leg, and patent leather black shoes. His black slicked down hair matched his ebony black skin. He introduced himself as Second Assistant Secretary of the Treasury Department of his Government (none of us knew what that meant) and then began to harangue us about the need for Australia to take many more people from his overcrowded and very poor country. This went on and on until we were beginning to run short of time for others to speak. Someone had to stop him, so I suggested he might like to continue his 'demands' over dinner or at some later time. He was not pleased to be interrupted in full flight, but others began to pressure him also and he stopped. I became very friendly with him over the duration of the course, and it turned out that he was a very senior public servant. Part of his role was to determine what portion of foreign aid was directed to infrastructure development within Bangladesh and what went towards purchasing food supplies for the starving millions. He told me that for every additional dollar he allocated to infrastructure development he knew another Bangladeshi citizen would die of starvation; however, making this decision caused him little concern. Of course, he and his family lived in quite palatial circumstances in a compound for the elite. He continued to harangue us about the need for Australia to take up to thirty million of his people, and we kept telling him that although Australia was a huge country it was mainly desert in the interior. He did not believe this until he and other overseas students had taken a four-day bus tour to the north-east of South Australia during the Easter break. When he returned, he was shocked by what he had seen and commented that no one could live out there. The same guy had never heard of a barbecue prior to his visit to Australia, but after the first experience he was keen to have one every lunchtime, weather permitting.

Val and our four children came down from Sydney by train to spend time with me for the Easter break at the mid-point of the course. We rented a unit in St Kilda, and the bank very kindly lent me one of their limousines for the four days. I had, for the first time in my life, grown a moustache in the three weeks that I had been at the college, and Val and the kids were all shocked to see me when I met them at the railway station. The kids couldn't stop looking at me and laughing, and Val thought it was odd too. Once they had seen it, I couldn't wait to shave it off as it really annoyed me. During those four days, we were able to see the sights around Melbourne and tour down the Great Ocean Road. Also, Des Dwyer who lived in Melbourne and was one of my fellow syndicate members invited us to have lunch with him and his wife at Cockatoo Restaurant in the Dandenongs. The kids had the greatest smorgasbord lunch ever, and both Paul and Mark remember it even today. Regrettably, the restaurant was destroyed a few years later in one of the area's many disastrous bush fires.

I was at the Australian Administrative Staff College at Mt Elisa when the public announcement was made about the merger of the Wales with the Commercial Bank of Australia. It caused quite a stir amongst the course attendees, as there had been no such mergers amongst the major banks in Australia for very many years. For me, it was a relief that the matter was out in the public arena and there was now no possibility that I might inadvertently 'spill the beans' as it were.

A month or so later when I was running a training session for the managers of my region and was in the middle of a presentation, I was interrupted and asked to take a phone call. I sent a return message to say that I was speaking to a group of managers and that I would return the call as soon as I finished the session. The messenger came back and said that I was wanted 'now'! The caller turned out to be Alan Thomas, the general manager for New South Wales, who told me that I had been appointed to the newly created position of State Manager, Western Regions, New South Wales Division. I was absolutely shocked once again by such a major appointment, and as I returned to the training room, my managers wondered what had happened. They saw the look of shock and disbelief on my face and the same expression registered on their faces when I told them the news.

The new Western Regions' State Division had been introduced by the bank in order that the enormous task of merging the businesses of the two banks in the massive New South Wales Division could be more effectively implemented. Western Regions encompassed the areas immediately beyond my old Parramatta region including the Sydney suburban areas of Liverpool, Penrith, Windsor and Richmond. Also included were all areas due west through the Central Highlands to the Northern Territory border and all areas west of the New England Highway up to the Queensland border. The new Western Regions' Division had no staff and no administrative premises, so I had to set about begging and borrowing, and in some instances I think we might have stolen items from other divisions to be able to establish all the required administrative structures and acquire the appropriate staff before the merger took effect on 1 July 1982.

There were many country branches as well as metropolitan branches in the Western Regions, some of which were very isolated. Not only did the isolated manager and his/her family suffer the lack of good shopping, entertainment, schooling, social intercourse, atrocious roads, and the harsh environment of the location of these branches but also they quite often were required to contend with other anti-social issues which are common to some of these outback towns. I spent a reasonable amount of time visiting branches so that I was in touch with the grass roots of the organisation, and on occasions I took Val with me on trips to the country. Initially, she thought it would be wonderful to travel around, enjoying lunches and dinners with customers, branch managers, and their spouses. She could also socialise with managers' wives while I was visiting the branches and talking with the staff. She soon found that the schedules were gruelling with lots of travel, meeting lots of people who were mostly very nice, long days, and early mornings. It was very demanding for her in addition to her very heavy household duties, and she was pleased to be able to opt out on occasions. She, like me, also found that it was always great to get home from trips to sit down to a sandwich rather than the official lunches and dinners that had been the order of the day for the past week.

The wives of the managers really appreciated Val's visits and she was a great unpaid ambassador for the bank. She had experienced life as a country branch manager's wife with a family of four young children (which always threw them), and she handled all occasions very competently and diplomatically. Quite often, she noted issues that a manager's wife had divulged to her, which the husband was loathe to speak about to me or his regional manager. Usually they were issues which were either impacting quite adversely on the harmony of the family or preventing the manager concerned from performing his duties to the best of his ability. I was usually able to carefully resolve these issues behind the scene and make a difficult life more agreeable for those involved.

Many country branch managers lived in a rent-free and very well-furnished residence situated above the bank premises in the town's main street. In normal circumstances, this was a highly acceptable arrangement; however, the background of conflict and misbehaviour in some small western towns meant that some of these people and their families were virtually prisoners in their own homes. Children could not go into the street without an adult escort and the bad behaviour, noise, foul language, and worse at night when the pubs closed had to be experienced to be believed. In all such instances, I was able to direct part of the division's premises budget towards buying a nice home in a quiet part of the town and shifting the family there. I was also able to have the bank introduce a policy of providing isolated branches with 4WD vehicles so that the manager did not wreck his own private car on the unsealed and usually ungraded gravel roads he had to frequently travel when undertaking bank business. Many managers were required to carry out rural property inspections that could take them hundreds of kilometres away from the branch on shire and station property 'roads' that left a lot to be desired at the best of times and which became positively treacherous and boggy with the slightest bit of wet weather. Communication facilities in those areas were almost non-existent and passing traffic very infrequent, which meant that should a manager's privately owned 2WD vehicle become disabled in these parts he could wait for assistance for very many hours. Later in my career, I was delighted to be able to have this same policy extended to isolated branches across the whole of Australia.

Paul was young for his class when he entered the New South Wales school system halfway through year 11, but he settled in well, and we were very proud of him when he matriculated in 1982 with exceptionally good results. It was during this phase in his life that he became interested in speleology (exploring and studying caves) with the Barker College Speleology Club. They frequently headed off to various areas of the State to investigate caves and their contents, and we were very relieved when they returned safely. They tramped and crawled through bat manure, underground creeks, and squeezes and came home with overalls that stunk to high heaven and which were caked in bat excrement. Val insisted that Paul hung the overalls on the clothes line and hosed the bulk of the mess off before she would put them in the washing machine. It was also during this time that Paul's 'green' interests surfaced strongly, and these were reinforced during his years at university where he also acquired a leaning towards small 'l' liberal politics, which moderated somewhat in later years. Paul elected to study arts law at Sydney University, I believe mainly due to some urging from us. However, after the first year he dropped the law component as he could not reconcile what he saw as the self-serving interests of lawyers being the priority taught at law school, with his personal principles which leant firmly towards providing help to others and maintaining the environment. He matriculated with very sound results in a Bachelor of Arts Degree and went on to do another year for a Masters in English literature where he achieved Honours. It was a proud day for Val and I to be present to see him presented with his degree at a ceremony in the Great Hall of Sydney University. Soon after this, he moved to Tasmania to work in the environmental field. He became an active participant in the campaign to save the tall eucalypts, which resulted in the addition of 200,000 ha of forest into the Tasmanian South West Wilderness World Heritage area. Although he hasn't given us too much detail of what he was involved in, and it is probably better that we do not know, it is clear that he spent extended periods living in shelters in very high trees in order to prevent destruction of the forests, also that he was arrested together with lots of other demonstrators on several occasions but did not have any charges recorded against him. He remains a fervent supporter of the environment today and is extremely proud of his work with the World Wide Fund (WWF) in Vienna where he is now a world authority on carbon issues and where his work is aimed at maintaining the world's environment as a place where it is safe for humans to continue living well into the future.

CHAPTER 16

The Big Time and Bad Times Arrive

I n May 1983 I was appointed General Manager for New South Wales Division. I am unable to fully recall how the news was broken to me, such was the shock, but I do remember within about twelve months of my taking up my then position of State Manager, Western Regions, New South Wales Division, Russell Leitch, Chief Staff Manager at the head office, called me to his office to tell me that Alan Thomas, General Manager for New South Wales Division, had been diagnosed with cancer and was to retire immediately. Russell said that the board had determined to appoint me in his place. However, I was to be given the opportunity to consider the situation before I decided either way so that I was comfortable in accepting all the responsibilities of such a demanding position and one that was so crucially important to the bank's success. He also mentioned that I could be in the position for up to seven years. I was absolutely stunned to say the least.

New South Wales Division is the jewel in the crown of Westpac, and it then comprised some 45 per cent of its entire Australian retail banking business. It was a multi-billion dollar business, contributing a huge proportion of the bank's overall annual profits, spread over some 465 branches, and employing more than 10,000 staff. I recall I had a number of mixed emotions pass very quickly through my mind; did I have the skill, fortitude, and experience to be able to handle such a mammoth role? It was unheard of that a forty-three-year-old should be trusted with the future of such an immense slab of the bank's business and particularly one who just three years previously had been a middle-grade ranking officer in the Queensland administration and was still relatively unknown in the organisation. When I had recovered sufficiently to respond to Russell, I told him that I had on many occasions during recent years made statements along the lines of: 'If only New South Wales Division could be made to perform more efficiently, the bank's profits would be enhanced considerably.' Of course, Russell's retort was 'Well, here's your chance to make it happen.' I told him that if he, Bob White, and the board were confident that I could do the job well and trusted me to such an extent, then I would be honoured to accept the role.

Alan Thomas already knew who the bank had in mind as his replacement and was waiting to see me when I returned to my office. When he told me what the salary was, I couldn't believe my ears, but he warned me that I would earn every last cent of it. How true that statement was! However, it did change our financial position markedly and Val was able to cease work at Masada Pre-School. Alan also informed me of the very important and demanding social side of the role that came with the position. He did not exaggerate, and I was to encounter an official lunch about 80 per cent of all business days for the next seven years. Additionally, there was usually a dinner or maybe two per week, many of which were preceded by an unrelated cocktail function— also frequent speaking engagements.

Val was required to be involved in a lot of the dinners and other events and at times had to endure some mindless twaddle from boring old matrons and pompous men who thought that they were the centre of the universe. Some of it was fun for her, but it was hard work looking after the needs of the family at home before rushing off to another bank function. Fortunately, the bank supplied a driver for such occasions, and he was able to collect Val at home, then collect me at work, deliver us to the door of the function, and then drive us home afterwards. Alan Thomas urged me to move closer to the city, predominantly in order to shorten the lengthy travel time to Wahroonga late at night. Fortunately, I took his advice, and after months of house-hunting again, Val located a home that suited us well in East Lindfield for $222,500. We sold the Wahroonga house for the same amount we paid for it and increased our debt to the bank by about $100,000, which was rather breathtaking for us at the time. The move cut my travelling time to work to half to about twenty minutes each way. I found that if I left home about 6.45 a.m. I missed the bulk of the traffic congestion and could be parked in the garage in the basement of Westpac Plaza building on the corner of George and Margaret Streets by 7.10 a.m. and at my desk soon thereafter.

I was under no illusion from the outset about the extreme difficulty I would face in the job, and it proved to be so. However, I enjoyed the huge challenges that it presented, and the results spoke for themselves. We gradually improved the overall performance of the business, and there was enthusiasm within the 'big' division as we began to show results that were superior to other State divisions across all segments of the business. I must admit that I got a certain amount of satisfaction out of seeing my division's contribution to the bank's profits, amounting to hundreds of millions of dollars, projected on to the screen at general managers' conferences. As the years in the role went by, my experience grew and I was able to, with the support of my very good top team, develop and promote to my then Australian retail banking boss Stuart Fowler many innovative changes. These were for eventual implementation across the retail bank and led to better customer and staff satisfaction as well as a better bottom line result. I also had my share of failures. Unlike others who were in the role of divisional head for a few short years, my stay of seven years allowed time for my discomfort over some of my decisions. I learnt a lot from these mistakes and am certain that I became a better leader as a result.

In 1984 during the early phase of my term as General Manager, New South Wales Division, I received a phone call from Westpac's Managing Director Bob White, who asked that I accept a position on the Board of the Royal Blind Society of New South Wales (RBS). I pointed out to Bob that I was already working about eighty hours per week and didn't really need any additional involvements to keep me occupied. He insisted that it would be good for my future development, and I responded that I might not live to have a future if I took on any more workload. We talked about it for quite a while and fortunately Bob ended up winning the day, and I eventually had fifteen very worthwhile and fulfilling years on that board.

I had no sooner joined the RBS board than I was elected Chairman of the Finance and Planning Committee, which of course meant at least one other meeting per month. Then the new president, Max Roberts, decided that he and I should set about modernising the management structure of the RBS, improving the salary structure, and employing high-quality people who were expected to perform to a high standard. This meant gradually moving away from the old mentality of a not-for-profit organisation paying its employees 'peanuts' and so expecting little by way of performance in return. The organisation prospered under Max's guidance, and in 1992 he introduced the idea of forming a national blindness agency by merging the major State-based blindness organisations in Victoria, South Australia, and New South Wales. A meeting of the presidents of these organisations was arranged to take place in Melbourne, and Max asked that I attend, together with him, as the representatives of RBS. Parochialism was very much to the fore and it was easy to see that the majority were hell-bent on retaining the status quo, for their own self-centred gain, rather than seeing the benefits that might accrue to the many thousands of blind and vision-impaired clients of these organisations.

Soon after the Melbourne meeting, I learnt why Max took me to that gathering. He announced to me that he was retiring and that I was to take his place. Bob White agreed that I should take on the role, and I subsequently spent seven years as president of that great organisation. It was a very rewarding moment for me when it was announced in about 1997 that RBS had been judged by the Productivity Commission to be the best run not-for-profit charitable organisation in Australia.

I determined to run with the 'merger' ball that Max Roberts had started rolling and sought the support of my board to do so. I must say that their initial response was lukewarm, and some told me that the dream was unachievable. I guess I have always liked a challenge, and my response to my fellow board members was along the lines of: 'Where there is a will there is a way. I have the will and expect that with the board's support and assistance, we can find the way. It might take twenty years to achieve the union of these big organisations, but if we don't commence the merger process sometime there is no hope of it ever happening'. The strength of my conviction hit the spot and I received unanimous support from the board. When I retired from the RBS in 1999, significant progress had been made with the Braille and Talking Book libraries having been amalgamated and already substantially better service to blind and vision impaired readers being provided throughout the eastern half of Australia.

The entire merger was consummated within fifteen years and the new national body known as Vision Australia is now able to speak to governments, Federal and State, on behalf of its clients in one very big voice. A few years after I retired from the Royal Blind Society, I was surprised and delighted to be awarded a Member of the Order of Australia (AM). The award was published in the Queen's Birthday honours list on 10 June 2002 for: 'service to the community, particularly through the development of programs and delivery of services through the Royal Blind Society of New South Wales'. It was a proud day for me to be accompanied by my dear wife, my mother, and son Mark to Government House in Sydney (there was a limit of three guests) to have the medal presented to me by the Governor of New South Wales, Prof. Marie Bashir. Upon leaving the Royal Blind Society, I did not lose contact with some of the people that I had worked closely with. Regrettably, Max Roberts died in 2009, but Prof. Frank Martin, an eminent ophthalmologist and a strong board member supporter of mine, Jon Isaacs, an excellent former CEO of the Society, and our respective wives, together with Max's widow Janet, have continued to meet socially a few times a year.

We were extremely proud of our daughter Lisa when she successfully completed the Higher School Certificate in 1985 after two years at Barker College. Her disability made school life and study doubly difficult for her, and we had reservations that she might ever be able to achieve at this level. Not only did she prove us wrong but she also went on to a business college at the beginning of 1986 and graduated with very good results in the middle of that year. Even more exciting for us, and no doubt for her, was the fact that she obtained a job with a computer company immediately thereafter. It was heart-warming for us to see Lisa so pleased with her achievements, and her confidence grew enormously as a consequence. She had obtained her driving license and sought my advice as to her purchasing her first car. She was a careful and sensible driver, so I encouraged her to proceed but suggested she should get a personal loan to cover the gap in the purchase price and learn how to manage its repayment for herself, with my close supervision of course! She chose a new Ford Laser and was so proud of it. She had matured into a beautiful young woman with a warm and engaging personality and had the confidence of one who knew exactly what they were going to do with their future life. A very good example of her bright (and, at times, rather quirky) personality is encapsulated in Appendix VI, a letter she wrote to my mother on 29 March 1982 when she was fifteen years of age. Mum recently found it in a 'bottom drawer' that she was cleaning out, and we feel so fortunate to have it as a treasured memory.

Some years earlier, we had successfully fought a court case on Lisa's behalf against the insurer of the drunken driver who had injured Val in a car smash while she was carrying Lisa. A precedent for a court award, involving injury to an unborn baby, had been published in the papers around that time, and it was this publication and advice from a Brisbane neurologist that prompted us to take action on Lisa's behalf. As a consequence of the win, Lisa was awarded a sizeable sum of money with me appointed by the court as her trustee. With Lisa's input, we purchased a very nice townhouse in her name at Artarmon with the thought in mind that Lisa could very comfortably live there when she felt like moving away from home. In the meantime, it would earn a nice rental income. We also purchased an investment unit at Lane Cove for her, and she had tenants in both properties. Although she still suffered her disabilities, for the first time in her life she had been able to demonstrate to herself and others that she could overcome them to a major degree and she looked forward to a successful and relatively normal family life.

However, this was not to be. In the very early hours of the morning of 24 January 1987, the blackest day of our lives, up until then, arrived with the appearance of two young police officers on our doorstep at East Lindfield. They came to tell us the dreadful news that Lisa had been fatally shot during the previous evening.

The murderer was arrested by the police a few days later, and we subsequently learnt that he was a drug-crazed schizophrenic. Lisa was nineteen and a half years old at the time. She had gone to her twin girlfriends Jenny and Kirsty McGregor's home that evening to ensure that the girls were properly organised for their planned trip to the Central Coast for the coming long weekend. Lisa had a heavy cold and intended staying for a short time only. Apparently, at about eight that evening there was a knock at the door of the McGregor's home. Lexie McGregor, a younger sister of the twins, opened the door and the murderer immediately shot her. He then proceeded to shoot the twin sisters and Lisa, all of whom were sitting in the lounge room. All girls died instantly from shotgun blasts. When arrested, the murderer Richard Maddrell claimed that Jenny was controlling his mind, and the only way he could stop her was to kill her. It seems that Maddrell was a distant acquaintance of the girls, having met them some time previously through mutual friends. It seems he was infatuated by Jenny, who had no interest in him whatsoever. At the time, Jenny was attending Wollongong University and one strand of her course was psychology. Maddrell is said to have believed in way out practices, and in his drug-crazed state, it seems he believed that through her psychology studies she had learnt to control his mind. Regrettably, he killed all four girls who happened to be in the house at the time. Fortunately, the girls' mother was not at home, as the police later said that he would have shot her and anyone else who came on the scene. There can be nothing worse that could possibly happen in one's life than to lose a child and possibly more particularly so due to a senseless murder. The hurt and heartache was almost unbearable for me, and I know Val, as the mother, felt the pain much more severely. That pain does not lessen over the years—one simply learns to better live with it, but it remains there every hour of every day.

The impact of Lisa's death on the family as a whole was profoundly detrimental in the long term. The dynamics of the family had changed forever, and now the boys had no 'big sister' to confide in or to go to for support if they weren't getting their way with Val and/or me and of course we no longer had a precious daughter. There would be no wedding for Val to enjoy the thrill of being able to fuss over the details with her daughter or for me to be able to proudly escort my daughter down the aisle. There would be no daughter for Val to confide in over the years ahead, nor to provide that loving care in our older years. The pain was almost crippling for both of us. However, Val and I quickly came to the realisation that we could not bring Lisa back no matter what we did and that we had to do our best for the boys and each other. We supported each other in our grieving and determined, perhaps wrongly, that we did not need counselling at that time. The pressures of work took my mind off my grief to a certain extent, but Val had no such distraction. She had always loved drawing and sketching and decided to take up painting in an endeavour to immerse herself in some pastime that gave her pleasure and took her mind elsewhere. She took regular painting lessons and made amazing progress. Her paintings now grace the walls of both our North Shore Unit in Sydney and our home here in Mudgee, and they regularly create great excitement and elicit very complimentary comments from visitors when they discover the name of the artist. Painting was a great therapy and very helpful to Val's well-being at that time, and she really enjoyed the company of her classmates. Regrettably, it is now some years since she put a brush to canvas.

Val remembers:

Is this a nightmare? It can't be real? I am going to wake up and all will be fine. It's not true!

But no! It has happened. It was true. Our precious Lisa is no longer with us.

I felt numb. I would shut my eyes and I could see her. I could not believe that our Lisa was dead. Who could have done this to her and her three friends? Four beautiful, innocent girls—or should I say young women.

Paul arrived home from Hobart. It was special to have him with us again just weeks after we had spent a wonderful family Xmas holiday together at Burleigh Heads on the Queensland Gold Coast—the six of us—as well as a lot of the Chatterton family. Lisa was on vacation from her work at the time and had two weeks' holidays. Mark and Andrew were on school holidays. Our last holiday together.

How were we going to cope with this dreadful tragedy? It all seemed like a blur—people coming and going. The police were absolutely marvellous. Relatives, friends, neighbours, and people we hardly knew called, dropped in cards, casseroles, other assorted foods, and flowers. We could not believe the kindness and generosity of so many people. It was all most unexpected but so very much appreciated.

John and I were sleeping very little, so around dawn each morning we would go for a walk for an hour or more to try to relieve some stress pressure. As time went by, we found that exercise was the greatest stress reliever.

We had to face the trauma of Lisa's funeral in the days ahead, but we endured because we loved her so very much and were so proud of her. Paul wrote and delivered the most beautiful eulogy for Lisa. It was very difficult for him, but he was able to do so, with much love for his sister. We were very proud of him. Mark and Andrew, like John and I, were still in an enormous state of shock.

After Lisa's funeral we had to start thinking about moving ahead, as difficult as it was going to be for us all. John had taken a couple of weeks off, but it was time to resume work. Paul had to return to Hobart and his work and Mark and Andrew to school. We all felt so very sad but had to try as best we could to return to some measure of normality. Our lives would never be the same again. Instead of our family of six, we were now just five. Lisa had been the centre of our family with her three brothers.

Mark and Andrew were back at school, and only a week or so later I was rostered to help other mothers at the school tuck-shop. It was difficult for me to attend for the first time after Lisa's death, but I felt that I must to support the boys. When I arrived, the other ladies had a beautiful flowering gardenia plant for me. It was very thoughtful of them. At morning break and lunch, both Mark and Andrew came to see me to buy some food as usual, but on this occasion both came back to see me two or three times, more for assurance. I was pleased that I had made the effort to attend and support them in our efforts to support each other. They were both finding it very difficult to concentrate on their studies and this was Mark's Higher School Certificate year. Paul was in Hobart and told us that he had some very good friends he was able to confide in. We spoke often to him by phone, but it was not the same as him being with us in person.

I had not only lost my only daughter but my best female friend. How was I going to learn to live with this enormous emptiness in my life? I somehow had to learn to live with my loss and be able to support John and the boys, as well as I was able to. They were all suffering enormously and we had to work together in supporting each other.

Grief is a very complicated state of mind and is experienced in different ways by different people. Understanding the various stages of grief helped me to comprehend the process. Some of the many stages were such a learning curve to understand and indicated why my feelings were quite normal under the circumstances. Over time, I learnt that my feelings were part of the grieving process. While at home I was able to grieve in private. When I initially had to attend functions that were personal or related to John's work it was very difficult, but I learnt to steel myself, put on my 'public face', and move forward to support John in his work or our sons in their activities. It was very difficult for us all.

To try to help myself move forward, I decided to commence art classes again. Painting was something that I had always thought I would enjoy, but throughout my life I hadn't had the opportunity, the time, or the money to try it until I undertook two terms in watercolour classes soon after we arrived in Sydney. I loved it, but I had to cease classes as circumstances required me to recommence working. After Lisa's death, I was able to commence classes in acrylic painting. I found it very difficult to concentrate but persisted. A few years later, I started learning to paint in oils. It took some years to be able to concentrate fully on my subject and lose myself in my work for those few hours. It was of the greatest benefit for me to have something which I learnt to love doing and to focus on.

How Lisa died became less significant as the years passed. I have lost my precious daughter and that pain will stay with me, and I will miss her and grieve for her for the rest of my life.

Paul was twenty-two years of age at the time of Lisa's death and was living and working in Tasmania. He did not display his grief openly, but we could see that he was hurting terribly. He wrote and delivered a wonderful eulogy (Appendix VII) at the funeral service on behalf of the family, for which I was so very thankful. As much as I would have loved to be able to do so, my emotional state at the time would not allow me to deliver a eulogy without breaking down completely and creating great embarrassment for myself and the family.

Mark was seventeen years of age and attending Barker College in his final year. Andrew was approaching fourteen and also at Barker College. As time went by, it became clear to both Val and I that neither Mark nor Andrew was coping well with the aftermath of Lisa's death, and we arranged counselling. This seemed to produce little benefit, particularly for Andrew, and we eventually arranged individual counselling for them both. This seemed to have some beneficial effect for Mark, but Andrew was never able to open himself up to the counsellor despite our trying a few different practitioners. Both boys needed a distraction, but we didn't know quite what to do.

Having come off the land as a youngster, I had harboured a desire for a number of years to own my own small farm and quite often broached the subject with Val only to be told, 'Go ahead if you want to live by yourself.' When feelings in the family were at low ebb in early 1988, I once again raised the prospect of buying a farm one Friday evening when I arrived home from work. To my great surprise, Val made no objection and actually agreed that we should go looking the next day. She shrewdly saw it as a good opportunity to provide the boys with a distracting interest and also as a means of getting me away from the bank for a while. Where should we go looking was the next question.

I recalled that soon after we arrived in Sydney in 1980 I had taken my mother, who was then in Sydney holidaying with us, and the family for a drive up a very pretty valley that ran west from a town on the Central Coast, the name of which I could not recall. I identified the town from a map as Wyong and the valley as the Yarramalong Valley. So off we set the very next morning. We decided that we wanted a property that had a house or weekender on it, so that we could use it as a weekend retreat. We found that there was only one listed property in the valley with any form of accommodation built on it. That 'accommodation' turned out to be a worthless shack. The same property also had a small cemetery near the front gate, and that quickly ruled out any interest once and for all.

We went home feeling deflated but went back to Wyong again the next day to look for vacant blocks. The only one available was a 40 acre block (16.2 ha) in Stinsons Lane about a kilometre off the main valley road and across the Wyong River by way of a reasonably sturdy wooden bridge, which also served three other properties. We inspected the land with an agent from Wyong, and I was sold on it almost immediately. We left the agent, and then Mark, Andrew, and I walked the boundaries or what seemed to be the boundaries as the fences were mostly missing. Those fences that were evident were not all that serviceable as a consequence of repeated flood and fire damage over the years. It was a picturesque block with a nice site for a house, so we made up our minds on the spot to call on the agent and make an offer. I wanted to get an agreement quickly before Val could change her mind. Unbelievably, the property was owned by a Japanese company that also owned and operated a turf farm next door, and we had to wait days before they accepted our offer.

Once settlement had been effected, we repaired and replaced sufficient fencing to make the block stock proof, and the first cattle that we purchased arrived on the property on my fiftieth birthday in 1989. I later leased the property next door and ran cattle across the two properties. Our initial intention was to build a large garage and fit it out so that we were able to live there on weekends until we built a home some years later. However, the first taste of winter arrived before the shed was finished, and we immediately decided that we would build the house and enjoy the luxury of some warmth in winter. This we promptly did, and we spent almost every weekend there over the next eight or so years. During that time, we had lots of our friends and relations come and stay and enjoy the tranquillity and scenery.

Mark was very keen to buy a motorbike to ride on the roads of Sydney. Having lost one child, this thought terrified us, so we bought both him and Andrew dirt bikes in the belief that they would be safer riding in the Watagans State Forest which almost adjoined the farm. We later heard some frightening tales of their escapades along the forest's logging tracks and they sometimes limped home with themselves and/or their bikes injured or broken. We saw photographs, which were totally hair-raising, of some of their jumps, and it was a relief that we saw them after the bikes had been sold.

We found the farm to be a great relief valve. It was beautiful to wake up and look across the sparkling and tranquil valley each morning and to sit on the front veranda in the late afternoon with maybe a glass of wine and listen to the various kookaburra clans of the area signing off for the day in their familiar loud voices. Mostly, I had to spend the better part of Saturday clearing my weighty briefcase of bank work, but I always got an opportunity to do some cattle work or to get on the tractor and do a bit of slashing and the like, all of which were great stress reducers. We paid a local chap Ross Murray, a small retainer to keep his eye on the cattle and house during the week. He also did any of the heavy work like chopping the firewood or doing fence repairs, so I was what is called a 'Pitt Street' farmer. I loved every moment of the time we spent there; it served to keep the boys with the family and Val enjoyed the breaks.

I was shocked when I came home from work one day, and Andrew told me that he had promised that I would sell Barker College a young steer for the school's agriculture students to rear and train for entry into the New South Wales Schools Champion Steer Competition at the Royal Easter Show later that year. I knew some of our calves were good quality, but I felt that Andrew may have well and truly overstepped the mark. He had promised his agriculture teacher that they could go to Yarramalong and inspect the steer in a few days, but because of work commitments, I was not able to accompany them. I described to Andrew the particular steer that I would nominate, and to my surprise the agriculture teacher was more than happy. They transported the animal to the school and the 'fun' started almost immediately. The steer jumped his yard fence the first night and cleaned up all the agriculture students' vegetable gardens. They built the fence higher, but still he escaped.

Andrew was called out of class one morning to assist in the retrieval of the steer. It had been located at Pymble about three kilometres down the Pacific Highway in the backyard of a house. At one stage during the previous night, the police had seen it walking down the Pacific Highway but had lost it when they went for assistance. The old chap whose house yard it was located in said he had noticed that the leaves of the plants in his vegetable patch had disappeared overnight, but he first blamed it on rabbits. Later in the morning, he had seen something large move amongst the trees and shrubs down the back of the overgrown yard, so he called the police. The school had a big, high-sided trailer, and they had to determine how the steer could be enticed into it as they had no way of loading it via cattle yards with a loading ramp or the like. The steer had not been handled previously, and fortunately I had arranged for Ross, our caretaker at the farm, to insert a ring in the steer's nose before he left the property in order to make him easier to control. Andrew was able to get near enough to the steer by tempting him with a handful of lucerne hay to be able to slip a rope through the nose ring when the steer was reaching to eat the hay. Apparently the steer went berserk for a while when he felt the pressure of the rope on the nose ring, and he flattened the poor chap's small trees, shrubs, and garden before Andrew could get him into the trailer. To Andrew's great delight, the good news was that the steer went on to win the New South Wales Schools Championship at the Royal Easter Show and also the carcass competition later when all the entrants were slaughtered and judged. I felt fairly chuffed also, and my only regret is that Andrew didn't get chosen to lead the steer in the parade. I am told this was because Barker College had a policy that their entry in the Champion Steer Competition was led by someone from the grade lower than his.

Mark completed his secondary schooling in 1987, the year of Lisa's death, and although he did reasonably well his results clearly reflected the effects of that dreadful occasion. He did not want to progress to university and didn't know what he wanted to do otherwise at the time. He worked in various fields such as insurance, bar work, and the building industry for short periods of time over the next two years, and eventually, with the help of a career guidance counsellor, he decided that he would like to study television and sound production. Charles Sturt University at Wagga Wagga offered a bachelor degree course in this subject and Mark's application for entry was accepted, and he commenced his studies there in 1991.

In his endeavour to support himself financially at university, Mark did cleaning and bar work. Like most of the young people there, he also had time to join in the many parties that occurred on campus and in town. We were very proud of him when he gained his degree, and he later used his new skills at Channel 9 and in freelance staging. Since coming to Mudgee, he has used the knowledge he gained from the photographic strand of his studies to work as the photographer for the local newspaper and freelance as a photographer for functions and weddings. He is very interested in cooking, and in 2009 he decided to enter into a partnership with a local chef and restaurant owner to manufacture and market items such as balsamic vinegar, sauces, nougat, and the like. Regrettably, after a few years they amicably determined to go their separate ways.

Back at Westpac, Bob White had announced his retirement in 1987 and Stuart Fowler assumed the mantle of Managing Director. Internally, this appointment was unexpected as Warwick Kent was thought to be the favoured contender. I had reported to Stuart while in London and he was also my boss for some of the time when I ran New South Wales Division. We had our disagreements from time to time and Stuart would get very heated; however, he calmed down quickly and never held a grudge. He was very good to Val and I around the time that Lisa died and sent us to the Sheraton Mirage Resort at Port Douglas for a week to ease the stress levels after the very daunting murder trial was concluded.

The court's verdict was 'not guilty on the grounds of mental illness'. This decision meant that the perpetrator could possibly be released from a psychiatric facility within a short period of time as a man without a single murder conviction to his name, let alone four. Neither family of the deceased girls nor many of the public could believe the outcome. To us, the way the case was conducted was a farce—it happened in an environment which completely disregarded the families who were left to grieve their losses. One's initial reaction is to fight on, but after deep consideration, I determined that all such an action would achieve would be to bring further hurt to the family. Although I was unable to forgive Maddrell for the heinous crimes he had committed, I decided that to pursue the matter or continue to maintain the rage would probably damage me more than him, so I attempted to put the matter behind me as best I was able to. Our son Andrew was not able to follow suit and he vowed to get square with him in due course.

Simultaneous with Stuart Fowler's appointment as Managing Director, Frank Conroy was appointed Chief General Manager, Australian Retail Banking, and was to become my new boss. As General Manager for New South Wales Division, I had a great relationship with Frank and was able to assist in accomplishing some positive changes in the retail bank as a consequence of his cooperation. Stuart Fowler was intentionally a short-term appointment pending the final grooming of Frank as the next managing director. This appointment took place in 1st October 1991, and at the same time I was promoted to the newly established job of Chief General Manager, Australian Banking, and became a member of the six-member executive committee. This newly structured position was a first for Westpac and was an amalgamation of the whole of the retail bank and corporate bank in Australia under the one banner. This was so that these two businesses could be managed on an integrated basis. Whoever dreamt up the idea must have thought I was Superman, but they overlooked including the magic cape together with my appointment. The areas of responsibility were so diverse, broad, deep, and complex that it would have been an impossible task, even in good times, for someone who not only had a deep knowledge of the retail bank, as I did, but who also had a deep understanding of the corporate side of the business, which I didn't.

With hindsight, it seems possible to me now that I was one of a very small group of people whom Bob White had singled out in 1983 as prospective future leaders of the bank. Although such an eventuality was mooted by the media from time to time and also by many in the bank, it was never my desire to occupy the top job. It was pleasing to think that one was thought of in such high regard. However, I was never a very good speech writer or presenter, because of my slight dyslexia, and I was not one who was good at speaking off the cuff; all of which are qualities required in abundance to be successful as head of one of Australia's major banks. I felt that my paucity of tertiary education left me at some disadvantage, and as a consequence I felt that certain sections of the media and others would, given the right opportunity, attempt to crucify me in the top job and possibly embarrass Westpac as a consequence. My loyalty to the bank would not allow for this possibility. Also, I could see that my honest and forthright approach would probably get me into difficulties at times with the press and politicians. I certainly did not need that additional stress in my life, nor did Val and the boys, so I made my position known to Frank Conroy.

I arrived at the head office just at the time when Westpac was beginning to reel under the weight of bad debts, primarily as a consequence of poor property development lending in its major subsidiary Australian Guarantee Corporation Ltd (AGC) and to a lesser but still substantial extent in the corporate banking area. The economic downturn at the time had also resulted in increased losses in the retail bank (including New South Wales Division) but nothing like the magnitude of the other two offenders. As a member of the executive committee, I was one of the top team responsible for framing a recommendation to the board as to how it should deal with the huge losses that were accruing in virtually all quarters of the bank's business (AGC's losses alone were in excess of $1.0 billion). We resolved in 1991 to advise the board that a write-off of some $1.6 billion was required and a huge recapitalisation of the bank was necessary. As CEO, it was Frank Conroy's job to alert the board to management's views. However, it is my understanding that the then board chairman rejected Frank's recommendation before it got to the board in the mistaken belief that commercial property values would rebound quickly and the bank would be able to recover its position. Apparently, he would not accept that the cost of carrying such a huge load of non-income earning and value-depleted assets would cripple the bank entirely. This situation led shortly afterwards to an arranged meeting between the board and the executive team at Leura in the Blue Mountains, where Frank gave a masterly presentation, which finally allowed board members to understand the enormity of the difficulties the bank was facing at the time. Fortunately, the remainder of the board members agreed to the proposed write-off and the raising of additional capital. The rest is history.

After about six months as the head of the mammoth Australian banking experiment, it was agreed that it was not workable. The planning 'boffins' and the board agreed that corporate banking should again be split off and that the retail bank should now be split into Retail Distribution Group with me as its head and Retail Banking Product Design under Geoff Kimpton. This structure also proved to be difficult, and we later switched back to an amalgamated Retail Banking Division.

My final training course was a six-week senior executive development course in June 1985 at Imede, a highly rated senior executive training college in Lausanne, Switzerland. Again, there were about sixty participants from all over the world, all then senior executives in their own right. We stayed at the Beau-Rivage Palace Hotel on the shores of Lake Geneva. It was quoted as a five star hotel, but like a lot of European hotels it was old and needed a good refit. However, that did not detract from their ability to charge astronomical prices and to attract the royalty of Europe to stay and dine there. After having one meal in the dining room and on seeing the cost, we decided to eat at street cafes from then on.

I had been at Imede for only a few days when I was called out of a session to take an urgent phone call from Australia. The caller was Warren Simmonds, Westpac's Senior Security Officer, and he was calling to tell me that Val had received a threatening letter in the mail the day that I had left Australia. The letter was mostly composed of bits and pieces cut from magazines and pasted on a blank sheet of paper. The message was convoluted but quite threatening and extremely worrying to Val and me. I felt totally helpless being on the other side of the world and immediately determined that I would return home, but Warren dissuaded me and assured me that he had matters fully under control. Val agreed with this decision.

Knowing the quality of Warren's work, I agreed to stay as long as he kept me informed of any progress in their investigations. Warren had put security precautions into place at our home, and the children were being escorted to and from school and Val was being well supported and chauffeured wherever she wished to go. Warren then proceeded to put me through the third degree: 'Was I having an affair with another woman? Had I been gambling and accrued unpaid debts? Did I know anyone who might want to harm me or the family?' And there were many more similar questions. I recalled that a customer of one of our Sydney city branches had recently written a weird letter to me in my capacity as General Manager for New South Wales, complaining of the treatment he had received in relation to a small loan he had guaranteed for some organisation. At the time, I investigated the matter and found that the branch manager had acted entirely responsibly. I replied to the client in that vein and had heard no more of the matter. However, the tone and style of the letter led me to believe that the customer may have been somewhat unbalanced and could be a suspect. On my return to work, I consulted Warren about the issue, and he assured me that they were fairly confident that they had identified the letter sender and that there would be no more letters, and there weren't, but he wouldn't divulge how he could be so certain of this!

It was the custom at Imede to invite the partners of attendees to an upmarket final dinner on the last evening of the course. Warren assured us that the threat had passed and that he would continue the tight security at home with the kids. We determined that Val should accept the offer, so she enlisted the services of a highly recommended local lady to become a live-in childminder until we arrived home. Val was escorted to the airport by the security team; then she flew by herself via Rome to Geneva. I met her there mid-afternoon on the day of the final dinner only to find that her luggage was missing. Fortunately, she had put a change of outfit in her hand luggage, and with a little assistance from the hotel laundry she was able to make herself reasonably presentable amongst the glamour of the night's occasion.

Maybe what I have written above could lead the reader to believe that these senior management development courses were fun. The situation for me was quite the contrary. Undoubtedly, attendance at these sessions broadened and deepened my knowledge base, but as in my school years, I found the study part very difficult and the light burnt brightly until the small hours of the morning on the majority of nights. Although I might have been awarded an 'A' for effort, I felt that I was never able to excel under these circumstances.

CHAPTER 17

Westpac In and Out of Trouble

———⟫●⟪———

T he early to mid-1990s was a very difficult financial period. An economic downturn affected most of the world including Australia, and Westpac too was not immune.

In 1992, the bank's share price had fallen below $3 (approx. $2.65 was the lowest recorded sale), and Kerry Packer, a billionaire media baron, saw an opportunity to grab control, install his man Al Dunlap (nicknamed the chainsaw) at the top, break up the bank, and sell off the component parts at a handsome profit. Fortunately, some of the board members had the fortitude to stand up to him and send him on his way. One good thing to come out of the issue was a review of the membership of the board and five directors, including the chairman, resigned.

An unfortunate flow-on from Packer's involvement was that he had demanded that the managing director be replaced. He believed that because of the magnitude of the task ahead in restoring the bank to good health, an incumbent who had been part of the institution all his working life would not be able to take the many tough business and personnel decisions that were necessary during the recovery process. The board followed his proposed course of action, and although Frank Conroy already had a very good board-sanctioned rescue plan in place and was in the process of implementing it, he was asked to resign. When Frank told me, I was shocked and very angry, as was the staff of the bank in general. He was a very popular leader who was well trusted and had the confidence of all.

When the Reserve Bank heard about the news of Frank's dismissal, they rang to gauge my reaction, as for me to resign in protest would have been a further destabilising influence on the bank. Board member John Uhrig had taken the chair of the board after the chairman's dismissal and also became Acting CEO, pending the hiring of a replacement for Frank. Uhrig called the top team to his office and told us why the decision had been made; it had nothing to do with a lack of satisfaction by the board in Frank's leadership, but they felt compelled to take a drastic action to send a message to the marketplace in order to turn things around and get the share price moving in the right direction again. Frank was the sacrificial lamb. I had cooled down somewhat by this time, and although I expressed to Uhrig my disappointment at the board's action, I recognised my duty in having to help steady the ship.

A group of us senior executives, some of whom were also Frank's close friends, organised a farewell function for him so that the staff of the bank, who were within travelling distance from Sydney, were able to show their respect for him and wish him farewell. I was one of the principal organisers and speakers at the function, which was held in the Sydney Wentworth Hotel. It was a very emotional and memorable occasion for the huge crowd of attendees and particularly for Frank and his wife Jan, the latter having been severely injured by what she saw as the extreme injustice of Frank's dismissal. I recall expressing my views in regard to the board's actions quite forcefully on the night in question, to the delight of the staff in attendance, and I expect that some board members present may have felt a little uncomfortable at the time although none of them ever raised the issue with me later on.

The 1990-1993 period was a severely challenging time at Westpac, and those of us in the top team were really operating in a mode of 'save the bank'. As a means of cutting the operating cost of the bank at the administrative level, a restructuring was undertaken whereby the Technology Division was rolled into the Support Services and I was appointed its Chief General Manager. The technology people were not only incensed that they no longer had their own separate division, but to rub salt into the wound, they were now required to report to a retail banker who had never had any real experience in managing technology issues. Not only did I have to attempt to dampen down the angst of some 'prima donnas' and bring them into the fold but also I had to get my head around the huge technology issues where hundreds of millions of dollars were spent on developments annually. Additionally, I had responsibility for the bank's multi-billion-dollar property and premises portfolios, its stores, furnishings, stationery, printing, cars, and so on. As an aside, I was asked to cut $100 million in operating costs from the Support Services' expense budget within six months.

Dealing with the technology people was the most challenging personnel issue I ever had to overcome in my entire career. Virtually all the people were information technology specialists. They had been hired directly into the Technology Division and had no real contact with the business divisions of the bank, nor did most of them want that contact in any shape or form. They were generally very highly paid, highly skilled, and very well educated. They did not want to be part of the Support Services, possibly seeing it as beneath their dignity, and they told me so loudly and clearly in both words and actions.

Fortunately, the head of Technology, Jack Stenning, was a very capable, fair, and level-headed individual who had been in the bank for about thirty years. He had spent some of his early years in the branch network before becoming involved in the technology area when the bank first introduced computers in the early 1960s. I also had an excellent personnel manager named Chris Pierce-Cooke, who was able to give me sound guidance and support in dealing with the issues. It took a couple of months of frequent meetings and workshops with the hundreds of technology people involved plus lots of two-way communication in order to achieve the turnaround, but when it did come I saw it as one of my biggest and best career achievements. Many technology people who had been vehemently critical of the initial restructuring were now openly supportive of me and my efforts. I recall that at the last meeting we had, I very emotionally addressed an audience of many hundreds, and with tears in my eyes and a shaky voice, I told them how proud I felt of them and the changed stance that they now took.

In whatever senior management role I became involved throughout my career, I met formally with my top team each week, having pre-circulated an agenda the previous day. The meetings were scheduled on the same day, time, and place each week so that everyone could reserve the appropriate space in their diary well in advance of the meeting dates. Even though I say it myself, I was a competent chairperson, who ensured that the meeting started promptly on time, that everyone was involved and got reasonable airtime, that proceedings were controlled, and that meetings finished within the allotted time limit. Furthermore, minutes were kept, and any actions arising were allocated appropriately amongst team members and monitored to ensure completion in a timely manner. My top team in the Support Services was an eclectic group of eight people, whose responsibilities ranged from technology, stores and printing, property and premises, cafeterias, the bank's car fleet and garage, personnel, financial management and reporting, technical support to branches, and last but certainly not least the coordination of the 'save $100 million' programme. Their areas of responsibility had little in common, and initially they showed little interest in each other's issues. However, they soon got the gist of my leadership style, which was to strive to make each of them successful in their individual roles, as I saw this as being the only way that I could successfully get my job done; simply put, I had to work efficiently and effectively through them to achieve the results expected of me. They cottoned on to the fact that if each of them in turn cooperated to make all their peers successful, then they had a greater chance of being successful themselves. The end result was a team that was so united and empowered that they steadfastly supported each other and me and saw no problem as being too difficult to solve together.

My Support Services role bore some similarity to the last job I had before leaving Queensland Division as Manager, Administration, but at a much higher level of complexity and responsibility, so it did not take long to get on top of all except the high-level technology issues that I knew I would never master. The challenge to wipe $100 million from the division's expense base gathered pace quickly and the desired result, and more, was achieved within the set time frame. Some of the rationalisation that I approved raised the eyebrows of my colleagues on the executive committee, and I recall one instance in particular. All the members of the executive committee were provided with a fully serviced motor vehicle at a cost to their personal salary packages. For example, if one owned, say, a Jaguar vehicle, the leasing and maintenance costs were debited against that individual's overall remuneration package. Because of the service provided by the bank's garage, I never lifted the bonnet of my vehicle from one year's end to the next, and I only found the petrol filler point when I went on holidays. All of the maintenance and cleaning work was done at the bank's garage at Pyrmont.

The bank also had a fleet of cars and chauffeurs, which senior management and staff could utilise for business purposes rather than having to hire taxis. At an executive committee meeting soon after I accepted the $100 million saving challenge, I warned my fellow members that, other than for the managing director and chairman of the board, they had better find out how to look after their own cars as I was about to sell the bank's garage premises, dispose of the bank's car fleet, and pay off all the mechanics and chauffeurs. They were initially horrified. However, as I pointed out, these were exceptional times and we were working to save the bank. This would require us to make lots of hard decisions in the near future that impacted adversely throughout the bank, and some of those hard decisions need to be seen to be impacting adversely on the top echelon also. I didn't get any more gripes, but the feedback from those in the field was very positive.

An American named Bob Joss was the successful candidate chosen from a worldwide executive search to replace Frank Conroy as Managing Director. He was fifty-three years of age, extremely well educated (PhD), and a very bright guy with a laconic, easy-going, and very likeable style. He had been hired from the position of second in charge at Wells Fargo Bank in California. He subsequently brought a few Americans whom he knew into Westpac, and in the main, they were good operators. He made other senior managerial changes and took great personal care to hire what he termed 'world-class professionals', spending an enormous amount of time with each of them in a number of pre-hire interviews. These people were generally on large salary packages and mostly added value to the organisation. In my view, a few were there for the self-serving purpose of getting the name 'Westpac' on their CV and spending a lot of time being 'apparently' effective and reinventing the wheel, all at great expense to the bank. They then made sure that they had moved on, together with their bonuses, before the 'proverbial', which they had created, hit the fan.

About a year after Bob Joss arrived at Westpac, he asked to see me and offered me the position of Chief General Manager, Managing Director's Office. I immediately saw this as an attempt to get me to take early retirement without being direct about his intentions or without offering me a redundancy package—in other words saving face for me and a hefty sum for the bank. I immediately told him what I was thinking and that if he thought I should go then all he had to do was say so. He was shocked. Neither of us knew each other well at that stage, and he opened up to me and explained that he had found the job far more difficult than he had expected and needed my help. He had not, nor could he have, understood that the 'BIG 4' banks in Australia were inexplicably intertwined in the economic, political, and social fabric of the nation whereas the situation in the United States was totally different. He explained that as the CEO of a bank like the Bank of America or even Wells Fargo, he would not be widely known publicly. He would rarely be asked for a media interview or to make major speeches at conferences or functions, nor would he be sought out by the equivalent of our Prime Minister or Treasurer for advice. Further, he would not be quoted in the media at every turn nor be expected to appear on TV frequently and face often hostile questioning. In addition, he said that he was struggling somewhat to come to grips with the complexities and nuances of the Australian culture and its banking practices, and this was impeding his ability to identify and prioritise some of the real urgencies. In his words, he said, 'I am having wheelbarrows full of all sorts of issues pushed at me from every direction. All are said to be extremely important and urgent, and I can't be completely sure which ones I should deflect in order to be able to concentrate on the truly important and urgent ones.' He said he had canvassed the need for this type of assistance amongst other advisers in the bank, all of whom had singled me out as having the trust and respect of the bank's staff generally, the knowledge to do the job, and the fortitude to tell him like it was rather than what I thought he might like to hear.

Because I did not know him well enough at that time, I was still not sure whether to trust him. I agreed to think about his offer overnight and get back to him the next day. At this subsequent meeting, we talked a lot more about what he expected of me in the role, and eventually I decided that he was being honest with me. I agreed to take the job with two provisos: (1) that I would contribute to his speeches but would not write them for him and (2) if he asked for my advice and then disregarded it, without providing a reason that was acceptable to me, I would leave immediately. He had no hesitation in accepting my terms, and I must say that the next eighteen months I spent working with him were very enjoyable, although I must also say that I missed the interaction with a team of my own.

Bob was very generous in his announcement of my appointment to the bank's staff when he wrote:

> I'm very pleased to announce that I am appointing John Chatterton as Chief General Manager of Managing Director's Office.
>
> John, who is currently Chief General Manager, Support Services, Retail Banking Group, has unrivalled knowledge and experience of Westpac's branch network and of Australian banking generally. His leadership, integrity and team-building skills are well known to all of you.
>
> John's high-level support and his unique knowledge, experience and skills will be invaluable resources to me

and my office as we go forward. John will also represent me to various organisations and on various boards.

I know you will all join me in congratulating John on his appointment.

Bob was always true to his word to me. Our offices were side by side with an inter-connecting door which always stood open. There were no airs and graces about him. He simply sat down in a chair in front of my desk and then in his laconic drawl would say something like: 'John, I've got a problem that I need help with.' We would talk about it until we both fully understood the issue/s, then I would tell him what I would do in the circumstances; maybe we would debate the issue a little longer, reach agreement, and he would return to his office, pick up the phone, ring the executive concerned, and tell him/her what he wanted done. I could hear his conversation from my office, and it was always spot on. I never wrote a speech for him, nor did he write them or have them written for him even though he delivered hundreds. I used to give him 'dot' points to emphasise in his speeches, and he simply added a few dot points to mine and spoke brilliantly off the cuff. His memory was almost photographic, and I was extremely envious of his capabilities in this regard. I used to have to sweat over speeches for hours and hours and then still found it difficult to deliver them really well and mistake free.

Bob Joss had a very different style from previous Westpac managing directors and spent a lot of time with those who reported directly to him. He was more inwardly focused on the detail of the businesses of the bank whereas the old Westpac style required huge external involvement by the managing director. He had an extensive knowledge of all facets of banking and initially worried the heads of the various business units when they found that within a few weeks he already knew more about the details of their business than they did. He coached and cajoled them and wherever necessary applied sufficient pressure to get those things done that he saw as important. All of his team soon welcomed the one-on-one time that each spent with him every week. Generally, those who reported directly to Bob respected my position well. Although he had given me the authority to act on his behalf in any manner that I saw fit, I was always very careful to exercise such authority judiciously. However, there were occasions when some executives were reluctant to accept my position and things got a little tense.

CHAPTER 18

The Time Has Come!

———>◦◦◦<———

Three or four months before my fifty-fifth birthday, Val raised the subject of my retirement. The rules of the Westpac Staff Superannuation Plan, of which I had been a contributing member since the day I joined the service, allowed for this eventuality. In my own mind, I had intended continuing on working for at least another few years, but she was very keen to see me finish up and take things a little easier. She pointed out to me the number of deaths that had occurred amongst recent retirees or their wives, and I found it hard to argue against her logic. It was clear to me that I was not going to get another job in the top echelon and I really didn't expect one in view of the fact that I had ruled myself out of selection for the top position, but I was still mostly enjoying my work. The part that wasn't so enjoyable was dealing with the influx of senior executives from outside the organisation, some of whom clearly had set their own interests ahead of the bank's. Additionally, some of them were highly political which was an issue that I had not had to deal with previously, and I found such behaviour to be distasteful in the extreme.

We agreed that financially we should survive in reasonable comfort in retirement if we did nothing too risky with regard to investments. I did not particularly fancy the idea of spending my time managing investments and playing the stock market during my retirement, so I set about finding a reputable investment adviser, with whom Val could also feel totally comfortable and whom we both felt we could trust implicitly. We settled on Jim Clegg in 1994 and remained with him until he retired in June 2009. The relationship between Jim and us was one of mutual trust and respect, and both Val and I believe that his advice and guidance has been excellent. Like almost everyone else, we suffered as a consequence of the world economic downturn in 2008 but nowhere near as badly as many others, due to Jim's care and competence.

A real concern for me at that time, should I decide to retire, was how I was going to keep myself occupied. We had the farm at Yarramalong and I was fairly heavily involved as president of the Royal Blind Society, but would that be enough? I was still quite fit and energetic and needed to be making things happen. I was concerned that a game of golf each week and perhaps a few lunches would not fill the gap. I thought that perhaps I might snare a board position or something else might turn up unexpectedly, which would fulfil my need to keep busy, so the commitment was made to Val that I would retire soon after my birthday.

I wanted to give Bob Joss plenty of notice of my intention to retire, so I told him within a few days of making my decision that I planned to finish up work on 19 January 1995 after thirty-nine years with the Wales and Westpac. He was horrified and initially thought it was a bad joke. He said I was far too young and in his view had too much to add to the organisation to be thinking of retiring. I reminded him that he was the same age as me and that I knew that his mother had been harassing him from the United States for months about him considering retirement. That did not stop him from continuing his attempt to talk me out of it. I told him that I had made a commitment to Val and if I reneged on it I would find it impossible to look at myself in the mirror. He asked me not to tell anyone of my plans as he wanted me to reconsider overnight and we would talk again in the morning. I did not change my mind, and he kept trying to overturn my decision the following day. When he realised his efforts were futile, he gave in and wished me all the best. We parted on very good terms when I finally retired, and I was pleased to see that his reign as Managing Director was very rewarding both for him personally and also for the shareholders of Westpac.

John Uhrig, Westpac Board Chairman, and his fellow board members were very gracious and hosted a black tie farewell dinner for Val and me on my retirement. There was also another very memorable function for those staff who wanted to bid farewell to me. The whole family was invited to this latter function, and it was lovely to see Val, Paul, Liz, Mark, Andrew, and Hallee there in support of me. As Val and I arrived at the function, a senior female executive said words to Val to the effect, 'John can't retire. We need him.' Val retorted, 'The bank has had him for almost forty years. Now it is time for him to spend time with me', turned her back, and kept walking. These were lovely words of encouragement to my ears. The function was arranged by my good friends Bruce Alexander, Tony Aveling, Chris Hard, Mike Burdett, and some others. Bruce and Tony both spoke on the occasion and said some very nice things about me and also 'bucketed' me a bit as was to be expected. In addition to other memorabilia that they gave me on behalf of the gathering, they presented me with a Bronco's jersey (Brisbane Rugby League team) emblazoned with the word "MAFIA" across the chest; the significance of this was that Bruce, Mike, and Tony were also amongst a small group of Queenslanders who had been transferred to Sydney in the mid-1970s to mid-1980s and who had gone on to become very senior executives in the bank. Per capita, we Queenslanders disproportionately outnumbered New South Welshmen and officers from the other states in senior head office appointments, and the group attracted attention as a consequence. In order to encourage a reaction, we started calling ourselves the 'Queensland Mafia'. Naturally, that sort of behaviour went down like a lead balloon with the locals and didn't do anything at all to endear us to some of them. It was all in good spirit and none of us lost any sleep over it.

So began another phase of Val's and my life together. Val had been warned by the wives of some other retirees that I could become a nuisance to her around the house, invade her space, and even want to go shopping with her. Val was actually looking forward to having me home, and I do not recall either of us experiencing any anxiety as a consequence. Soon after I retired, I was in my home office at East Lindfield one day when Val came hurrying down the internal stairs on her way to her car, popped her head around the door, said she had left my lunch prepared in the fridge, wished me goodbye, and was off to some function. I reminded her that I was retired and could get my own lunch on these occasions. She has since allowed me to do so on some occasions!

I must say that contrary to my expectations I never missed the bank for one day after retirement, although I did miss some of the camaraderie of my bank friends. Right from the start, I was immersed in the paperwork that one encounters when establishing a super fund, investment portfolio, and the like. It simply never ceased, and I had to arrange a double-sized post office box to accommodate all the endless mail. I was still heavily involved in the RBS, played golf one day per week, and we went up to Yarramalong for at least a few days each week.

In the first six months of my retirement, we had been working on arranging a major trip to Africa. I had always wanted to see the

African animals in their natural environment, and although Val was not as enthusiastic as me about the idea, she agreed we should go. I looked upon the trip as a treat to both of us for our hard work and as a sort of reward for what we had endured. We spared no expense and in August-September 1995 we visited the following places:

- Tanzania—safari camps in Tarangeri National Park, Serengeti Mara National Park, and Ngorongoro Crater, plus a day visit to Olduvai Gorge.
- Kenya—Nairobi, Mombassa, and Mindi, plus a safari camp in Masai Mara Game Reserve.
- Zimbabwe—Harare, Victoria Falls, Zambezi River Lodge, plus a day visit to Livingstone and a local village in Zambia.
- Botswana—Maun and Chobe National Park, plus safari camps in the Okavango Delta named Shindi Island, Machaba (Fig Tree), and Pom Pom (Mosquitoes).

Within a year or so of retiring, my good friend Dick Watson asked me to join him and some other friends in an annual snow skiing trip to Blue Cow in the New South Wales ski fields. The only skiing I had done previously was on water, but Dick assured me that I would find the experience really enjoyable. He had commenced skiing only a few years earlier and was a very competent skier despite the fact that he was about five years older than me. I did learn to ski reasonably well and continued to enjoy the annual event for about ten years. When the snow coverage was good, the skiing was exhilarating; however, snow seasons in Australia are very unpredictable, and on a few occasions when there was little snow or whatever coverage was there was mushy, it became hard work but enjoyable all the same. In 1997, immediately before Paul and Liz were to marry, Val was petrified that I would sustain an injury while skiing and have to attend the wedding in a plaster cast or worse. Luckily, I never suffered any breaks or sprains from any of the very many falls I suffered throughout the whole time.

Not long after we arrived home from Africa in 1995, my then income tax accountant rang to tell me that he had a good investment opportunity, which he would like me to consider. When he told me that it was to buy shares in a vineyard development, I reminded him that I had previously told him that I was not interested in crazy investments like ostriches, tea tree oil, and the like. Nevertheless, he sent the proposal to me and it looked interesting. Being retired and freed up from the strictures of a full-time job, Val and I drove down to Yenda in the Murrumbidgee Irrigation area of New South Wales where the project was to be launched in order to meet the two principals of the venture and discuss the project in detail. Although we were impressed with the two individuals and their obvious capabilities, I eventually decided against investing in the project as I would have no control over how they would spend our money. They then issued an invitation that I should become a director of the company, representing the interests of all outside shareholders, but this did not sway my decision to not be involved. Shortly after our visit to Yenda, I attended a retirement farewell lunch for Bob Newman, my long-term friend, whom I had known from London days. One of the other guests at our table happened to be the Westpac officer who was the account manager for Rosemount Estates Wines. We talked about what I had been doing in retirement, and he insisted that I should meet Bob Oatley, the principal shareholder of Rosemount. I reluctantly agreed, and a few days later we were on our way to their Denman operation in the Northern Hunter Valley of New South Wales to spend most of the day with Bob and his son Sandy.

We were accompanied by my very long-term friend Col Walker and his wife Pat from Brisbane, who happened to be spending a few days with us at the time. I first met Col when I was in the bank in Chinchilla in 1958, and we have been good friends ever since. When I relayed to Bob Oatley what I had been contemplating doing in the Murrumbidgee Irrigation area, he told me to forget that option and go and buy about 100 acres at either Broke in the Hunter Valley or Mudgee and then hire an old farmer as the vineyard manager and run my own show. He said Rosemount would lend technical support and purchase my grapes under contract. Val and I mulled over this advice and decided that Broke was out of the question. It, like Yarramalong, is only a district with no decent town nearby, so we were left with the option to look at Mudgee. I had been to Mudgee twice previously on business trips when I was General Manager for New South Wales; however, I did not really know what the town and district were like because in that type of busy job one really flies in, attends to the business needs of the occasion, and flies out again.

At about this time, we had arranged to accompany Dick and Anne Watson and Kevin and Jan Holm (ex-London friends) on a 4WD expedition from Broken Hill in New South Wales up the Strzelecki Track in north-west South Australia to Birdsville in far Western Queensland and back down the Birdsville Track to both Maree and Adelaide in South Australia and then home to Sydney. Val and I left Sydney a few days before the others and visited Mudgee. We were impressed by both the town and the natural beauty of the area, so we looked around in earnest for suitable land. An assured irrigation water supply was my number one priority, and although the various real estate agents we dealt with were usually quite loose in their comments and assurances on the 'ample' availability of water, when questioned deeply about the matter, the outcome was invariably an inadequate and/or uncertain supply. We eventually determined to leave the property purchasing project to a later date and met up with the Watsons in Nyngan and the Holms at Broken Hill for the start of our trip.

After our outback adventure, we returned to Mudgee to continue our hunt for a suitable grape-growing property. Each time we passed the property that we eventually purchased, I told the agent who we were with at the time that I would like to purchase it, but I was always told it wasn't for sale. We had exhausted all other opportunities and were on our way back into Mudgee from inspections with the last agent in town when I suggested that he make an offer to the owner of the property that we fancied for the purchase of 100 acres (40 ha) fronting Cassilis Road. This was promptly done, but the response was negative. We went back to Sydney, and I felt quite disappointed. I mulled the issue over in my mind for a week or so and eventually decided to write to the owner of the property and tell him a bit about us and why we wanted to purchase the property. It worked because two days later he rang and invited us to have morning tea with them when next in Mudgee. This eventually led to our exchange of contracts for the purchase of almost 100 acres of very nice cattle property in July 1996 with the settlement effected in April 1997 after the necessary subdivision had taken place.

I began planning the establishment of a vineyard with a local viticultural services contractor about September 1996, and we were able to commence the implementation of the plans soon after settlement. Some 16,000 posts were erected and about 120 kilometres of wires strung as trellises. A drip irrigation system with a state-of-art electronic irrigation controller and electronically operated valves together with soil moisture measuring equipment were installed. Fifty-six thousand grape vine rootlings were ordered well in advance from suppliers in South Australia, and Val and I visited these establishments to check on the quality of the rootlings that we were buying. Planting of the Shiraz, Chardonnay, and Merlot varieties commenced in September 1997, and the last of the Cabernet Sauvignon vines were planted in November 1997 due to hold-ups with the supply of the last few thousand posts. We were travelling back and forth between Sydney and Mudgee virtually every week for the first year and stayed at the Country Comfort Motel a few hundred metres down the road from our property at least one night per week. We always had the same very nice end room, where we were able to tie our dog Gemma to an external post during the day when we were at the motel and put her in the back of the Toyota Land Cruiser to sleep at night. Later, we decided to rent a home in Mudgee until we had the vineyard fully established, and then we would concentrate on the construction of a home on the vineyard. This arrangement proved to be convenient for us, and our son Andrew was able to reside there while he was working on the establishment of the vineyard.

We now had the farm at Yarramalong, the house at East Lindfield, and a property in Mudgee. In order to ease the pressure of maintaining lawns and gardens and visiting among each property, we decided to sell the farm at Yarramalong in mid-1997 and shift all our possessions from there to either the rented house in Mudgee or the large work shed I had erected on the vineyard land. In order to further reduce the pressure of maintenance and security, we sold the East Lindfield home in early 1998 and bought a home unit at Killara on the North Shore, where there was no outside maintenance required of me and the security concerns were greatly reduced.

A thorny issue arose soon after settlement with the vendor of the Mudgee property, which we now owned. The irrigation water supply for the vines was to come from two wells, both of which were located a short distance inside the boundary of his remaining property. During our purchase negotiations, he was not prepared to sell me the extra bits of land around the wells. However, with written approval to our planned approach from the head of Water Resources Department in Dubbo, we had agreed and put in place, via our respective solicitors, appropriate easements which provided unfettered access to the wells for me and my heirs solely in perpetuity and for the extraction of up to 150 megalitres per annum of irrigation water in terms of the licence I acquired with the property purchase. Shortly after settlement had taken place, the department advised that the regulations had been changed by the State Government and they were no longer able to recognise and register such an arrangement involving easements. This left me in the most precarious situation with a newly planted vineyard requiring lots of water to establish the vines but having no control whatsoever over the ongoing access to the actual water supply. Even worse, the new Government regulations now forbid an arrangement whereby a property owner pumped water from a neighbour's well or bore, which was exactly the unfortunate situation I now found myself in.

Despite my having a written authority from the head of the Water Resources Department to proceed as we had done, the area manager of the department insisted he now had no authority to allow the position to stand and advised that the only way that I could obtain absolute certainty of control of the water supply was to own the land on which the wells were situated. My vendor was not at all cooperative initially in resolving the issue and it took a period of calm negotiation followed by my having to tell him I would see him in court before he realised that I was deadly serious about resolving the water supply issue in my favour immediately. A few hours later, we had agreed that a small area of land around each well would become mine and be amalgamated into my land title; thus, I became assured of the total control of my own irrigation water supply. I felt quite aggrieved at having to pay the additional inflated price that was demanded for these tiny pieces of land as the value of the water supply had already been factored into the initial purchase price of the land. However, I was not prepared to go to court over the issue or have continuing unpleasantness with my neighbour.

About two years after we commenced the establishment of the vineyard, we had all the approvals and preparations in place to commence building our home on a spot that we had especially selected. Val had lots of ideas for the floor plan. We agreed on them together, and Val drew them up roughly for the final attention of a professional draftsperson. The building process proceeded very smoothly and we moved into the house in September 1999. We spent virtually all of our time there, with occasional stays at Killara for a night or possibly two each three or four weeks. We retained the unit at Killara for our convenience when we visited Sydney and for the family to use. Also, it was seen as a base for Val to move back to, if she so wishes, should something untoward happen to me.

We established a major garden at the vineyard house with considerable and very expensive assistance initially from professional landscape gardeners. Later, Val set about rearranging parts of the gardens by having me transplant many of the shrubs and plants in order to get the colour coordination and symmetry correct and the outcome was a great credit to her. Pruning a number of quite big hedges regularly and all shrubs twice a year was a major job. On these half-yearly pruning occasions, we paid a helper to follow along behind me to pick up and dump the prunings on the waste heap. Water was in ample supply from our own wells, and the large lawns were well irrigated and consequently always seemed to be in need of a trim. Although the garden demanded considerable attention regularly, we both gained a lot of enjoyment from the work, and it was a great way to relieve our stresses.

In April 1996, I became involved with the Walter & Eliza Hall Trust in an honorary capacity, which I have mentioned earlier in these writings. Eric Tait, my former Westpac boss, was a trustee of this charitable organisation and invited me to join the Board of Trustees. The trust was founded in May 1912 by Eliza Hall, with a sum of £1,000,000, in memory of her late husband, Walter, who died during the previous year. Enquiries of the Reserve Bank of Australia lead trustees to believe that in today's inflation adjusted terms that sum would approximate to $111 million. Walter Hall arrived from the United Kingdom as a young man with few assets, and through hard work, shrewd business dealings, and successful investments in organisations such as Cobb & Co's Australian operations and the Mount Morgan Gold Mine, where he and other family members were major shareholders, he became extremely wealthy and a major philanthropist together with his wife. The 'Mountain of Gold' as the mine was known paid absolutely huge dividends to its early shareholders, and in the year 1889 alone, the total was £1.1 million (approx. $143 million in today's inflation adjusted terms). Coincidentally, Mount Morgan was the place of my birth, and the town has a suburb called Walterhall named in Walter's honour. The objects of the trust are the relief of poverty, the advancement of education, the advancement of religion in accordance with the tenets of the Anglican Church, and to generally benefit the community by way of grants from the income derived from the trust's investments.

Walter had been a director of the Mount Morgan Gold Mining Company Ltd for a number of years, and in 1911 his close friend and business partner, Mr R. G. Casey, became the chairman. Casey was obviously well regarded by Eliza Hall also as she appointed him as one of the founding trustees of the Walter & Eliza Hall Trust. He was one of the driving forces behind the trust in its early years of operation, and current trustees believe that it was through his efforts and foresight that the trust provided the seed money which led to the formation of the now world-renowned Walter & Eliza Hall Institute of Medical Research based in Melbourne.

R. G. Casey's son, also R. G. Casey, was a mining engineer at the Mt Morgan mine in 1914 and later became a very prominent and successful Liberal Federal politician. In recognition of his many great achievements, he was offered and accepted a life peerage in 1960 from the British Government and so became Lord Casey. In 1965, he was appointed Governor General of Australia.

A year after joining the trust's board I was elected Chairman of Trustees. After a short settling in period, I set about modernising the management of its operations, which at that time were quite Dickensian. Today the trust is a highly efficient operation that now owns its office premises and has seen its investments grow from about $2.5 million in 1996-97 to in excess of $20 million. A recently received bequest of about $12.3 million from a deceased estate added greatly to our future ability to assist the needy. As a trustee, it is really rewarding to be able to say 'yes' to the majority of the many and varied heart-rending applications for grants that we trustees see. At the time of writing this story, I remain the president of the trust and am proud to be able to say that with the assistance of my fellow trustees, the secretary, and an historian, we were able to celebrate the trust's centenary by launching a very well-written and interesting history of the trust 'A Remarkable Gift' on the hundredth anniversary of its founding on 24 May 2012.

During my early time with the trust, our son Paul was courting a young lady, and on 14 September 1997, he and Liz (Elizabeth) Dwyer were married at Ball's Head Park fronting Sydney Harbour on a balmy evening. Paul had been working in Tasmania for a number of years when he was invited to a friend's wedding in Sydney. He met Liz there and found that she was studying and living in Sydney but came from Launceston, Tasmania. He moved back to Sydney, and they lived together for about six years before they married. By then, Paul was working for WWF. They purchased a unit at Coogee, which they still own and have tenanted while they are absent overseas with Paul working for WWF. On 22 July 1998, our first grandchild Lauren Chloe was born ten weeks prematurely and weighed in at the tiny size of approx. 1.35

kg (3 lb). Both Liz and Lauren were extremely unwell initially, and it was a very worrying time in the first few days for Paul and both families. Liz began to pick up health-wise towards the end of the first week while Lauren fought on and began gaining weight. Lauren is now a very healthy, athletic, intelligent, and loving young lady whom we adore.

In the 1990s, Paul undertook a number of short-term environmental consultancies in PNG and was very attracted to the area—its flora, fauna, and its people. On one occasion, he spent a fortnight living in a tribal village in the Hunstein Range at the headwaters of the Sepik River. The staple diet of the village people was mainly sago palm supplemented with a small amount of smoked fish and a few home-grown vegetables. Paul was quite slim then and really couldn't afford to shed much weight, but he lost about four kilos in those few weeks on this low-calorie diet. He was quite amazed and disturbed to find that the village had no medical supplies whatsoever; simply, it was too poor to obtain such luxuries, which we in the Western world take for granted. He was distressed to see a number of villagers suffering from large open ulcers for which there was no hope of local treatment. Paul became friendly with a healthy young PNG national who guided him on the Sepik River trip, and he kept in contact with him on his return to Australia. A few years later, while again in PNG, Paul enquired about his national friend, only to be told the shocking news that he had recently died from malaria.

Paul acquired the cerebral form of malaria on one of his early visits to PNG and as a consequence almost died a few weeks later. In this form of malaria, the brain is attacked by the malaria parasites in the bloodstream, and unless medical attention is accessed promptly, death follows soon after. Fortunately, Paul was home in Sydney by the time the parasites had incubated in sufficient numbers to sicken him to the point where he was having hallucinations, and he was able to be quickly taken to the Infectious Diseases section of Royal North Shore Hospital for urgent attention. Once the appropriate medication was provided, recovery was quick and there appears to be no adverse after-effects. Paul suffered two more such attacks later in his stay in PNG, and one has to wonder what long-term damage is done to the brain as a consequence. Treatments such as this are simply not available to the masses in PNG, and many thousands die annually from the various forms of the disease. If one survives from a cerebral malaria attack, it does not recur unless one is again stung by the appropriate parasite-carrying mosquito. Other forms of malaria repeat themselves in debilitating bouts of illness for the rest of one's life.

In March 2001, Paul accepted a position with WWF in PNG based in Madang on the northern coast of that country. Liz was pregnant at the time, and because of her previous difficulties with Lauren's birth together with the extremely poor health system available in PNG, she and Paul wisely determined that she should remain in Sydney until the baby was born. Our first grandson, Jack Ashur, was born on 5 September 2001. Fortunately, Liz retained her good health throughout the pregnancy, and Jack was born a very healthy little fellow and remains so today. Liz moved to PNG when Jack was six weeks old. He is now a very confident and articulate young man, who has all four of his grandparents under his spell. Paul established his WWF office in PNG in premises situated on a resort named Jais Aben, which is about twenty minutes drive north of Madang on the north coast of the island. Jais Aben is an internationally known scuba diving resort and hosts divers from many parts of the world, who are attracted to the nearby Great Barrier Reef, which extends up the Queensland coast and beyond Madang. His job responsibilities were primarily directed towards saving very large tracts of pristine PNG rainforests from logging by foreigners who frequently had no approval from the Government but were able to proceed to ship huge quantities of beautiful and valuable coach timber overseas due to the rampant corruption within the Government. When such large-scale illegal operations came to Paul's notice during his field trips, he reported them to the relevant Department of Forestry. Usually, the outcome was for no action to be taken other than that Paul sometimes received a warning to mind his own business.

The Jais Aben resort has about thirty fairly basic accommodation cabins, three large adjoining home units, a beach bar, dive shop, and a restaurant, all of which are located in this gloriously scenic position among the coconut palms overlooking the sea. Conveniently, one of these rather large three-bedroom units became available at the same time as Paul established his office at the resort. The family lived there for the next six years until 2007, when Paul accepted another position with WWF in Vienna, Austria, as International Director responsible for projects in places as disparate as the Amazon, Congo, Mekong, Danube, Borneo, and Indonesia. A few years ago, he contracted with the WWF head office in Switzerland to write the WWF worldwide policy on carbon issues from his location in Vienna and is now the deputy leader of very large international projects.

When his latest employment contract expired, we hoped that schooling issues would bring the family home to Australia. This did not eventuate, and since then Paul has gone on to complete the first half of a diploma of management at IMD in Lausanne, Switzerland. Regrettably, we are not able to see anywhere near as much of Lauren and Jack and their parents as we would like because of the distances involved, but we talk with them on the phone regularly and now are able to also see them via our webcam; also, we visit them in Vienna at least once a year. The family have been offshore for almost thirteen years now, and one never knows what further great opportunities might disrupt their plans for returning home. They are currently experiencing all the delights of Europe, and the children, who attend schools offering Viennese German for the majority of the day and English for the remainder, are now highly proficient in writing, reading, and speaking the German language. Paul and Liz are also quite competent in the language but not to the same depth as the kids. Despite the fact that PNG is a truly Third World country and that Liz had to conduct home schooling for the children at Jais Aben, both children did well in terms of their education and gained enormously from the multitude of wonderful PNG experiences and the interaction with the local people that they encountered and mixed with daily. The entire family became proficient in the Pidgin language, which is used widely throughout PNG as a means of communication between the 820 plus different language groups across the length and breadth of the country. On a recent visit to Vienna, the children told us that regrettably they have forgotten their Pidgin due to their inability to practice it.

CHAPTER 19

Another Dark Period

D ealing with the issues of one of your children addicted to drugs is difficult at the best of times. When there are two of your children involved, the situation is almost impossible.

We are not clear as to whether it was Mark or Andrew who first started using cannabis, but we are certain of the fact that the commencement of such a disastrous habit was at least partly due to Lisa's death and the trauma that it brought into their lives. At the time, we had no knowledge whatsoever of drugs and were completely innocent of what was happening around us. It wasn't until Andrew was about fifteen years old when he started to display really erratic behaviour in his final years at Barker College that we began to suspect the problem, but it was already too late. The next dreadful event to darken our doorstep had arrived—that is dealing with children who are addicted to drugs.

Anyone who has not suffered the terrifying experiences of dealing with the issues of a drug addicted child is not able to comprehend or even begin to understand the overwhelming feeling of helplessness that one faces as a parent. Effectively, you are no longer able to reason with your once loving, honest, stable, cooperative, and sensible child. You are suddenly required to not only contend with a teenager filled with anger and grief at the loss of his sister but also a person who is now controlled by a drug-addled brain, which rarely enjoys a moment of reality and who mostly thinks and acts irrationally. We had two such cases at the one time, both of which were serious and both of which added considerably to our continued hurting from the loss of Lisa. We sought help, both for ourselves and the boys, from doctors, specialists, and Government agencies, only to find that advice was mostly non-existent, or if available, the provider seemed to have no sense of the urgency of the situation. Despite the huge known problem that drug addiction is in the general community, we found that Governments, both State and Federal, mostly pay lip service to its solution and treatment and that their agencies really do not want to know you or the sufferer. As a consequence, uninitiated parents are left with a feeling of utter hopelessness as to how to deal with the situation and desperation as to how to go about rescuing their child from what could be a path leading to death.

Mark was the easiest to deal with (if one can call anything easy in dealing with people who are drug addicts), and we believe that he stayed with cannabis use only. This drug is often talked about by professionals and others as a relatively harmless 'recreation' drug. As a consequence of our dreadful experiences, we are very firmly of the opinion that there is no such thing as a safe 'recreation' drug—all drugs are evil, and we saw the diabolical impact that cannabis had on Mark's brain and on his behaviour and health. It is insidious in its ability to completely warp the human mind, and without doubt it has a permanent effect when used in excess as happens in addiction. Eventually, Mark, who was then in his early thirties, was able to accept and admit that he was addicted and that he could not kick the habit by himself. Until he was able to make this admission to himself, he was not able to begin the recovery process. To his great credit, he accepted an offer to undergo rehabilitation in a programme run by the Salvation Army. He was in the programme and away from home for ten months. Not one day of it was easy, although he came to believe that the light at the end of the tunnel was getting much brighter towards the end of the programme. He was about to give up on many occasions, but fortunately we were always able to convince him of the benefits of sticking it out, even if it took us very long discussions on the phone, as it sometimes did. Mark proudly graduated as one of less than 10 per cent of programme clients who eventually finish the programme at their first attempt and now recognises that the programme gave him back his life. We were very proud of him. During Mark's time in rehabilitation, many addicts were directed to the programme by the courts. They were given the option of completing the programme or going to jail. Most immediately opted for what they believed to be the easy way out and commenced the programme; however, almost every one of them lasted no more than a few months and then elected to go to jail, as they found the drug-free and self-examination aspects of the programme too difficult for them to be able to handle.

The one single thing that disappointed Mark greatly about the programme, which almost led to his departure from it on many occasions, was the dishonest behaviour demonstrated by some of the Salvation Army's own people. This was swept under the carpet and never investigated or corrected. While in the programme, Mark worked and lived in St Peters in Sydney, where the 'Salvos' had an absolutely huge receiving depot, sorting operation, and retail shop. People like Mark were given jobs such as sorting into various categories all the myriad of clothing, furniture, jewellery, books and the like that come to the 'Salvos' via deceased estates or by way of gifts. One of Mark's roles was to sort out and price for sale in the shop all the jewellery and bric-a-brac. Some of these items were extremely desirable and valuable. Mark often found that a lot of the good items had been stolen while he was at lunch, and it wasn't only the other addicts who stole them.

Salvation Army people had the job of collecting household furniture and other contents from deceased estates. If, for instance, a wardrobe in apparently very good condition was brought back to the depot but was found to have a loose door hinge, it was simply tossed into 'Magumba', the big crusher, and destroyed. No attempt was made to simply tighten the screws in the hinge and raise much needed funds from its sale. When Mark raised these issues with the senior Salvos person in charge of the facility, the response simply was that they were people of the church and didn't have the capabilities for controlling or managing the issues he raised. Mark is scrupulously honest, and these happenings disgusted him almost to the point of despair. I must say that it worried us greatly also, but I still retain a very soft spot in my heart for the 'Salvos' because of the way they treated us at Sunday school in the War Memorial Hall at Struck Oil when we were kids, and this has been reinforced by what their rehabilitation programme did for Mark. They are one of the very few who cared enough about the drug problem to devise and offer a real solution, and in Mark's case, most thankfully, it was successful.

In addition to our ongoing support, Mark was also strongly supported during this troubled time by his then long-term partner Kelly Spice. They had met in early 1996 when Mark was working on the Gold Coast, Queensland, installing Pay TV cabling in unit blocks and private homes. She gave him a great deal of love and assistance during and after the time when he had a major motorbike accident in June 1996. Mark always loved motorbikes, and when his university mate Andrew Olsen and a friend brought their newly acquired motorbikes around to show them to Mark, he took one for a spin around the block. Regrettably, he did not take time to put on a helmet. The bike got out of control in loose gravel on a corner and Mark was thrown head first down the footpath. Andrew Olsen applied pressure to the head wound and stopped Mark from bleeding to death.

We received a call from the local Southport Hospital to tell us Mark had been involved in an accident but that it wasn't serious and there was no need to come to Southport. We immediately arranged for Val to get on the first available plane to the Gold Coast so that she could assess the situation for herself. Before she got to the hospital, I again rang the hospital to check on Mark's progress only to be told that he was in surgery having a 'brain scrub'. Apparently, this was a procedure to remove the gravel and bone chips from the major depressed fracture Mark had suffered to his forehead. Val got to the hospital to be told that he had about seven fractures of the skull, including the roof of the mouth where the cranial fluid was leaking. He was very ill, but he checked himself out after five days as he felt he could not get the sleep he needed because of the continual noise. Kelly looked after him, but he was suffering excruciating head pain. An incorrect medical prescription from the local medical centre exacerbated the situation terribly. We got him to Sydney to see a specialist as soon as he was well enough to be able to fly and were told that he was not only lucky to have survived the accident but also that the prescribed medication could have killed him. Kelly came to Sydney soon after and continued to look after him.

Regrettably, Andrew's situation was far more serious than Mark's. We did not see a lot of him during this period and at times did not know where he was, although he usually contacted us weekly. On occasions when he visited or we visited him, we thought that we may have seen him alive for the last time as he looked so desperately drug impacted. Like most addicts, he always felt that he could kick the habit if he really wanted to, but of course in reality he couldn't.

When I told Andrew that we had bought property at Mudgee and were going to set up a vineyard, he was ecstatic. He had always excelled in agriculture as a school subject and had a great understanding of plant biology. He was about twenty-three years old at the time and immediately decided that he would move to Mudgee and gain experience in the establishment and operation of vineyards with a view to managing our vineyard in due course. He first lived at a caravan park but later lived in the house that we had rented in Mudgee. He initially worked on the establishment of a 400-acre vineyard for the Filipino owners of a large rural horse breeding and farming operation named Gooree Park near Gulgong. He didn't have a car, so he purchased a pushbike and initially daily rode the twenty plus kilometres to and from work. He later was able to get a ride to work with another of that vineyard's employees. It was extremely hard work in stifling summer temperatures, but Andrew loved every minute of it and thrived. His use of drugs subsided and his health improved tremendously. When I commenced the establishment of our vineyard, Andrew began working for me. Hallee Keegan, his girlfriend, moved in with him and worked with him at the vineyard also. All seemed to be going well, and his drug use appeared to be quite minimal; he loved the vineyard work and was fairly much on the road back to normality.

However, he began to get quite ill on a regular basis, and medical tests showed that he was allergic to the sulphur contained in vineyard sprays used to control mildew. This was a hereditary issue passed down from my mother. Specialists warned that continued exposure to the sulphur spray particles in the air and on the vine leaves was life-threatening to Andrew, and yet it was virtually essential that I and all other viticulturists in the area continued to use this spray to prevent the entire loss of the grape crops. The allergy was so severe that Andrew began to feel unwell as he came into the Mudgee Valley after returning from Sydney or elsewhere outside of the region. He was devastated by this news from the specialist as were Val and I. His hope for his future had evaporated before his eyes, and my hope and intention for his future management of the vineyard on behalf of the family vanished also. Andrew had no option but to leave the industry and the district as there was no known cure for his allergy, so he and Hallee went to Sydney and lived with Hallee's parents for a time. He had a very fine palate for judging the quality of wine and obtained a job working very successfully for Coles Ltd in their Quaffers liquor store.

Our delightful granddaughter Jessica Lisa (named after Andrew's deceased sister) was born on 13 October 1999 in Sydney. In January 2000, soon after Jessica's birth, Andrew, Hallee, and Jessica went to Cairns in North Queensland to live, where Andrew again obtained employment running a suburban liquor store. The relationship between Andrew and Hallee eventually broke down nine months later, and Hallee returned to Sydney with Jessica and resumed living with her parents.

A couple of years later, Andrew began a relationship with Joanne Croden in Cairns. He seemed to be infatuated by Joanne and was unable to see that her own personal problems and erratic behaviour were going to bring him nothing but much heartache and stress, whereas what he really needed was someone who could give him a great deal of support to conquer his addiction. He married Joanne in our garden at the vineyard in August 2002. Rather than her providing the support that he needed, all he received from being with her was a lot of hurt and anxiety. Clearly, he was back into using drugs at the time, and we were eventually able to convince both him and Joanne to undertake a drug rehabilitation programme. Joanne soon bailed out and went back to Cairns to her parents. To his credit, Andrew commenced the course but gave up after a few months and also went back to Cairns to be with Joanne. In between leaving the programme and going to Cairns, Andrew spent a few days with us at the vineyard before Xmas 2002, and we were terribly concerned for his future. He was under great stress, yet there was little we could do to help other than show him our continued love and support. Val arranged all sorts of medical appointments in the hope that someone would be able to help him, but we were again left with the totally depressing feeling that society provides no real assistance to those very many people who find themselves in a hopeless situation such as Andrew's.

On New Year's Day 2003, we were told by Joanne's father that Andrew had taken his life. He had not given us any real indication that he was contemplating suicide when he spent time with us prior to Xmas, although he was very depressed and we were extremely worried about him. However, after the dreadful event had taken place and upon reflection, we were able to see signs of his preparations for this eventuality and one cannot help but blame one's self for not recognising the 'signals' at the time, as muted as they might have been. Since Andrew's death, we have noted many similar cases—parents blaming themselves for not being able to recognise the signs before the event and thus being unable to provide the support that just might have resulted in a changed outcome.

Because suicide was involved in Andrew's death, the police were required to investigate matters in order to ensure that foul play was not involved and an autopsy also had to be undertaken. It was a terrible time for us all while waiting for his body to be released some nine days later and flown to Sydney so that a funeral could be held. The service was conducted at the Northern Suburbs Crematorium and Memorial Gardens Chapel, and Andrew's ashes were later deposited in our family plot together with those of Lisa during a small family gathering. Val has been able to control her emotions much better than me in recent years, and she undertook to deliver a lovely eulogy in Andrew's memory with me standing by her side (Appendix VIII). Mark wrote and delivered a heartfelt poem (Appendix IX), Paul delivered a loving eulogy (Appendix X), and Andrew's good friend Adam Rumble also spoke in Andrew's memory (Appendix XI).

Val remembers:

1 January 2003—we could not believe that tragedy had hit our family again.

I understood that Andrew was in a very depressed, vulnerable state of mind from the way in which he had talked to me on the phone from Cairns prior to entering the rehabilitation centre in Sydney. The repeated offer by us of seeking various medical options to help was not accepted by him as he felt that he was unable to take that course. When we said 'goodbye' to him before he flew back to Cairns a few days prior to Xmas I knew that his mind was in a most precarious state, but he would not be convinced to stay; after all he was twenty-nine years old. We spoke to Andrew on the phone on New Year's Eve with our best wishes for the New Year. He didn't speak for long, was his usual polite self but appeared to be distracted. Within hours of our conversations, he was dead. Our beautiful son, damaged in his mind beyond repair by tragedy, was unable to carry on.

From an early age, Andrew had an engaging personality. He was loving, helpful, smiled a lot, and enjoyed company and chatting to people. Lisa's death, at a very vulnerable age, had a dramatic and adverse impact on his life. From when he was a little boy, she had been like a 'second' mother, and now she had gone under such tragic circumstances. He missed her terribly.

Fortunately, Paul, Liz, Lauren, and Jack were holidaying with us from Papua New Guinea when we received the dreadful news. Mark was at Merimbula on the New South Wales South Coast on a travelling holiday which he cancelled and came home so that we could all be together to face yet another tragedy. Paul, Liz, and Mark were very supportive and it was comforting to have them with us. We were all in deep shock with very dark days ahead.

Was it any easier for the second time? No! Definitely not!

We still had to go through the same grieving process, but 'perhaps' we now knew a little of the path that lay ahead. Lauren and Jack were a welcome distraction, but they would soon return to Papua New Guinea with their parents. We had not only lost Lisa but now our precious Andrew as well.

Some nights later, I awoke from a fitful sleep in the early hours of the morning—I must have been dreaming— thinking about what should be said to explain to everyone 'why' Andrew had taken his life. The words were going through my mind. I knew that I wouldn't recall all of the words in the morning, so I got out of bed and started writing. I wrote and wrote and had the basis for the eulogy that I felt I needed to deliver at Andrew's funeral. When I later rewrote the eulogy from my notes, the message changed very little. At the time, the words came with such fluidity I felt that I must have had someone helping me. My mission to follow this path meant that I had to try to put my grieving on hold until after the funeral, but my need was strong to explain why we were there that day to say goodbye to our beloved Andrew.

Grief can have a detrimental effect on any relationship as statistics show. John and I were fortunate that we had a very strong bond, supported each other, and tried to understand

and share in each other's grief. It was not easy for either of us, but we managed to survive this dreadful time again. However close a couple is, each partner has to deal with a big part of the grieving process alone. John had his work, which was his greatest distraction, whereas I guess my best way of dealing with my grief was to think of others—John, Paul, Liz, Mark, Lauren, Jessica, and Jack. How are they all coping and what might I be able to do to relieve their suffering?

I was fortunate to have some wonderful female relatives and friends who would call often to 'check on me' after our loss of both Lisa and Andrew. On a bad day, and there were very many, their presence and thoughts helped enormously, and I will always be grateful for their support.

We felt very sad that Jessica would not remember her father, Andrew, or his love for her as she was only three years old. We feel so blessed that we still have Jessica in our lives to see and to love. She has some of Andrew's mannerisms. At times when she smiles or turns her head like her daddy, the resemblance makes me feel happy to see, but also very sad that he is not here as well to share in her life.

We now have four beautiful grandchildren: Jessica, Lauren, Jack—in 2010 we welcomed Mark and Katrina's gorgeous little son, Ashur. We now have them as the next generation to look forward with together. They bring such joy to our lives.

Andrew's pain ended on 1 January 2003, but I had lost my precious son and my pain will continue, and I will miss him and Lisa and grieve for them for the rest of my life.

Once again, the remaining family had to contend with another dreadful dark spot in our lives. Fortunately for us, Paul and Liz were holidaying in Sydney at the time, and the family is forever indebted to Liz in particular for the calm and compassionate counselling that she so lovingly provided for us. She has a great natural skill in this regard, and we are so fortunate to have her as a daughter-in-law. Andrew's loss doubled our inconsolable hurt, and we continue to deal with that hurt daily. Their birthdays and the anniversaries of Lisa's and Andrew's deaths come and go and heighten our stress levels at the time, but the loss is there constantly day and night. I know that both Paul and Mark also miss Andrew greatly as they used each other as sounding boards and the void which was created cannot ever be filled. Hallee was very upset by Andrew's death. Jessica was three at the time, and although she missed her father badly, she was not really able to understand the ramifications of his death. Fortunately, Hallee has been able to move on with her life and has found another partner whom she recently married and whom Jessica calls Dad. Jessica now has a little sister Chloe, whom she adores. We consider ourselves very fortunate that Hallee continues to allow us to be involved in Jessica's life, and Jess loves spending school holiday time here at Mudgee. She is now almost fifteen years of age and is growing into a lovely young lady who is very bright academically and gifted with natural athleticism. We love her dearly, and as with Lauren and Jack, we regret that we are not able to see a great deal more of her.

A minor disappointment to me in my retirement is that I never received a serious invitation to join a company board after I retired. I received a number of offers to take up very well paying CEO positions in companies that needed resuscitating. However, I had no interest in these as they meant returning to full-time very demanding work and long hours. This defeated my reason for retiring from my role in Westpac, which I liked and which was to reduce the stress levels and to be able to spend more time with

Val and the family. Despite the meteoritic promotions I received from time to time in the bank, they always came to me totally unexpectedly. As a consequence of my rapid rise through the ranks after I came to New South Wales where the bank's head office is situated, others often said things such as: 'Gee, you're lucky' or 'Who do you know up there?' My response was always along the lines: 'It seems that the harder I work the luckier I am.' I believe this latter statement to be true in that I never saw myself as ambitious, but I certainly worked hard, was always honest, forthright, and firm in my decisions, endeavoured to be fair to others, and aimed to do the best job that I could in all circumstances.

I have found in Mudgee that there is a great void of experience such as that which I acquired in my banking career and that the boards of all types of local organisations are calling out for assistance. If I wanted, I could be on a dozen or more boards; however, to do a director's job properly takes a lot of time and involvement. Although I employed a manager to do the day-to-day work in the vineyard, I nevertheless had to devote a reasonable amount of time daily to the overall management of that business. Currently, I am the treasurer of the executive committee of the Owners' Corporation of our block of home units at Killara, and this involves a reasonable amount of input from time to time. There are twenty-eight units in the complex, mostly occupied by older people, few of whom are either capable of or prepared to manage the day-to-day operational issues of the facility on behalf of all the residents. As with any other premises, there are maintenance issues of various magnitudes arising from time to time, and there are some 'interesting' times obtaining consensus from such a group of owners.

A few years ago, I was approached by the chairperson of a small State Government funded private organisation here in Mudgee to assist them recover control of their business. It provided support services to young, intellectually disabled adults and respite to the parents of these young people; also, it provided a permanent fully serviced home twenty-four hours a day every day of the year for up to three young lads between the ages of twelve and eighteen years with severe intellectual disabilities. These were boys who had been rejected by their parent/s or they had been found to be unmanageable. I agreed to take on a board role as adviser for only as long as it took to get the board pointed in the right direction again. I found the board to be in complete disarray with not one member having the skills necessary to effectively contribute to the management of the business. Fortunately, in a financial sense, the organisation was healthy, although the board did not know this due to their total lack of financial management skills and non-existent financial reporting systems.

Although the organisation was small, the task that confronted me was huge. It was like starting from scratch with the addition of a totally dysfunctional board acting like 'lead in the saddlebags'. We were also dealing with a group of non-committed, non-responsible, and non-responsive public servants in the State Government agency that funded the organisation, and that did not make the task any easier. It took almost two years of effort to completely reorganise matters, install efficient management, financial processes, and practices, and strengthen the board membership to the point where I felt the business was again in good hands. When I stepped aside, it gave me great pleasure to know that the funding Government agency had recognised the much improved efficiency of the business and granted the board the sum of $700,000 to buy or construct a five-bedroom home with office and staff facilities and thus overcome the need to constantly shift premises when the current lease expired and could not be extended.

I was also approached by a local not-for-profit aged care facility to assist its board in the management of the business and in particular the financial overview of the $6.5 million contract that they were about to enter into for the addition of a further thirty single rooms with en suites plus a complete remodelling of the majority of the existing building housing fifty beds. Although its board membership was much more competent than the one I had previously dealt with, this one too lacked much of the expertise that a business of its size and complexity required for efficient control and direction. I am pleased to be able to say that although the project ran about six months behind schedule and approx. $0.5 million over budget, the latter primarily due to board-approved plan changes during the building phase, it is now clearly seen as the premier aged care facility in the region. We have been able to recruit additional expertise to the board and also engineer some major changes in the attitude of the board members towards the business and the style of management the organisation requires. Financially, the organisation is now strong with quality management and a capable board.

I have witnessed the same lack of expertise in the management of my golf club and also at the local lawn bowls club where Mark is a member. Not only are young people reluctant to take on the responsibility of board positions, thus hastening the ageing of boards in general, but the lack of essential skills in country areas also works to the detriment of the organisations concerned. Also, one finds that the 'old guard' cling to their positions on the various boards and are reluctant to invite new blood to participate. I would dearly love to assist a few other local organisations; however, each role requires a lot of time, and in retirement Val and I have a lot of other things we want to do while we are still fit and able. Also, it seems to take longer to do things as one gets older!

After Mark completed his rehabilitation programme in 2002, he and Kelly lived in a unit at Lindfield, Sydney, and Mark worked in the building industry as jobs became available. He eventually determined that it would be easier for him to get ahead if he moved to Mudgee, so in 2004 he made the move and we supported him in the purchase of a home. Kelly was hesitant to make the move, but she eventually followed him. Mark became the photographer for the local newspaper *The Mudgee Guardian* and did freelance photography in his own time. The relationship between Mark and Kelly began to deteriorate, and eventually they reached a point in 2006 when they decided to separate. Mark and Kelly have since gone their separate ways after spending twelve years together. She stuck by Mark through those very difficult times in rehab and went to see him most Wednesday evenings and Sunday mornings, the only visiting times allowed. This was a great comfort to Mark as he saw that few other inmates had anyone visit and show them support. Kelly knows that Val and I greatly appreciated her demonstration of loyalty to Mark over the years they were together. Mark has since focused on renovating his house with the assistance of a young local carpenter, and the outcome is a great improvement. The installation of the garden is completed and the place looks very good indeed. Mark can be proud of what he has achieved. As a consequence of the head and brain injuries, Mark now suffers from a severe disability of short-term memory loss which impacts quite adversely on his capability to remember things and organise his life.

Mark later commenced a relationship with Katrina Odgers, a school teacher whom we see often and enjoy her company. On 25 January 2010, Ashur Robert Chatterton was born at the Mudgee hospital. He was a very healthy baby and some five years later is an extremely bright and energetic youngster with fair curly hair. We see him frequently, and he is always keen to have one of Nana's meals and a special treat. Mark and Katrina lead separate lives but share the caring for Ashur. Mark lives in Mudgee and Katrina and Ashur some forty-five minutes by car from Mudgee on a bush block, where she enjoys the peace of the countryside and her lovely garden. Mark and Katrina are good friends and see each other frequently, and Ashur quite often stays with Mark who adores him. Ashur is the only one of our four grandchildren within close proximity and Val loves to spoil him. We have recently been told the exciting news that Katrina and Mark are expecting a daughter in May 2015.

Since I retired from Westpac, we have done a lot of travelling and intend doing more while our health allows. In addition to the wonderful trip we did to Africa soon after I retired in early 1995, we have done between two and three trips by car each year back and forth to Queensland to see the family. We also visited PNG about ten times during the six and a half years of Paul and Liz's stay there. We have also enjoyed numerous other overseas trips and cruises, and as a consequence we have now visited at least fifty-five different countries around the globe.

CHAPTER 20

Has Retirement Finally Arrived?

When I decided to enter the viticulture industry in 1996, I determined that it would be great for me if I was able to have a second 'career' for say ten years or so. By then, I would be about sixty-seven years of age and probably starting to slow down a little, assuming always that the health of Val and I held up in the meantime. Over those years, we created a first-class vineyard with an excellent reputation, built an extremely nice home where we enjoyed wonderful views over the vineyard and the valley beyond, and developed an extensive and beautiful garden. It was country living at its best.

Since about 2004, the grape-growing and wine-making industry was largely unprofitable primarily due to depressed grape prices caused by a worldwide wine glut. Another contributor to the problem in Australia was the actions of some major Australian wineries. They had no hesitation in importing huge quantities of cheaper grape juice from overseas for manufacture into wine and sale in Australia and elsewhere, thus reducing the demand for locally grown grapes. One such company also commenced satisfying the supply needs of its overseas owned wineries such as those in the USA by importing juice directly to them from South America and other countries where production costs were much lower than in Australia. Many local vineyards were forced on to the market but could not find a buyer, and quite a few were mothballed and may never be reinvigorated. Large-scale removal of vines has been the outcome for the industry.

We always knew that we could not maintain the vineyard indefinitely, and in an endeavour to broaden its appeal for eventual sale, we decided to attempt to obtain the council's approval for a tourist-type development on 4.2 hectares (10.2 acres) of vacant land situated on the main Cassilis Road frontage of the property. After two gruelling and very expensive years of continuous hassles with the council's planning personnel, who repeatedly moved the goalposts, we obtained development approval for 10 ′ one-bedroom and 10 ′ two-bedroom high-quality tourist villas plus a cellar door sales area/gift shop and a bistro/restaurant.

I would have preferred to excise the area in question from the remainder of the vineyard property and obtain a separate title for it as it was already virtually separated from the rest of the vineyard by way of a right of way entry road to a neighbouring property. The council's planning staff would not agree to this idea, nor would they under any circumstances contemplate a proposal which involved additional housing development of any type in the immediate area. When I initially established the vineyard, I took particular care to ensure that the vineyard's service road actually ran down the centre of the survey line, which denoted the split of the vineyard into two equally sized blocks. As an additional means of enhancing our future sale options and concurrent with obtaining the council's approval to the tourist development, I also obtained its approval to formally split the vineyard into two equally sized blocks so that two titles could be issued in due course with the second block having entitlement to the construction of a house. Again, my dealings with the council on this matter were not one that I am able to recall as being pleasant.

In early 2007, the wine industry appeared to begin to mount a recovery, and we decided that it was probably the right time for us to sell and move on to the next stage of our lives. I was not at all convinced that the upturn would be long-lasting; on the contrary, I was of the view that the industry would soon continue its downwards slide with no clear picture available as to when viability may return. My previous banking experience told me that agricultural pursuits in Australia in the long term seem to go through peaks and troughs over a period of about ten years on average, but these periods could be significantly shorter or longer. We determined that if we were to decide to wait to sell when the wine industry was next about to peak I could be in my late seventies or even older, and that could possibly be an unwise decision. Accordingly, in September 2007, we placed the entire property on the market for sale by tender, that is, by inviting bids from interested parties within a set period of time—in this instance within seven weeks. In view of the then history of almost total lack of interest in the purchase of local vineyard properties, it was my belief at the time that it could take a year and possibly two or more to find the buyer who was interested in the approved development in addition to the vineyard and who was also prepared to pay our asking price. Fortunately, we quickly had two very determined buyers and had exchanged contracts for the sale to one of them within the seven weeks of listing. This was at our nominated price with the 10 per cent deposit paid and settlement arranged to take place at the conclusion of the harvest of the current grape crop in approximately April 2008. The actual settlement for the sale was effected on 21 April 2008.

It was a surprise to us that our neighbours were interested, and they became the eventual buyers. Unbeknown to me, they had recently sold a large hotel in Newcastle and were looking for investments outside the hotel industry. He told me later that he intended to play hardball on the price he was offering. However, the other interested party came to agreement on both the price and the terms of sale quickly. The difficulty with this possible purchaser was that his funds were tied up in trusts in New Zealand, and he was required to have his trustee from New Zealand inspect the property before the legal wheels could start turning in preparation for exchange of contracts and eventual settlement, assuming all went well along the way. Although this second interested party had signed an expression of interest to purchase at our price, it would have taken many weeks to achieve exchange of contracts and the whole deal could have collapsed during this process. Really, our neighbours were the most promising buyers, and via the agent, who had informed them that another interested buyer had agreed to the price, we gave them sole rights until 5 p.m. on Friday 16 November 2007 to meet the asking price, exchange contracts, and pay the deposit. Failing completion of this arrangement, the other party would be given a similar sole option period to exchange contracts. In the event, contracts were exchanged and the deposit paid by our neighbours on the allotted day.

Soon after they acquired our vineyard property, the purchaser stood in the local Council elections on the ticket of one of his friends, who was a serving councillor, and was elected. Within weeks of this eventuality, he made application to the council to have the property added to the draft Local Environment Plan with a view to early subdivision into what was said to be 60 × 1 acre rural residential lots, 2 × 10 acre lots each with house sites included, and the house and gardens split off on a separate 1 acre lot. He has since been elected mayor of Mid-Western Regional Council. I am told that recently approval has been gained for him to divide the 60 × 1 acre lots into 120 half acre lots. His experience with grape growing was not rewarding. Low prices and disease issues led to very disappointing returns, and he arranged for all vines, trellis posts, wires, and irrigation lines to be removed from the site after a few years, at considerable cost. The wheel has turned a full circle and the land is again used for cattle grazing as it was when we purchased it.

Once contracts for the vineyard's sale had been exchanged and the deposit paid, we were faced with having to finally make a decision as to where we were going to live after settlement took place in four months' time. Val was interested to move to our unit at Killara which would give us better access to our many close friends in Sydney and better access to medical facilities for both of us—the latter being more important as age creeps on. However, I felt that I was not yet ready for such a lifestyle even though the unit had a large outdoor terrace area and garden. Other options that we explored were the likes of Bowral in the Southern Highlands of New South Wales or the Central Coast of New South Wales, but again neither of these appealed to me greatly.

We were driving to Brisbane to see my mother and other family members in early December 2007 when Val saw an appealing-looking home advertised for sale in the *Mudgee Guardian* newspaper. She rang the agent and made an appointment for us to inspect the property on our return to Mudgee a week later. Upon inspection, we both liked a lot of things about the home, but a walk-through from the main bedroom, through the walk-in wardrobe/dressing room, then the en suite to the second bedroom, was unappealing to us, and we turned our attention to inspecting other Mudgee houses. A few weeks later, we had another inspection of the initial house with the walk-through, and Val decided that the addition of an en suite to the second bedroom and the closing of the doorway from the en suite to the second bedroom would resolve our issues with the house. With Paul, Liz, and the children living in Vienna and Mark our only other family living in Mudgee, we decided to purchase this Mudgee home and exchanged contracts on 21 December 2007 with settlement due in conjunction with the vineyard settlement.

It was a somewhat sad day for me when we vacated the vineyard property on 21 April 2008; however, this was yet another move amongst many for us, and both Val and I were certain that the decision to sell was the correct one. Both the sale process for the vineyard and the purchase process for the house proceeded smoothly and amicably, and we were able to arrange the settlement for the vineyard to be followed the next day by the settlement for the house. No sooner had we moved into our new house than we were flying to Vienna to see the family. Because there were a lot of changes that we wanted to get underway at the new house, we stayed in Vienna for only two weeks. The end result of all the improvements is a lovely, comfortable home in an excellent location within two blocks of the centre of town and directly opposite a large riverside park with an Olympic-sized swimming pool. When we purchased the property six years ago, our aim was to live here in comfort until age dictated otherwise, when we would possibly move to our Sydney unit. Regrettably, that time has arrived. We have made the decision to relocate to Sydney, and that unit has been fully renovated in anticipation of the move. Our Mudgee home has been placed on the market, and the move to Sydney will be effected when its sale has been concluded. I will resign from my board position at Pioneer House Aged Care, but keep myself occupied to a degree by continuing with the chairmanship of the Walter & Eliza Hall Trust for at least a little while longer and possibly also as treasurer of the Owners' Corporation of our unit complex. Hopefully, I will have more time to read the very many books that I continue to accumulate faster than I am able to read them and also to play a game of golf regularly.

As I write this final paragraph of my life's story, I do so in the knowledge that I have celebrated my seventy-fifth birthday and am now in my twenty-first year of my retirement from Westpac. Fortunately, I remain in good health, but some health issues are pressing on Val. I prefer not to look back in time due to the hurt of the memories of the very dark periods in our lives; however, if one was able to overlook these times, then I think I could say that it has been a very diversified, interesting, and rewarding journey, which I trust will continue for some years yet. I must say that writing this story has forced me to take a very detailed look at the past, and as a consequence, I am astonished by the almost incomprehensible changes that have taken place during my short lifespan. I expect that if we were all given a second opportunity to relive our lives we would all make some different choices on the way through. However, there is no such thing as a practice run. We are all living the real thing here and now without a 'How To Do It' manual and can only strive to do our best, guided by the limited knowledge that we possess at the time. When I ask myself the question: 'How does one judge whether one's life has been successful?' I believe the answer lies somewhere in the realm of whether one can claim to have added value during their stay on this planet. In my mind, I believe that on the whole I can justifiably answer that question in the affirmative, and for that reason I am truly satisfied. The real highlights of it all have been the wonderful memories I have of the times I spent initially with my parents and siblings (we still see my four siblings regularly) and those very many enjoyable times with my darling wife, our children, and now our grandchildren.

Son Mark, Me, daughter Lisa, sons Paul & Andrew, Val, mother-in-law Mary Bennett - Southampton Docks, England - April 1974

Me, son Andrew, Mum, daughter Lisa, sons Mark & Paul - Bromley, Kent, England - July 1974

Mum, Me & Val - dressed for Queen's Garden Party
at Buckingham Palace, London - July 1974

Mum - Theddlethorpe, England - 1974

Mum's 70th birthday - with extended family group -15 March, 1985

Son Paul & daughter-in-law Liz Dwyer - Master of Arts graduation
with Merit in Anthropology - Development - Sydney University - 1992

Son Mark, daughter Lisa, son Paul, Me, Val
& son Andrew - November 1985

Me and family at Burleigh Heads (a few weeks
prior to Lisa's death) - January 1987

Yarramalong farm house with Bert the bull and other cattle - 1995

Son Mark - Charles Sturt University Graduation Ceremony -
Bachelor of Arts - TV & Sound Production - April 1994

Bridge over River Khwai - Machaba Safari Camp,
Okavango Delta, Botswana - August 1995

Light Aircraft refuelling "Serengeti style" Tanzania - August 1995

Pom Pom Safari Camp accommodation, Okavango
Delta, Botswana - August 1995

Me & Prince Phillip aboard "BOUNTY", Sydney Harbour - 1992

Val and Me - Val's 60th birthday - 8 December 2001

Me & friend Richard (Dick) Watson, Sandfly Point,
Milford Track Walk, New Zealand - 1995

Son Andrew & granddaughter Jessica Chatterton -
Vineyard house pool, Mudgee - March 2001

Sons Andrew, Paul & Mark Chatterton - December 2001

Sons Andrew & Paul, Val, Me, Son Mark -
Paul's wedding - 14 September 1997

Aerial view of portion of Bonnyview Vineyard,
house & garden - December 2006

Son Mark - pointing vineyard posts, Bonnyview
Vineyard, Mudgee - 1997

Bonnyview Vineyard house garden, Mudgee - 2007

Son Andrew (far right) planting grapevines, Bonnyview
Vineyard, Mudgee - September 1997

Friends Anne & Dick Watson and Jan & Kevin Holm &
Val - Strzelecki Track camp, Central Australia - 1996

Friends Kevin Holm & Dick Watson attempting repairs to
Kevin's vehicle - Strzelecki Track, Central Australia - 1996

Cousin Tom Chatterton & Me - 2 Nov 1997

Me - retirement function with "Bronco's" jumper &
Akubra hat presentations - 15 December 1994

Son Paul Chatterton & daughter-in law Liz Dwyer -
prior to United Nations Ball, Vienna 2010

Son Mark, Hallee Keegan & son Andrew, Me, Val, daughter-in-law
Liz Dwyer & son Paul - retirement function 15 December 1994

Hallee Keegan (Jessica's mother) with granddaughter Jessica
Chatterton (1 yr) & son Andrew Chatterton - 2000

Granddaughters Lauren (15) & Jessica (13) Chatterton - Jul'2013

Grandson Jack Chatterton (13) - Vienna 2014

Member of Order of Australia Medal (AM)

Order of Australia presentation by New South Wales Governor
Prof. Marie Bashir at Government House, Sydney - 2002

Me & Val - my 70th birthday aboard RHAPSODY
OF THE SEAS - 30 November 2009

Son Mark & grandson Ashur Chatterton - 3 months

Mum, Me, son Mark & grandson Ashur Chatterton - April 2013

Grandson Jack & son Paul Chatterton, daughter-in-law Liz Dwyer & granddaughter Lauren Chatterton - walking through France - 2014

Granddaughter Lauren Chatterton - 16 yrs

Grandson Jack Chatterton - 14 yrs

Son Mark Chatterton & Katrina Odgers - 2014

Granddaughter Jessica Chatterton - dressed
for High School Formal - 2014

Grandson Ashur Chatterton - April 2015

Daughter-in-law Liz Dwyer & Son Paul Chatterton with
grandchildren Lauren & Jack - February 2015

Friends Group - Bryn Harris, Howard Dudgeon, Allan Wright,
Me, Val, Jan Conroy, Eve Wright, Frank Conroy, Bruce Alexander,
Alma Dudgeon, Wendy Alexander & Helen Harris - Nov'2014

Friends Group - Ian & Marie Grieve, Richard & Anne Watson, Val
& Me, Pam & Robert Newman, Val & Vern Brockman - c2005

FROM THE BUSH TO BANKER AND BACK
EPILOGUE
CHAPTER 21
Sentimental Visit to Struck Oil

I was prompted to add the following words to my life's story as a consequence of a very touching coincidence that happened in early 2016 and which then led me to enjoy a number of subsequent nostalgic events.

My nephew, Michael McMillan (Valmai and Graham's son), was asked to stand for the position of Mayor of Rockhampton in that year's mayoral elections. Amongst his many promotional speeches was one that he delivered to the residents of a retirement village in the North Rockhampton suburb of Park Avenue. Incidentally, this is the area where I used to deliver the Sunday paper as a schoolboy.

When introducing himself to the residents in attendance, Michael mentioned that his paternal grandfather was born in Rockhampton and lived there all of his life. He also mentioned that his father was born there, and his mother, Valmai (nee Chatterton), although born in nearby Mt Morgan, lived in Rockhampton for a number of years prior to her marriage. At this point in his speech, a woman in the audience began to cry and continued to do so throughout the event.

Puzzled by what he might have said to offend the woman, Michael approached her after his speech, apologised for upsetting her and asked what he had said that had caused her upset. She told Michael that her name was Eileen Matheson (nee O'Brien) and that, as a young girl, she used to mind his mother and her siblings when they were babies at Struck Oil. She told Michael that she and my mother Mavis (Michael's maternal grandmother) had kept in touch until my mum's death in January 2015; also, that she was simply delighted and overwhelmed by learning that Michael was Valmai's son, hence her crying.

Michael passed his account of this event to me via his mother and I immediately determined that Val and I should go to Rockhampton in the not too distant future to meet up with Eileen.

Val and I had previously agreed to spend two nights at Rainbow Beach (on the Queensland coast near Gympie) and three nights at Noosa with five other couples, who were long term friends, in mid-June 2016. So, we extended these plans and decided to drive to Rockhampton first, spend three nights there and then meet up with our friends at Rainbow Beach.

I wrote to Eileen and told her of our plans to call to see her. She was extremely excited and insisted that we come for afternoon tea. I sent her a copy of my book and she thoroughly enjoyed reading about our years at Struck Oil and her caring for us in the very kindly manner that I had described. Following is a brief excerpt from her thank you response to me:

"It was just simply amazing to catch up after all these years and it (the book) brought back all those happy memories of 1940 to 1944. I loved your Mother John, very dearly. She was such a wonderful person and I kept in touch every year until the day she died. Your father was also a very special person."

Val and I drove to Rockhampton and arrived on 16th June. We called on Eileen in the afternoon, as had been arranged. She was as spritely as can be, almost 91 years of age, and in full control of all her faculties. It was really lovely to meet with her – she is still the same very kind person but her face reveals that she has had a hard life. Her husband Pat passed away in 1979 and she kept her home going until a few years ago when she realised it was getting too much for her.

Eileen had arranged for her three daughters to be there to meet us. One is named Merle after my oldest sister and Eileen's only son, who was not present, is named Colin, after my younger brother. They had gone to great length in preparing a lovely afternoon tea – when finished, there was almost enough food left over to share as afternoon tea with the residents of her entire retirement village.

While there, another surprise was the arrival of John Johnson and his wife to meet us. They are residents of the same retirement village as Eileen and she had invited them to join us. John was in my class at Mt. Morgan State School and also lived at Struck Oil and travelled into town daily with me on the school bus. We had a lot to catch up on after some 65 years since we last saw each other.

The following day, together with my brother Colin and his wife Sharon, whom we had arranged to meet up with in Rockhampton, we drove to Struck Oil for one last nostalgic visit to the farm. Colin was only 3 or 4 years old when we left the farm so he has no memory of it at all and was pleased that I was able to point out features and relate happenings to him while on the spot.

Some weeks prior to our visit to the Rockhampton area, I had attempted to contact the current owners of the farm but had been unsuccessful. Regrettably, the owners were not there when we arrived so, without their permission, we were not prepared to walk around the paddocks. The spot where the farm house is located is relatively elevated so we were able to see for a reasonable distance in all directions. What we saw was extremely disappointing indeed. The fact that the season had been dry and the grass was withered and brown detracted further from the picture before us.

The cow yards, milking shed, bails and cattle dip were all totally dilapidated. The barn had been demolished. The invading regrowth of lantana, trees and bushes made it impossible to determine precisely where the boundaries of the cultivated blocks used to be. We could see a few beef cattle and horses in the distance and I expect the carrying capacity of the property had been severely diminished over the years. The only maintained structure was the 'new' house, which is now some 75 years old. When one recalls that my parents worked so hard to build a highly productive dairy farm, they have to be seriously admired for their achievements. However, in doing so, Dad ruined his health and subsequent owners of the property gained more benefit from his outcomes than they did. He would turn in his grave if he was able to see the state of his once prized possession.

When driving from Rockhampton to Struck Oil, I was able to show Val, Colin and Sharon where Dad and I rode our horses down part of the Great Dividing Range to the Bouldercombe district to collect and drive home the two 'scrubber' cows, which Dad had purchased from Sammy Richards. Sammy's 'humpy' has been replaced with a number of modern homes and now there is a sealed road past his old place to the base of the range. Interestingly, the range is still as steep as I remember it being and the lone narrow track up its side is still clearly visible.

Many changes have taken place in the Struck Oil district since I was last there about 30 years ago. A large proportion of the roads are now sealed and further roadwork improvements continue.

Many homes have been erected on small rural blocks and electricity and telephone services are now available.

The road access into the district divides before the third crossing of the Dee River – the right-hand fork of the road leads on to our old farm and the left-hand road leads to where the corrugated iron-clad Memorial Hall still stands and where the school used to be. It also leads to the property where Dad was raised as a youngster and which he later acquired from his Father's estate.

After visiting the area of the farm where I lived as a young boy, we backtracked to where the access road to the district forks, then drove up the left-hand road and gained access up to the northern boundary of that part of the old property where Dad grew up. We were then standing on the bank of the Dee River where alluvial gold-mining took place many years ago. One of the McDonald boys, whom we kids used to hide from when rounding up the cows of an afternoon, was still living in their old neighbouring house.

From where we stood, we were able to discern the site on which my paternal grandparents' home stood those many years ago. The very old and very overgrown orchard of mango trees could also be seen a few hundred metres away. A portion of this part of the property has been sold and an attractive new home has been constructed.

We then drove to where the left fork of the road terminates at the top of the Range. This is the spot where, many years ago, Dad and I, on horseback, commenced following the track down to Sammy Richards' place at Bouldercombe to collect the two 'scrubber' cows.

Speaking of Bouldercombe reminds me also that soon after my book was published in 2015, an old lady named Mrs Hinchliff contacted me. She had lived her entire life at Bouldercombe and recalls the dances that used to be held in the hall there when she was a young woman. She knew my Dad and his siblings and was able to tell me that on moonlit nights they used to walk down the Range track to the Bouldercombe dances, change into their dance finery when they arrived (ladies to the left, gents to the right) as was the custom of those days, then reversed the procedure before later heading home.

While talking to Eileen the previous day, I had mentioned the name Sammy Richards and her eyes lit up. As a child, she first lived on a rural block, which the family called Sammy's. We kids well remember the paddock we knew as Sammy's from where, on weekends, we frequently rounded up and guided the cows home to be milked. Eileen's father later sold that block to Dad and they moved to another rural block location on the left-hand fork of the Struck Oil road. It was while living at this latter location that Eileen began working for my parents as a nanny to us very young children.

After the visit to Struck Oil, we visited Mt. Morgan and were agreeably surprised by what we saw. Although the gold mine has not functioned for many years, the population did not appear to have reduced and many homes were now painted externally and their rusty rooves had been replaced. Tourism drives the economy with the old mine and railway station being a major attraction. We had lunch at what used to be George Mullins' cafe. I mentioned to the waitress that the cafe used to be owned by Mr. Mullins some 65 years ago but she was unaware of this fact. She did tell me though that she lived with her husband and children on a small rural block at Struck Oil and loved the environment. The family grew their own vegetables and the kids loved the freedom of the outdoors.

After lunch we visited the district cemetery, which is located in the suburb of Horse Creek. We located the grave of my paternal grandparents, which is still in quite reasonable repair; the cemetery being well maintained as a whole. Horse Creek is also the location of the school my father attended in his early years. The area has changed little from what I remember it as – an unattractive and relatively depressed area.

We decided to take an alternative road when returning to Rockhampton. The route took us via Razorback, Kabra and Gracemere. Razorback is so named because of its sharp drop-off over the Range down to the plains of Kabra and beyond. I recall Razorback as being very difficult to negotiate for the low-powered vehicles of the early days– it is now a steep but well maintained sealed road and presents no difficulty to modern cars. Trains were originally required to engage their 'rack and pinion' gear in order to negotiate Razorback due to the steep gradient, otherwise their steel wheels could not maintain traction and simply spun on the steel rails while the train remained stationary. A new line, with a lesser gradient, was eventually constructed. This upgrade overcame the need for the 'rack' but the line has since been closed.

Kabra is a cattle grazing district with a very small local village. It is the district where my parents agisted their dairy cows on Mr. McEvoy's property over 80 years ago when their farm was suffering very severe drought conditions.

Rockhampton is noted as the 'beef capital' of Australia and is a major cattle selling centre, and known as such both nationally and internationally. A very substantial selling facility was erected there in the near past and we decided to visit it in the hope that cattle sales were in progress. We saw the last few of some young stock being auctioned and in the relatively short time that we were there, viewed the loading and unloading of hundreds of head of cattle. This activity continues almost non-stop day and night. It is an extremely efficient operation and my love of cattle made it a real treat for me. Val, Sharon and Colin also found the experience interesting.

The following day, to round off our trip, we visited the towns of Yeppoon, Emu Park and surrounding areas, all of which have shown considerable growth over the years.

CHAPTER 22

Another Move

I believe it is fortunate that we are not able to see what the future holds for us. It seems to me that, to a large extent, certain events in our lives, whether good or bad, determine our future direction, and at times, where we are to reside. For instance, in the case of Val and myself, we knew that ageing would eventually determine our return from Mudgee to our Sydney unit, where quality medical care was readily available.

Although our son Mark was still living in Mudgee, we determined that we should make the move back to Sydney in October 2015. We engaged the same removalist, John Williams, who had previously moved our furniture and effects from the rented house in Mudgee to the new vineyard house in 1999. In 2007 he moved us from the vineyard house to the house in town, then to our Sydney unit in October 2015.

The move from Mudgee to Sydney was particularly challenging for Val in that we (mainly she) had to determine what furniture from a fully furnished 4-bedroom home in Mudgee would fit into an already fully furnished three-bedroom unit in Sydney and at the same time, determine which furniture would need to be disposed of. Val loves working with house plans. She knew the measurements of the various rooms in the Sydney unit and set about measuring all furniture to determining a suitable location for each. There was much furniture to be disposed of and the hardest part of all of this planning was disposing of it, even at give-away prices, despite the fact that it was all in very good condition.

The Sydney unit was very comfortable, having been only recently fully renovated – we enjoyed the environment there and the company of our many friends. However, it wasn't long before we commenced discussing how we intended to cope with advancing old age. Our initial thoughts were that we would move into a retirement village in the northern suburbs of Sydney and dispose of our unit. Visits to a few of these soon dissuaded us from this approach.

Around this time my sisters Merle and Valmai and their husbands had moved to retirement village accommodation in different suburbs of Brisbane. On a visit to that city in 2016, we inspected each of their units and were particularly impressed by the one occupied by Valmai and Graham McMillan. Internet enquiries led me to find that the operator of this village was also building multi-storey accommodation units at Holland Park in Brisbane, which were scheduled for completion in July 2017. We were fortunate to acquire one of these 3-bedroom units and moved here in October of that year. In addition to its relatively central location and proximity to shopping centres and major hospitals, we were influenced also by the fact that there was an established, fully functioning high-rise 141 beds aged care facility on the same site.

Again, Val got to work with her tape measure and determined where our furniture from the Sydney unit would fit. She found that if we attached the TV to the loungeroom wall of the Brisbane unit, the only item which would not fit was the TV stand. We leased the Sydney unit and the tenants were happy to have the TV stand. John Williams again very competently managed another self-inflicted move of all of furniture and effects, this time from Sydney to our present retirement village unit in Brisbane.

CHAPTER 23

Family Affairs

In 2014, Katrina, with whom Mark continued a casual relationship, found she was again pregnant and prior to giving birth, without any consultation with Mark, took their son Ashur, who was then around 5 years old, to Brisbane to live with her mother. Isabella was born in Brisbane on 1st May 2015.

In 2017 Claire came into our lives and our family. She is the daughter of a woman with whom Paul had a very brief liaison whilst at Sydney University in the mid-1980s. Her mother had returned to Tasmania and Paul had no contact thereafter. Claire had been searching for her father and in 2017 met up with him by arrangement in Munich, Germany where she was then studying Linguistics. We met her soon after on a trip to Vienna to see Paul and his family. She has since returned to Hobart and we have greatly enjoyed having her stay with us here at the unit. She is a delightful young lady who recently joined the RAAF. She has now graduated as an Aircraftwoman from eleven weeks of basic training at Wagga Wagga in NSW and was awarded the prize for the most improved recruit. She now is in the process of undertaking a further eleven weeks of special training in Adelaide,

S.A. to become an Intelligence Analyst – seemingly, her previous Linguistics training fitting her well for this particular role. We look forward to seeing much more of her in the future, wherever that may take her.

On leaving Mudgee in 2015, I resigned from the Board of Pioneer House Aged Care, after some ten enjoyable years assisting in the management of what are commonly known as notoriously diffi- cult facilities to manage successfully and profitably. At the time, I was proud to be able to say that Pioneer House had an excellent reputation within the population of the district.

Also, in 2015, having served as a Trustee/ Director for 19 years and as Chairman since 1997, I resigned from the Walter & Eliza Hall Trust. Although I was still enjoying my role at this wonder- ful organisation, I was now 76 years of age and realised that it was time to leave when the organisation was in sound shape.

The 'hole' created in my work day by these board retirements was quickly filled by arranging an interstate move and all that is connected therewith; also, by the fact that our retirement vil- lage home was brand new and thus did not have any organised operating structure for residents, which is essential for enjoyable and inclusive community living. My past experience on the Strata Committee of our Sydney unit for 20 years served me well in introducing a constitution and establishing various committees to govern the day to day activities, function and events of the village. We are delighted to be able to say that we have found ourselves in a community of supportive and caring individuals and are enjoy- ing our lives here.

Like most people as they age, we have had our share of health prob- lems since coming to Brisbane. Both Val and I have spent time on a few occasions in the nearby Greenslopes Private Hospital but have overcome the underlying issues and lead an active, fulfilling life. For many years we were reluctant to even consider returning to Brisbane to live because of the climate, which we recalled as being very humid in summer time. We have found this to not be so and really enjoy the summer (with some assistance of air conditioning on occasions) and the delightful winter weather. Another strong consideration in our decision to return here was the fact that my three sisters and my brother and their respective spouses all live in Brisbane – being here affords us the opportunity to see them more frequently.

We were reluctant to leave our very close bank friends in Sydney but the move has not prevented us from keeping in touch. A few couples from Sydney have spent time with us when in Brisbane and we have continued to holiday with the group each year up until now when the Coronavirus Pandemic forced the cancellation of our June'20 group booking for 5 nights at Daylesford in Victoria. We have been able to reconfirm this holiday for March 2021.

CHAPTER 24

Writing Begins Again

———⇒❧❦⇐———

The Coronavirus Pandemic has resulted in all sorts of restrictions being introduced by State and Federal Governments across Australia in an attempt to halt the transmission of this deadly virus. Most shops, other than food shops, were forced to close as were hotels, restaurants, clubs and the like. Social distancing, one from each other, was introduced and strictly policed; people were asked to stay at home and self-isolate unless it was absolutely necessary to visit a Doctor or some similar emergency. These restrictions have applied since March 2020 and it appears they will not be relaxed for some months yet. Australia's borders are closed to overseas visitors and it seems these restrictions may not be relaxed until next year at the earliest. This extended period of 'down-time' has prompted both Val and me to do some writing to fill in time.

By chance, I met the daughter of a couple who live here at the village. Nicole was visiting last Christmas from Nannup in Western Australia where she and her partner run a publishing business with the delightful name 'Pickawoowoo Publishing'. Some 40 years ago, Val wrote a series of children's educational poems about

Australian insects and has carried them around with us ever since, move after move. She spoke with Nicole and now Val has her poems published by IngramSpark under the title the 'Creepy Collection'. Not to be satisfied with that, she has now finished hand-writing the story of her life, which will also be published shortly by IngramSpark under the title 'Acceptance – A Memoir'.

All of this spare time has sparked me to also commence writing again but only to correct a few errors and to bring up to date that which I have previously written.

Paul and Liz remain in Vienna, Austria with Paul still working for WWF. Liz is teaching English as a second language to local and foreign students in Vienna at two different schools during the week. Lauren is now 21 and attending University in Vienna and is also working part-time. She has applied to attend university in Amsterdam next year to undertake Multi Media and Communications studies which are compatible with those of her senior school years. She is a very dedicated young lady. Jack is now 18 and is attending a select school as a boarder a few hours from Vienna. He is progressing very well and is looking forward to attending university next year. All four of them have felt the impact of the Government-introduced restrictions and the overall effects on Austria of the Coronavirus Pandemic; the university and schools are closed and Liz and Paul are having to work from home.

Our last overseas trip was to Tanzania and Kenya in Africa in August 2019, where we met up with Paul and his family. Mark accompanied us from Australia. Granddaughter Jessica (now 20) was to accompany us also but found she was pregnant a few months before we departed and disappointingly for both her and us, had to cancel. We are now the proud great-grandparents to Hunter Robert Hedditch and have welcomed his father Sam, Jessica's partner, into the family.

We have determined to not visit overseas again and will assist the family financially to allow them to visit us. Our travelling days are over, except for trips within Australia and possibly New Zealand. We now find the long haul trips too stressful and tiring and prefer to leave the challenge for the younger folk. We have thoroughly enjoyed the many wonderful overseas trips and cruises we have undertaken in the past and are satisfied with what we have done and seen. We were hoping to see Paul and his family this Christmas but the closure of Australian borders to overseas visitors due to the Coronavirus is unlikely to be lifted by then.

We have Mark and his children Ashur and Isabella stay each school holidays.

I celebrated my 80th birthday in November last and Val will celebrate her 79th birthday in December this year. We are in quite reasonable health for our ages and neither of us has any difficulty in filling our days. Val is planning a further series of children's educational stories – this time on Australian animals. I have no further writing plans and will continue in my role as President of the Residents Committee of the village until March next year when my three years limit as President is reached. I may decide to take a place on the committee, if so nominated and elected, and will continue to read the very many books, which I frequently buy faster than I am able to read them, on my Kindle device.

Life is good!

THE END

Paul, me, Val, Mike (guide), Liz, Jack, Mark & Lauren –
Ngorongoro Crater – Tanzania, Africa – 2019

Me, Jack, Liz, Paul, Lauren, Val, Mike – Tanzania – 2019

Claire – RAAF Graduation – 2020

Jack & me – Tanzania – 2019

Lauren – 2020

Jessica – School formal – 2016

Ashur & pet Bluetongue Lizard – 2020

Isabella – 3 yrs – 2018

Jessica, Sam and Hunter – 2019

Hunter – 1 year - 2020

APPENDIX I

World War I: Service Record Robert Chatterton

(Second Light Horse Regiment A.I.F.—Service No. 496)

Details of Grandpa Chatterton's Service Record and additional information obtained from the Australian War Museum in Canberra show the following:

- 25/08/1914—joined Queensland Light Horse 2nd Regiment at Rockhampton, Qld. Age: 38, Occupation: Baker, Address: Horse Creek, Mt Morgan, Queensland.
- 24/09/1914—embarked at Pinkenba Wharf, Brisbane for Egypt on 'STAR OF ENGLAND'.
- 29/03/1915—detention for 14 days (reason not stated).
- 09/05/1915—proceeded from Alexandria, Egypt, to join M.E.F. (Mediterranean Expeditionary Forces) at Gallipoli arriving on 12 May 1915. (The M.E.F. was the overall force responsible for the Dardanelles theatre of operations.)
- 18/12/1915—'Temporary B Class'—ANZAC Advanced Base at Mudros on the Greek Island of Lemnos. (Recent input gained from the Australian War Museum indicates

that he was medically assessed as 'B Class', meaning he was only capable of carrying out light or non-combat duties. I am told that this could have been either a temporary status whilst recovering from illness or wounds; alternatively it may have been a permanent classification given the units he was attached to after this time and his early discharge. The latter is the most likely. Family input tells me that he suffered shrapnel wounds to the leg and also suffered heart problems.)

- 10/01/1916—disembarked from front (Mudros) on 'AUSONIA' for Alexandria and Ghezireh Palace Hotel in Cairo. (This hotel was taken over by the 2ⁿᵈ Australian Battalion and acted as a general hospital.)
- 19/03/1916—embarked on 'DEMOSTHENES' for Australia on Escort Duties. (The Australian War Memorial personnel recently advised that he would have been engaged as a member of the escort staff during the voyage to Australia. He would have been employed in either tending the injured or possibly working as a baker, given his pre-war qualifications.)
- 19/05/1916—discharged 1ˢᵗ Military District.
- Awarded the following medals: 1914/1915 Star No. 3054, British War Medal No. 768 and Victory Medal No. 768. (The whereabouts of these medals is unknown to me.)

APPENDIX II

Brief Family History

One's life story has to begin somewhere, and I have chosen to believe that mine began as a consequence of Leslie (Les) Chatterton (my future uncle) marrying one Beryl Camplin in 1929, some ten years before I was born. This union most probably came about due to the fact that the Chatterton and Camplin families knew each other very well in Theddlethorpe, Lincolnshire, England, before their emigration to Australia. It seems that their close family friendship continued in Australia, where I understand that both my future paternal and maternal grandfathers attended the same school in the same class in Bundaberg, Queensland, in their early school years in Australia.

Les's brother, and my father, John Thomas (known as Jack), was amongst the official wedding party at Les's and Beryl's marriage, and there he met a younger sister of Beryl's named Mavis Aileen Camplin, who was one of the bridesmaids. Jack was then about nineteen years of age and Mavis was only fourteen. Some five years later, Beryl asked Mavis to go to Struck Oil, where she and Les operated a dairy farm. Mavis was to attend to home duties and mind the children while Beryl was in hospital having another baby. Mavis and Jack renewed their acquaintance, and when Mavis returned to Bundaberg my father actually wrote her a letter. He must have been really smitten by young Mavis as I cannot imagine my father having written a letter to anyone unless it was business orientated. At that time, Mavis worked for a Mrs Patterson in Bundaberg as a nanny looking after their three children. By coincidence, Jack's Aunt Alice lived next door to the Pattersons and from time to time he went to stay there, I imagine more so to continue his relationship with Mavis than to spend time with his aunt. In the interim periods, he and Mavis corresponded. Their love deepened, and they were engaged when Mavis was twenty years of age and they married on 25 January 1936.

My mother died on 18 January 2015 at the age of ninety-nine years and ten months and still fully in control of her mental faculties. However, I have not found it easy to learn the details of my forebears from her as memories have faded with time. All but one of my grandparents had died before my birth, and in those days, communication and family association was not as easily maintained as it is now. However, I have learnt a reasonable amount of detail about past family members, which I feel is worthwhile recording here as a family interest.

Mum's father was Charles Edward Camplin (known as Ted), one of eight children, seven boys and one girl, namely, Albert, George, Joseph, John, Cliff, Rose, and Enos. A ninth child, a girl named Blanche, died accidentally in infancy. Ted was born in Theddlethorpe, Lincolnshire, England, and arrived in Australia with the rest of his family when he was eight years old. They departed Plymouth on 6 January 1884 and arrived in Australia on board the 'SIRSA' via Cooktown and later disembarked at Rockhampton in late February 1884. It seems that the voyage may have been a very unhappy one in view of a report which appeared in the Brisbane Courier on Saturday April 5 1884. This report dealt with the outcome of an enquiry into the voyage by the Immigration Board in Brisbane, Charges were set out in a petition signed by some 300 of the passengers whose main complaints were as follow, in addition to several other minor complaints:

1. Overcrowding
2. Short issue of provisions during the early part of the voyage
3. Unwholesomeness of the bread through bad baking and bad cooking generally

The enquiry found that although the ship was authorised to carry 537 'statute' adults, she left Plymouth with 610 souls, or 531 'statute' adults, on board. The Board was of the opinion that she had a far greater number of emigrants on board than could be carried in reasonable comfort to the passengers, especially as they were in hot weather from the time of entering the Mediterranean until their arrival in the colony. The Board expressed the opinion that 400 'statute' adults was the maximum number that should be carried in similar circumstances. It also found that several days of heavy weather immediately after leaving Plymouth had contributed to complaint No. 2 and was also of the opinion that those ship owners contracted by the Government to bring immigrants to the colony should be compelled, under penalty, to provide competent bakers and cooks.

Ted Camplin became a dairy farmer at Branyan, which, in those days, was a country area about three miles from the centre of Bundaberg, Queensland, and is now an inner suburb of that city. The family milked about thirty cows by hand, and when the milking was completed it was then grandfather Camplin's job to deliver the fresh milk to households and cafes throughout Bundaberg by means of a horse-drawn cart. It was the job of Mum and her sisters to help with the milking, which started about 4 a.m. each day, prior to going to school. They attended Branyan Road

State School first and then moved to West Bundaberg State School when Mum was about twelve. After primary school, Mum attended Bundaberg High School by bicycle and played lots of tennis and netball. She was a good tennis player and once was runner-up in the Bundaberg Junior Female Championship. She was still playing tennis socially at about sixty-five years of age.

Elizabeth Jane Cunningham, Mum's mother, was born at Maryborough, Queensland, on 22 August 1887. She was married on 29 April 1908 at her parent's home in Charles Street, Maryborough. She died of kidney cancer at Bundaberg on 28 February 1921 aged just thirty-three years when Mum was only five years old. She was the oldest of six children, namely Alexander Robinson (known as Bob), Jesse, Jubilee, May, and Norman. During the school holidays, Mum loved to accompany her father on the milk run and visit the city of Bundaberg. She speaks of her father in glowing terms and has mentioned that after her mother died he used to take her and her siblings into town to buy their clothes and shoes.

Mum's maternal grandparents were Alexander and Jane Cunningham (nee Hardgrave). Alexander was born in Glasgow, Scotland, on 31 July 1859. How, when, and where he arrived in Australia is not known to me. Jane Hardgrave was born on 4 December 1857 at Sofala, New South Wales, a small gold mining town situated between Bathurst and Mudgee. The Hardgrave name is sometimes associated, incorrectly via a corruption of the spelling, with that of Edward Hargraves, who is credited with making the first substantial gold discovery in Australia in 1851 around Sofala and the nearby district that is now known as Hargraves.

Mum's paternal grandparents were William Taylor Camplin, who was born also at Theddlethorpe, Lincolnshire, England, and Rosa Marie Hall-Hyde who was born at Theddlethorpe, Lincolnshire, England. When the name Rosa Maria Hall-Hyde first appeared before me, it raised the question in my mind as to how such an 'Italian' sounding name came to appear in an otherwise very 'English' family. However, from the research work that my cousin Tom Chatterton has done on the family tree and very generously shared with me it is apparent that Rosa's father George B. Hall married Azubah Ann Hyde in Theddlethorpe, England, in 1853. George B. Hall's father was George Hall who married Mahalah Bartholomew of Gautby, England, at Theddlethorpe All-Saints in 1827. Both of these women's names appear to be of a Hebrew (Arabic) origin, and perhaps that explains the rather large nose that some individuals in the family exhibit today, including me.

My mother is one of five children, and in order of age, they were: Jean Mildred born 8 May 1909, Lillias *Beryl* born 12 January 1911, Iris *Valmai* born 16 February 1913, Mavis Aileen born 15 March 1915, and Jack Edward *Hall* born 11 May 1918. Hall inherited a family name through his paternal grandmother. Mum was born with a midwife in attendance at the home of her maternal grandparents Alexander and Jane Cunningham at Bolsover Street, Rockhampton. She lived all her early years in Bundaberg, and when her mother died, her spinster aunt, Jubilee Cunningham, came to stay with the family to assist Mum's father in the children's upbringing. Although Aunt Jube (as she was affectionately known) was very good to the children, Mum has often said how very much she missed her mother throughout her life. Aunt Jube stayed on until Mum's eldest sister Jean was sixteen, when Jean took on the entire responsibility, with the support of her father, for the rearing of the rest of the family and caring for the house. Hall, the youngest sibling, was still only seven years of age.

Dad's paternal grandfather, James Chatterton, was born in 1832 at Little Cawthorpe, Lincolnshire, England, which is only about thirty or forty kilometres from Theddlethorpe. Apparently, the family was quite wealthy and records show him and his family to have been farmers, butchers, and wool-buyers in Theddlethorpe, all at the one time. The family had previously shifted from further north, where they were watermen—river workers who transported passengers across and along the rivers in the Fens country. They acquired land when the Fens area was drained in the late eighteenth and early nineteenth centuries. It seems that James met with an untimely death in 1881 at the age of forty-nine years. He and his horse are said to have drowned in a roadside canal. Grandfather Robert Chatterton's mother was Ann Chatterton (nee Wilson). She was born at Theddlethorpe, Lincolnshire, England, in 1834 and was the daughter of a groom at the Chattertons' establishment. Apparently her marriage to James rested uncomfortably with the family. At the age of about forty-seven years, after her husband's unfortunate drowning, she was given the then very considerable sum of £1,000 by the family and 'sent' out to Australia with her seven youngest children. They departed from Glasgow on 21 September 1882 in the '*SHENIR*' and arrived in Maryborough, Queensland on 2 January 1883 and eventually settled in Bundaberg. The two oldest boys who were already apprenticed in trades stayed in England. Ann's mother was Martha Wilson nee Campling (then spelt including a 'g'), so history tells us that the marriage of a Chatterton to a member of the Camplin line probably first took place in 1853 and repeated itself seventy-six years later in 1929 (Les Chatterton and Beryl Camplin) and then again seven years later in 1936 when my father and mother married.

In the late nineteenth and early twentieth centuries, communication options were very limited (virtually only letters and telegrams—very few telephones even). Motor vehicles were in their infancy, very basic, and generally affordable only by those with some degree of wealth. Where roads existed, they generally were unsealed gravel surfaces and extremely rough. This meant that travel by car over long distances was slow, uncomfortable, and beyond the reach of most.

Like many others of their generation, few of the members of Dad's parents' families keep in close touch subsequent to their arrival in Australia. The only one of Dad's uncles that I knew when I was a youngster was my grandfather's youngest sibling Thomas (Tom), who was born in 1878 in Theddlethorpe and died in Rockhampton in 1948 at age seventy. He was a bachelor and a retired railway worker whom my parents visited on occasions when they undertook their monthly visit to Rockhampton on business. He lived with Mrs Malone, who I remember as a very nice old lady. Dad and Mum visited Uncle Tom and Mrs Malone most times they went to Rockhampton and obviously liked both of them. She had a sulphur crested cockatoo in a large cage out at the back under the mango tree. We kids were enthralled by this bird that could talk, swear, bite furiously, and drink by scooping water up in a small tobacco tin held in its foot from a big water dish on the floor of the cage.

Mum's family retained a little closer contact, and we kids knew three aunts and an uncle on the Cunningham side of the family. Jubilee and Norman died when I was quite young and I recall them only faintly, but Jesse and May became well known to my wife and me in our early married years when we used to call on them on our way through Maryborough where they then lived. May never married, and when we knew them she and Jesse lived together with Jesse's daughter Joan.

Jesse's husband, Edmund Samuel Flavelle (Ted) Woodhouse, was the manager of Katu Plantation on Kavieng Island, New Ireland, Papua New Guinea. When the Japanese entered World War II, all women and children were evacuated from PNG back to Australia—Jesse and young Joan being amongst them. Many of the men became coast watchers, spying on the movements of Japanese shipping and troops and continually moving to new hideouts in the jungle to avoid capture. Ted stayed behind in this capacity and sadly was never heard of again. Recently accessed records show that he was captured by the Japanese and killed (probably executed) with about twenty-one other POWs on either 18 February or 17 March 1944 on Kavieng wharf at the age of fifty years.

My paternal grandfather, Robert Chatterton, was the second youngest of nine children, namely, Edward, Charles, William, Susannah, James, Sarah, Alice, Robert, and Thomas. He was born on 3 July 1876 at Theddlethorpe, Lincolnshire, England, and died on 15 May 1938 from a heart attack while at my parents' home on the farm at Struck Oil. He is buried at Mt Morgan. Dad's mother was Minnie Sutton, known affectionately as Ma to us kids. She was born on 3 October 1879 at Dudley, a suburb of Birmingham, Staffordshire, England, and came to Australia via assisted passage on the *DUKE OF NORFOLK*, which sailed from London on 15 December 1900 and arrived in Brisbane on 16 February 1901. She was the daughter of George Edwin Sutton and Emma Ogden. It seems that she was born in a workhouse. The only other knowledge I have of any of Ma's relatives is that which she related to my mother, i.e. she had a sister Lily Jones and two step-sisters Edith and May—also that Lily had a son named Lawrence. Ma married Robert Chatterton on 30 June 1904 in Bundaberg and died on 26 November 1945 in Mt Morgan aged sixty-six years. She is buried in the Mt Morgan cemetery (Section 4, Row W) together with her husband. Dad was the fourth born of eight children, namely Leslie (Les), Victor (Vic), Doris, Jack, Olive, May, Sydney (Syd), and Edith (Edie).

Grandfather Robert Chatterton, like many immigrants who arrived from England, was fiercely loyal to the King and country. On 19th May 1902 at the age of almost twenty-six years and prior to his marriage, he sailed from Pinkenba Wharf, Brisbane, on the transport ship *CUSTODIAN* with 'A' Squadron (Southern Coastal District) of the Queensland contingent of the 7th Battalion Australian Commonwealth Horse as Private No. 39 to serve in the Boer War in South Africa. His unit arrived in Durban on 22 June 1902 and returned to Brisbane on 2 August 1902, seemingly without firing a shot in anger, and it was disbanded on 9 August 1902.

When World War I broke out in 1914 he again enlisted (then aged thirty-eight), this time as Private No. 496 in the 2nd Australian Light Horse. Ma was left at home with five children under ten years of age and another to arrive some two and half months after his departure. Dad sometimes spoke about the hard times the family endured when he was young, and one can imagine the difficulties, both work-wise and financially, that Ma and the family encountered during grandfather's absence. His unit was part of the 9th Battalion that sailed for Egypt from Pinkenba Wharf, Brisbane, on the *STAR OF ENGLAND* on 24 September 1914. After training near Cairo with the 5th Australian Light Horse, another Queensland Regiment, and cooling their heels for a while waiting for orders, they were eventually ordered into action on 12 May 1915, a few weeks after the initial landing at Gallipoli, which occurred on 25 April 1915. They joined the infantry to be decimated there. He was withdrawn from the front with shrapnel wounds to the leg and for medical reasons (heart problems) on 18 December 1915, just a few days before the Gallipoli campaign ended on 9 January 1916. After his discharge, in addition to suffering continuing heart problems, he, like many other returned servicemen, suffered from what was termed 'shell-shock' (more likely termed post-traumatic stress disorder these days), and he was said to never again be the man that he was prior to the War. History now tells us of the atrocious circumstances under which these brave men fought, and I feel enormously proud of my grandfather's participation but at the same time feel terribly sorry for what he and his mates suffered as a consequence—not to forget either those who were left at home to fend for themselves as best they were able.

In civilian life, Grandfather Chatterton was at various times a baker by trade, butcher, miner, and farmer. On one occasion, he was employed in the gold mine at Mt Morgan and on another he worked as a baker at Mt Chalmers, near Rockhampton, another small mining settlement. Dad was born there, and his birth was registered as 11 September 1910 although his birthday was always celebrated and believed to be on 14 September. We did not find out his 'correct' birth date until a copy of his birth certificate was obtained at the time of his death on 6 May 1968. Apparently the family moved to Horse Creek, near Mt Morgan soon after Dad's birth, I presume so that Grandfather could obtain work in the Mt Morgan mine. I understand that Dad started school there at the State School that opened on 16 November 1909 and which subsequently closed in 1972. One of his teachers was a Miss Kitty Hayman, who briefly came into my life many years later.

The marriages of Dad and his brother Les to Mum and her sister Beryl resulted in a very close relationship between the children of each family—we being double first cousins. Obviously, both families have identical ancestors, and my cousin Mervyn Thomas (Tom) Chatterton has expended quite many hours of dedication and care in researching the family trees of both the Chatterton and the Camplin lines. He was unbelievably generous in providing me with a copy of his research output recently, for which I am extremely grateful.

On the Chatterton side of the family tree, through George Chatterton's wife Rachell Coke (c1594-1653), my ninth great-grandmother, Tom traced our ancestors back to noble families in the United Kingdom and thence on to nobility in many other countries in Europe and Asia. The most distant ancestor he has recorded in the Chatterton line is my twenty-sixth great-grandmother Queen Anna Agnesa of France, Duchess of Kiev (Ukraine) (c1024 to c1076).

Through Ma's side of the family, Tom has traced our ancestors back to my thirty-fifth great-grandmother Alpaide Concubine of Austrasia (Belgium) (c654 to c705). She was the wife of Pepin Martel, second mayor of the Palace of Austrasia (Belgium) (c635 to c714). A number of other ancestors of noble birth were also recorded in this line.

On the Camplin side, he has followed the generations to my twenty-sixth great-grandfather King Henry De Longespee, the second king of England, 1133 to 1189. Also, through George Bartholomew Hall's wife Azubah Hyde (c1832-1913), he was able to trace her ancestors back to John Hall (1756) who married Isabella Neave, whose ancestors go back to Adam Neave (Naf) (1495-1571) of Switzerland.

In more recent times, both Chatterton and Camplin lines appear to have lived in Lincolnshire, England.

As was the case in those days, politically expedient marriages were made between the nobility and rulers of many countries in an attempt to gain security and allies for the future. Once Tom's search achieved a 'noble' link, where ancient but good records were maintained, the field expanded exponentially.

Although Tom has not had this information authenticated by a genealogical expert, he has consented to me publishing these findings with the proviso that the information is recorded as coming from records obtained from various sources in family trees found in the public domain of 'Ancestry.com'.

Appendix III

World War II: Service Record
Sydney Edward Chatterton

('C' Company, 2/15 Battalion A.I.F. ARMY No. QX8321)

Details from Syd's Service Record and additional information obtained from the Australian War Museum War Diaries show the following:

- 06/06/1940—enlisted at Rockhampton, Queensland. Single. Dairy Farmer. Religion—Church of England. Hair—Light Brown. Eyes—Brown. Scar on left knee and towards front of Right Tibial (shin). Tattoo mark left forearm.
- 18/06/1940—taken on strength 2/15 Battalion, Northern Command at Redbank, Queensland (located between Brisbane and Ipswich). Pay Book No. 55111.
- 01/07/1940—embarked on H.M.T.S. (His Majesty's Troop Ship) ZEELANDIA (this was later sunk in Darwin Harbour on 19 February 1942 during a Japanese air raid).
- 11/07/1940—disembarked and taken on strength 7 M.D. (Military District) Darwin, Northern Territory.

- 16/07/1940—admitted to Darwin Military Hospital (the reason being to have all of his teeth extracted and the provision of false plates).
- 20/07/1940—returned from Darwin Military Hospital.
- 25/10/1940—marched out of Northern Command, Darwin.
- 07/11/1940—Marched into Redbank, Qld.
- 11/11/1940—pre-embarkation leave until 21/11/1940.
- 25/12/1940—(Xmas Day) Departed Redbank Army Camp and boarded train at South Brisbane Station for Sydney. Detrained at Casino, NSW, for refreshments consisting of sandwiches and tea.
- 26/12/1940—arrived Gloucester, NSW, at 07:00 for breakfast (sandwiches and tea) then continued on to Darling Harbour where the troops were ferried to the 'QUEEN MARY' (fitted out as a troop carrier) for embarkation.
- 28/12/1940-2/15 Battalion—A, B, C, D and Headquarters Companies (total of approx. 990 men) sailed from Sydney Harbour in convoy with 'HMAS CANBERRA', 'HT AQUITANIA', 'HT MAURETANIA', 'HT AWATEA' and 'HT DOMINION MONARCH'.
- 03/01/1941—sailed from Fremantle, Western Australia.
- 12/01/1941—arrived at Trincomalee, Ceylon (Shri Lanka). and transhipped to 'INDIAPOERA' (Army No. HT311) a Dutch East Indies liner of 13,000 tons).
- 14/01/1941—'INDIAPOERA' joined a convoy of 12 other ships.
- 16/01/1941—convoy set sail for the Middle East.
- 28/01/1941—convoy arrived at Port Suez—all troops stayed on board.
- 31/01/1941—'INDIAPOERA' anchored in Great Bitter Lake within Suez Canal—food supply was running short.
- 3/02/1941—disembarked at Katara (near Jaffa), Palestine, to undergo desert warfare training.

- 28/02/1941—crossed the Nile Delta and headed West 290 miles by train to Mersa Matruh, Egypt, then onwards by land transport.
- 01/03/1941—battalion passed through Tobruk, Libya.
- 08/03/1941—arrived in Benghazi, Libya.
- 10/03/1941—reached battle front.
- 09/04/1941—battalion moved back to Tobruk.
- 29/06/1941—War Diary describes this day as: 'Blackest Day for D Company'. Syd was in 'C' Company where the situation appears to have been similarly dreadful.
- 29/06/1941—AWM 52, 2nd Australian Infantry Forces and Commonwealth Military Forces unit war diaries 1939-45 Item No: 8/3/15 2nd Battalion May—July 1941 at page 109 states: 'Tobruch Area (now Tobruk) 0430 hrs. Lieut Christie's patrol reported into E Coy. QX6230 Lieut E McW Christie wounded. QX8341 Pte Pinder P J, QX6950 L/Cpl Harper D G, QX8231 (correct No. QX8321) Pte Chatterton killed by booby traps'. (Lieut Christie, O/C of the Fighting Patrol from C Coy. later reported that, having lost their correct location due to miscalculation, the Patrol turned back and ran into an anti-personnel mine field. No one was injured in the initial explosion but Pte Pinder was badly wounded and Syd was wounded in the second explosion. Lieut Christie set out to carry Pte Pinder on his back while Pte Harper assisted Syd. Then there was a double explosion and both Syd and Pte Harper were killed instantly and Lieu Christie wounded by shrapnel in the calf of his left leg. Pte Pinder died when Lieut Christie reached his Platoon. Another secret report at page 122 of the same War Diary by the Battalion Commander on 'Operations in the Eastern Sector of the Salient' dated 8 July 1941, at point No. 5, described the Booby Traps and Mines as follows: 'When the enemy vacated the positions which made possible the advancement of our line, he left behind hundreds of 'S'

type anti-personnel mines. As an example of the thickness of the field, the following examples are quoted, viz:—(a) In front of the right Coy, they were reported by a patrol to be 3 feet [ninety-three centimetres] apart in four rows. This field resulted in four fatal casualties to a patrol. (b) When clearing a track for the laying of wire in the left sector 89 mines were removed in a length of 22 yards [the length of a cricket pitch]. (c) In the same area on the following night a (mine) field was followed outside the wire and 68 mines were removed. (d) A stack of 400 Teller mines were located (unplaced) in the new fwd area.)

- No date—buried in the field.
- 27/05/1944—re-buried at Knightsbridge War Cemetery, Acroma, Libya—Plot 15, Row B, Grave 8.
- Syd was awarded the Africa Star and 1939-1945 Star War Medals posthumously. These together with his Rising Sun Hat Badges and his watch are now in the possession of my cousin Mervyn Thomas (Tom) Chatterton.

APPENDIX IV

Sydney Edward Chatterton: Copy of Lieutenant Christie's Patrol Report

2/15 Bn HQ.
29 June 41.

REPORT OF FIGHTING PATROL from C Coy.

Date: Night 28/29 June 41.
Time out: 2330 hrs
Strength: 1 Offr 1 L/Cpl, 5 ORS.

Report: Patrol left R8 at 2330 hrs moving on a bearing about 10*
WEST of NORTH. A fairly strong breeze was blowing from a
northerly direction and made hearing difficult. After about an
hours slow progress in which a fairly wide sweep had been made,
sounds of digging were heard and also timber being used. These
sounds came from a bearing of 335* from Post R8. After further
crawling, figures could be seen moving about. The patrol swung
further to the left and were able to crawl quite close. The estimated
strength of the working party was about 60, working in three
parties and fairly close together. No isolated parties or straglers

could be seen and the strength of the party was too great for the patrol to attack with any hope of success. The patrol then moved back and owing to some miscalculations struck some sangars, which were mistaken for some on the right of R8. A tank was also visible which was mistaken for the one in the rear of R8. The patrol then went to move as it thought to R8 but immediately struck trouble in the form of anti-personnel mines. One exploded without doing any harm, but was shortly afterwards followed by another which severely wounded one and also wounded another. Placing the severely wounded one on my back and the L/Cpl assisting the other we tried to get out of the field, but had not moved far when I heard a double explosion behind me and found the L/Cpl and the other he was assisting killed outright. One pellet from the second explosion had entered the calf of my left leg. I now thought we had come too far WEST and that tank visible was the one on bearing of 285* from R8. It was impossible to distinguish the land marks, so I moved EAST thinking I would strike the wire close to R8, but after travelling between 500 and 1,000 yds the wire was reached in front of E Coy. The man severely wounded died on reaching 19 Pl HQ.

Moving out the patrol had the assistance of Green Verey lights fired by A Coy for direction. No flares at all were visible during the time we were trying to return to Post R8.

The enemy did quite a lot of firing their automatic weapons during the time the patrol was out, but were not fired on when the explosions occurred. The firing was taking place on our right.

Sgd. E.M. Christie Lieut. O/C Patrol

APPENDIX V

Sydney Edward Chatterton
Lieutenant Christie's Letter to Ma

(The following is my best endeavour to piece together the handwritten contents of a very frail and badly faded airmail letter card sent to Mrs M. Chatterton, Struck Oil, via Moongan, Mt Morgan, Qld, Australia.)

QX 6230 E M Christie,
2/15 Aust Inf. Br.
A.I.F.
Middle East Force
25 Jan (1942?)

Dear Mrs Chatterton,

I must apologise for my great delay in answering your letter. Firstly I was not quite certain of some things and have been trying to get some proof and lately I have been very . . . and not able to write.

Syd was killed well forward in enemy territory and was not buried immediately by us as we were withdrawn from that area a few nights later. This took place in the 'Salient' where he had made a bulge in our lines and we were moving our line forward to shorten it. One of my chaps went into hospital and there met some of the relieving Bn. who claimed that they had buried two Australian Soldiers when they moved forward in this area a little later. It is of this that I have been trying to get confirmation as to the best of our knowledge Syd and the other chap Harper were the only two we knew of out there.

I left Tobruk four days before the last Western push started and was not able to stay and have the opportunity of going over that ground.

As Tobruk is now relieved, all bodies around the perimeter would be transferred to the cemetery and re-interred there. The cemetery was being well looked after and all graves were being concreted over to make a lasting and permanent structure over them.

I am so sorry that I can give you so few details but should the opportunity occur to get a snap of the grave at any future date I will certainly do so and see that it is forwarded on to you.

I remain,
Yours sincerely,
EM Christie

Appendix VI

Copy of Lisa's Letter to Her Grandmother

(29 March 1982)

Dear Grandma,

How are you and everyone? We are all fine. I was going to write to you before now but I lost the letter somewhere under my bed. My room is an absolute mess. Just picture a rubbish tip and you know what my room looks like. If you are wondering why I am typing this letter, it is because I'm lazy. (wasn't I always, that is what Mum brought me up to think). Last Wednesday my grade had a history excursion and I don't take history so I stayed home instead. (I DID ALL THE WASHING, VACUUM, IRONING, AND THEN I HAD TO WASH THE SHOWER OUT AND I SLIPPED AND WAS SOPPING WET FROM HEAD TO TOE). That dog is so adorable but she is into everything that she can put her teeth into. When Dad comes home at night the first thing he says is 'Whats that stupid dog got into this time'. (but he uses much more severe words) She is so cute though. It is only five weeks till the May holidays (RIPPER). Mum and I went and bought all my winter clothes on Saterday. We spent about three hours at the shops and you would hate to know how much we spent. (Dad was horribly jealous) He is still the same old spiolt kid he used to be (sometimes I THINK he is worst). Paul went on a caving trip to Jenolan Caves and he was tickled pink when he came home. It was for the whole weekend (pity it wasn't for the whole year. Mum has finished 3 more stories and she ONLY has 6 more to do. She had an excursion today, she had to take the little monsters to Lane Cove park (not us kids, even though the boys are monsters, thats what I think of them even though you might think differently). Mark seems to like his new school, though I don't know why. (I'll be going there myself in two years). Creme Puff lives a luxurious life on my bed (I bet you never thought he'd ever get there). School is okay (I could be doing better things though . . . eg visiting you).

Mum says she won't write this week because I'm writing (talk about lazy) BUT SHE SENDS HER LOVE.

Thank Auntie Sharon for her letter, it came today. It was a pleasant surprise to hear from her. I hope Peter is feeling alot better soon. From your description he seems to be pretty sick. Last fortnight I hit my toe on a cement step and a couple of days later I had bruises all around my toe. I thought it felt worst than it should so Dad took me to the doctors and the doctor said I've cracked the bone. So that means that I can't play tennis for about a month. I had better finish off now because Mum is threatening me with a Pork Chop. HELP . . .

All my love
from Lisa

P.S. CAN YOU GET THE RECIPE FOR SWISS CHICKEN OFF AUNTIE VALMAI

P.P.S. DO YOU KNOW IF CHOPS STAIN

Appendix VII

Paul's Eulogy to Lisa

'To Lisa—With Love'

I would like to read you a poem I wrote on the day I heard of my sister's murder. I think it says better than anything what I feel.

I scream at the sky.
What more can you do
against this oceanic fact—
Cry at the anguish of stones
and try to breathe life into bones
bleaching on the sand?

Racking the logic of stars
Will not bring her back,
nor give reason to this fatal mistake.
Cruel as mountains.
Hard as a gunshot.
Silent as space.

But she will live still.
I will remember the smile,
her gentle, disarming look
that melts anger into apology.
Her soft humour
that turned no heads
but bent many hearts.

Her determination
that strove to make the impossible
look ordinary
and sought no applause.

Her beauty lives in my memory
And I will work to live that beauty
And she will live in my life.

Lisa was born 19 years and 6 months ago in Brisbane. She very nearly didn't make it into the world at all. While carrying her, my mother was involved in a head-on car accident and was rushed to hospital where she lay unconscious for a number of days. This could have been fatal for the unborn infant but thankfully she survived and was born without any obvious disabilities.

Her life since has been full of struggle. Initially to conquer this accident and its legacy. Then to come to terms with being the only girl in a family of four, especially with brothers like us. And then her schooling which for her as so many of us was a trial. Like my brothers and I, she went to a smorgasbord of schools, and though she never shone academically, she neither slackened her efforts nor complained. Her greatest strength has been her determination to defeat these obstacles and her calm acceptance of what could not be changed.

I think the best example of her courage was in her music. Of all the instruments she could choose, she chose the piano, the one that demands the greatest manual dexterity. I remember vividly, one day, listening to her play a Bach minuet. She played it well, but that wasn't what struck me. I guess all musicians need that determination, but for Lisa the achievement was that much greater since she had more to overcome than just the limits of the instrument.

My father and mother deserve a lot of credit for this strength of spirit. They always demanded the most of all of us and although that was hard sometimes we all appreciate it deeply.

Something that struck us all was the humour she managed to keep while facing all of this. I think we all remember her as a happy young woman and it is that image I will always carry with me. All of her school reports noted this humour and compassion and it's a pity that our society only rewards those who can remember the most facts or write the best essays. If they had exams for compassion Lisa would be in the top percentile.

The last year of her life has seen the most astounding change in her. I moved to Hobart a little over a year ago and when I left I remember Lisa as an uncertain schoolgirl, unsure of herself, her abilities and the direction she wanted her life to take. Over the year all that changed dramatically. She took up secretarial college and for the first time in her life she found something she could put her full efforts into, and something she could do well. After years of resigning herself to mediocrity she was suddenly faced with success and it made all the difference to her. She came first in every exam, she was first in her year to graduate, first to get a job. She positively blossomed in self-confidence and was moving closer and closer to the point where she could make of the world what she wanted.

I returned to Sydney this Christmas and at the airport to greet me was a very elegant and self-possessed young woman. I hardly recognised my own sister, the change had been so great.

That is how I will remember her. That and her humble courage, her soft humour, her gentle and contented nature.

I don't want to say anything about her death. You all know the details and they are best forgotten. As I was trying to say in the poem, Death is a fact. You can't alter it; we can't go back and change it. All Death ever says to us is 'that's it', nothing more. You can't argue and there is nothing to be learnt.

But life is something very different. Life says a million things and Lisa's was a particularly eloquent one. I find that every day I think of her I discover another thing she was saying to me in her quiet manner. In her gentleness she was telling me to be gentle, in her courage she was telling me to be courageous, in her contentedness to be contented. It took me a long time to learn what she had to say but ever since she has been a great teacher to me and I feel very grateful for that gift she has given me over such a short life.

I want to use this time not to commemorate her death but to celebrate her life and to celebrate life itself. You all knew her in different ways and I would ask you to meditate for a few moments on what she meant to you, what lessons she taught you. If we can all learn from those quiet lessons and put them into action in our own lives then the world will be a slightly better place because she has lived and that's the greatest compliment we can ever pay her.

Paul Chatterton, 23 January 1987

Appendix VIII
Val's Eulogy to Andrew

(7 March 1973-1 January 2003)

Sixteen years ago Lisa died.

She was 19 ½ years old and Andrew was almost 14 years.

Sixteen years ago Andrew's nightmare began.

Like me, John and Paul and Mark know how terribly her death has affected all our family.

Lisa was like Andrew's second mother—she was always there when he felt he needed her.

When she had gone part of his life had gone too.

Like all of us, Andrew so often put on his 'public face'.

He was happy-go-lucky.

He enjoyed life.

From time to time Andrew drew solace from the use of drugs and alcohol.

He thought it would help.

It appeared to help at first but as time moved on it only accentuated his pain.

We have all known Andrew in different ways.

Those of us close to him have known of this pain he has been living with.

We have all tried to help him in many different ways.

He has wanted help but the nightmare has been too great.

I will miss Andrew desperately for the rest of my life and I know John, Paul and Mark will too.

We who have loved Andrew all his life will always miss him terribly.

But I feel a peace in my heart that at last he has found peace and at last he has been reunited with Lisa.

His nightmare is over.

Let us give thanks for Andrew's life and remember our great times together—and there were many.

Let us give thanks for little Jessica—a living reminder and part of Andrew—that she will be able to enjoy a life filled with peace and love in Andrew's memory.

Val Chatterton (Mum), 10 January 2003

APPENDIX IX

Mark's Eulogy to Andrew

(7 March 1973-1 January 2003)

Many different lives Andrew had, with adventures far and wide,
People, places, situations, as changing as the tide.

A carefree child with open eyes, and mischief to be found,
A cheeky grin, open heart within, and love to share around.

School was a curse to waste his time, and work to waste his play,
To fix and organise, help and create, would take his time of day.

In growing up his heart did close, as rules of his game did alter,
A faster pace to hide the pain, and hope he did not falter.

Personal problems were kept inside, and medicated at will,
Raves and parties could mask the pain, to temporarily be still.

A different face was worn outside, to control the demons within,
As to open up and face his fears, was a battle he couldn't win.

Fishing was a passion he had, as was Tigger his loyal dog and friend,
A solace was found in nature and the bush, right to the very end.

Agriculture and growing plants, was an enjoyable release all times,
But an allergy to sulphur made him unable to work grapevines.

His knowledge was transplanted from vines to wines, in pursuit
   of the very best,
Through research and tastings, his expert knowledge put even
   professionals to the test.

His strength of will and determination, set goals for him to succeed,
Yet anger and frustration and learning to let go, were things he
   did not heed.

He tried one last time to face his demons, and deal with past inside,
But facing himself was the only thing he feared, and from his
   demons he had to hide.

Back to Cairns where he thought he could conquer, with love and
   Joanne his wife,
But the fear to face himself and his ghosts was too great and he
   took his own life.

But Andrew lives on here in the hearts of many and his daughter
   Jessica his child,
For she was for Andrew the apple of his eye, and I pray that she
   not be so wild.

His life was far different than most ever saw, and lived at a fast and
   furious pace,
But he would want us to celebrate the life that he had, and not say
   'oh, what a waste'.

Mark Chatterton, 10 January 2003

Appendix X
Paul's Eulogy to Andrew

I've struggled with the right words for farewelling my brother lying there.

But nothing expresses the misery I am feeling without him.

The only words that ring with some semblance of truth are just simply that:

I love you, Andrew—as a brother and more recently as a dear, dear friend.

What sense is there in this? As the world celebrated the beginning of 2003, Andrew was bringing his life to an end. As we all looked forward with the hope of a fresh New Year, Andrew had let go of all hope. That day he decided he was alone and beyond love—and yet look at us here, 10 days later. How much love can one man have stirred up around him? And the biggest irony is that you are going to miss out on the best party, mate.

His choice to die is so hard for us all to understand. I don't begin to comprehend it, but I do believe that we must remember one point.

Andrew alone bears the terrible responsibility for that choice. No one else is at fault. He chose this path. And for that I am hopelessly angry with him . . . and also horribly sad.

I have no way to know what he was thinking on New Year's morning. I can only presume that he must have felt too utterly alone. I wish I could have been there for him. I'm sure we all do. And I recognise with sadness that so many of them were there for him in so many ways. I think we have to realise that he chose to walk away from all that love.

The one lesson for me in this is to stay connected to those we love. Aloneness is our choice. Every day we have the choice to connect with those we love—or to cut ourselves off from them. We have the choice to receive that love—or to reject it. And to show compassion in how we deal with those around us—or to fail to find that generosity within us.

In Andrew's honour, let's choose love, life and compassion.

The one joy in this death is in the wonderful memory of his life.

You all have your experiences of Andrew. He lived in so many different worlds. But let me give you some impression from the last years of the Andrew that I knew.

I'll never forget a magical 1984 Leo Buring Riesling and his spaghetti bolognese in Cairns. His instinct for quality wine was remarkable and brought some of the happiest times in his life. We spent a lot of time just talking, sharing, delving, and trying to find a place in the world. And also dueling on the go-cart track or hooning around Cooktown or the back roads of Atherton.

Importantly, we spent a lot of time walking in the rainforest, swimming in mountain pools or exploring back tracks. We shared a belief in the spirit in nature and these walks for us both were like going to church. For him, fishing was a part of this spiritual practice. It was as much about communion as about consumption. Nature will continue to remind me of him.

For Andrew, there was also the strong desire to do what he did with quality and flair. His work in the vineyards, his walking in the bush, his cooking and his fighting were all done with extraordinary intensity and pride. He was a man of great strength, warmth, generosity and love.

I will so badly miss all of that.

I'm so pleased to see so many people here. Andrew left his lives in so many of us. Let's treasure that.

I treasure especially one person that he brought into my life—Jessica.

And I treasure also my parents who bear all of this with such extraordinary grace and goodness.

Goodbye, Andrew.
I love you.
I'll miss you horribly.
And I am a lesser man without you.

Paul John Chatterton, 10 January 2003

Appendix XI

Andrew Rumble's Eulogy to Andrew

To My friend—Rest in Peace

Good afternoon and thank you for sparing a few moments of your time to allow me to speak a few words about a very good friend of mine.

My name is Adam Rumble; I am a friend of Andrew's and his family. I first met Andrew at Waitara Public School 20 odd years ago and then again at Barker College after he did a small stint at East Lindfield Primary School.

I would have to say that Andrew has always been an adventurous person. If you could ride it, climb it or cross it then it presented a challenge to Andrew, it had to be conquered and he would go about doing just that—and as if that was not enough, he would then better his previous attempt.

There was a small group of us in High School who would go on outdoor expeditions quite frequently under the Duke of Edinburgh

Award Scheme; the fact that we were only interested in the opportunity to 'Go Bush' was not picked on by our peers until much later. Very rapidly we were taking the most extreme bush challenges, vanishing for days not content to follow the delegated walking tracks but preferring to go through dense scrub, down sheer rock faces and across remote areas. I seem to recall during one of these trips Andrew's famous 'No, let's go this way it's much better' words ringing in my ears whilst trudging knee deep in snow with full packs and frozen boots and knowing that there was another 50 kms to do yet.

Andrew's passion for the Australian outdoors combined with his desire to go faster and more extreme when he upgraded his meagre 6 speed KDX200 Kawasaki off-road bike for a 'climb a tree vertically' Yamaha YZ. It was faster, much more powerful and more importantly very loud. Soon after Andrew got this 'weapon on wheels' he regurgitated volumes of information on statistics, mechanical properties and some phenomenal physical capabilities and not having the foggiest what he was talking about I would just chime in with a 'really' or a 'no way' at the appropriate time; I didn't even try to attempt to fake my way through the conversation.

I refer to this bike in detail as I am going to tell you a story about an incident that sums up some characteristics about the kind of person I know him as;

The incident took place in Yarramalong where the Chattertons had a property for some time up near Wyong. From time to time I would visit and go motorbike riding up in the Wattagan State Forest with Andrew. On this particular day however we were in the neighbour's paddock. I believe Andrew had been constructing this jump for his bike for some time. Andrew had ridden his bike some 200 metres back from the jump and was careening towards an all-time best, I have to admit it was impressive—he reached his cruising altitude at about 80 km/hr, a good 8 metres above ground and touched down nearly 25 metres beyond the jump—the error was in the positioning in the air he told me in a matter of fact way as we got nearer to the hospital to get his leg cast; he would correct it next time.

Upon returning to the property and after a good berating, Mr Chatterton, John, thought it safe to go out for a while and that we would be quiet for the rest of the afternoon, Andrew's leg being how it was and all. No sooner had the dust begun to settle on the drive than Andrew was kick-starting his bike with his good leg and back across the paddock. I have kept this secret for nearly 15 years now but a good laugh is a good laugh.

When Andrew hit a tree and came a cropper the first thing that crossed my mind was John is going to belt us both. Andrew calmly stood up, collected himself and began unwrapping the bandage around his cast. I thought he was checking for damage but as it turned out he was simply turning the bandage inside out to hide the grass stains so Mum would not be concerned. I had to admire his stubborn persistence to not admit defeat.

My experiences with Andrew have seen us both fishing for Spanish Mackerel in crocodile infested rivers outside Cairns wondering who will get to the fish first, Andrew, myself or the croc; taking a run-up at a hill at high speed in Mark's wagon only to have it breakdown half way up and then us breakdown laughing on the way to Andrew and Hallee's place in the Gold Coast hinterland near Mount Tambourin; and watching him exit by helicopter after his wedding to Jo in Mudgee at the Vineyard. I have been camping with Andrew during 150 km/hr winds and horizontal rain at Marley beach whilst Turramurra was being decimated, camping during a hailstorm and had ice the size of golf balls rip through the tent at Crescent Head and have sat out a 3 day snow blizzard in Barrington Tops at a temperature of about 4 degrees C and then dig the tent out afterwards. These are unique experiences which have happened over time, memories which at the time do not seem important but when combined provide a history of understanding—in this case about a friendship.

I think there are people who come into your life and leave a permanent mark on you and who you are, both physically and mentally. Andrew has been there in my life to keep things in perspective; just when I think my existence might be getting a little mundane and predictable Andrew would pay another unannounced visit and lead me off on another adventure—it seems to me that life with Andrew was all about variety and a new challenge. Andrew has shown me that I need to keep injecting a little spontaneity into life; his companionship will be sorely missed.

Andrew was many different things to many different people. I have countless memories about Andrew and I am sure you all do too.

Thank you for the opportunity to speak today.

Adam Rumble, 10 January 2003